equi
suc

How Can We Equip
Our Children
To Succeed?

Empower, Enable and Equip Our Children
to develop the
Attitudes, Thinking and Behaviours
to Learn, Achieve and Be All They Can Be!

Beverley Burton

Published by

Education Innovation Ltd
Nottingham UK

Version 1.0

First published in 2013

Copyright ©2013 Beverley Burton

IISBN 978-0-9926678-0-1

*This book is dedicated to Harriet and George, who are,
and will always be, at the heart of my world:
the people I love above all others.
They have taught me so much and their faith has allowed
me to openly share aspects of our lives.*

Harriet

I taught Harriet throughout secondary school and have followed her progress in education and her career. Harriet always demonstrated a great maturity in all aspects of school life. She combined an excellent academic work ethic with a desire to train hard in sport. Her commitment and leadership were exemplary throughout her time in school and I know she took this forward to 6th Form College and University. Harriet's emotional and social skills meant she was able to be 'one of the crowd' whilst maintaining an excellent relationships with staff. Her positive attitude, willingness to tackle any challenge and push herself set her apart, as when she won the girl's prize in her year group in a Navy challenge and went on to win 'Best Girl' in the follow-up outward bound week. Harriet's academic grades and sporting achievements, both in and out of school, demonstrated her drive and focus. She was a pleasure to teach!

John Craven, Assistant Principal,
Bluecoat Academy, Nottingham

George

Throughout my time in professional sport, both as a player and a coach, I have had the pleasure of working with some great sportsmen, coaches and support staff. I have noticed, over the 25 years or so, that the one thing which defines how much a person can achieve is, in the main, their attitude. I have known George, Beverley's son, for several years now and on this front you cannot fault him. George gives himself the best chance to succeed in everything he does through hard work and application and a great self-awareness rarely seen in a young person. I am of the belief that this has been engendered from a very early age at home, through his relationships with family and friends and, latterly, in his time with the Academy at Nottinghamshire County Cricket Club. George embodies the equipped2succeed framework!

Chris Tolley, Academy Director,
Nottinghamshire County Cricket Club

Acknowledgements

I want to start by thanking my parents, Margaret and George, who have given me my roots and wings. Their disregard for the 9-to-5 mentality also modelled for me a 'get out what you put in' work ethic from a very young age.

A key person in our lives has been Karen (Simpson), who helped care for Harriet and George when they were young, resulting in a lifelong bond of deep friendship for us all.

There are so many people who have helped me develop the work shared in this book: those who have supported my relentless pursuit of improving ways to empower young people. Sarah has been with me through much of this journey, keeping me grounded with her challenge and keeping me going with her faith. Jeremy brought concepts to life for young people in energising, creative ways. Aaron and Errol deliver these concepts for young people in passionate, insightful ways. Andy has been constantly affirming. Gary Brazil's belief in the value of my work enabled me to work with young footballers, their coaches and parents at a time in football when mental skills were rarely recognised as something that could be integrated into young players' technical and tactical programmes.

Per-Olof Lindroth in Sweden, Dag Ofstad in Norway, Elizabetta Delle Donna in Italy, and Anca Colibaba in Romania have recognised my work and enabled me to embed the equipped2succeed framework into many of their development programmes across Europe. Nigel Akers, Richard Holloway, John Hudson and Paul Davies have recognised the value of developing enterprising, self-determining young people and I feel honoured by their faith and trust in me to develop programmes that have benefited thousands of young people.

My very good friend, Shelagh, has been there for me throughout the successes, trials and tribulations of life mentioned in this book. Sian has encouraged me with professional insight, and provided a retreat for me to write whenever I felt the need. Karen (Mellors) helps me in untold practical ways for which I am eternally grateful. I would also like to thank all those people who have taken precious time to read chapters for me – your feedback has been invaluable!

I would also like to acknowledge some of the places where this book has been written: in cafes where I got lost in writing, with accommodating staff who allowed me to sit for hours with a coffee, until my battery ran out or it was closing time: *The Little Deli* and *Le Mistral*, in Nottingham, *The Wild Poppy,* in Fremantle, *The Baths Café* in Brighton, Melbourne and *The Wilson*, in Hull.

I am indebted to Martin Fickling at Full Phat Design for listening, being patient with me and creating designs that just work. Laurie Bryant and Simon Wade at FAH Designs have been equally patient in the technical demands I have placed upon them to ensure all the downloads mentioned in this book are easily accessible on my website.

Jane Allcock has been the person I've trusted and relied upon above all others to help me realise this dream. Her amazing work ethic, thorough approach, proofing and editing brilliance, honest feedback and advice have been invaluable throughout the process. To work on a book with a friend whom I trust, professionally and personally, has been simply marvellous.

Finally, thank you to all those who have shared their life and work - in person, in writing and on-line - from whom I have learned and continue to learn.

As I was finishing this book, Nelson Mandela sadly passed on. His life and work has been a huge inspiration to me: as to many across the world. I quote him often: his vision, humility, wisdom, passion, clear thinking, focus, unparalleled positivity and ability to bring people together will continue to inspire for generations to come.

Contents

Why This Book? Why Now?

It's a thrill for me to be writing this introduction and an even bigger thrill to think of you reading it. Where do you start with an introduction?

My Motivation To Write This Book

I am passionate about learning and continuous self-improvement: to be the best we can be at whatever we want to succeed in. I am also passionate about removing the limits from our children's aspirations and enabling them to realise their potential. For over 30 years, in many and varied capacities, I have been pursuing ways to help young people achieve more. I have also spent the last 25 years in the most amazing relationships of my life, raising my own children, Harriet and George, to be all they can be. I am excited to share with you the insights I have gained, both from working with young people from varied backgrounds and communities, and from raising my own children.

I am passionate about empowering our children and young people to be 'rounded' individuals who are equipped to realise their potential. That has been the main focus in my work and with my children. I am driven to have the sort of education system where developing the core attitudes, thinking and behaviours to become self-determining individuals (where young people do not allow circumstance to limit their outlook or achievement), and to succeed personally, socially and economically in achieving goals, is as important as the other fundamentals. This is not only crucial for individual fulfilment, but also for society; how much better would our society be if more young people were in a positive, rather than negative, spiral? There are some people to whom these capabilities come naturally – they are driven and find ways to succeed, despite circumstances, environment and set-backs.

There are children raised in a way that develops some, or all, of these characteristics. There are children who go to schools that look to develop some, or all, of these characteristics. But they are not in the majority. I have sought to empower, enable and equip my children to develop these characteristics in all sorts of ways as we live our day-to-day lives, and from the examples I share in this book you'll realise it's underpinned our daily life; making conscious decisions about our attitudes, thinking and behaviours.

Making It Happen

I have been working on this book for years. Seeing my children as adults, living their own lives, thriving and pursuing their goals was definitely a catalyst to use what I've learned over many years of pursuing my passion for equipping young people to succeed. I'm confident that sharing what I have learned and developed can help parents and carers, doing their best for their children amongst the many demands they have. I believe that what I've learned can help young people realise their potential and achieve their life dreams, passions and goals. I'm also confident that the insights and tools in this book can help us enable our children, and the young people for whom we care, be all they can be.

What's in this book is grounded in vast experience and research: taking learning, knowledge and information from diverse disciplines and making it accessible, usable and helpful. I have my own longitudinal study: my children are now 25 and 21 and they have encouraged me to write this book for some time. They have taught me lots; our open relationship means they are very frank with their feedback and have been from a young age. Our debates, my parenting successes and mistakes, have been a constant learning process and I have their full permission to share some of our highlights and challenges.

Why Now?

Our world is uncertain, and constant economic, social and environmental imperatives mean we all need to be equipped to make the most of opportunities and handle challenges.

Over the past 50 years, old certainties have gone in terms of 'jobs for life' and being able to map out precisely what technical skills and knowledge we'll need for the future. More than ever, we need to be agile in our thinking and prepared to learn, unlearn, relearn as needs arise. We need to develop ourselves to make the most of changing environments and technological advancements. We also need agile, creative, enterprising, entrepreneurial minds that can help society address the challenges it faces economically, environmentally and socially. Changing our public bodies, large corporations and education systems is akin to turning the Titanic, but they all need to become more agile, creative, enterprising and entrepreneurial to avoid the failures of the past, and create a positive future. To do this, all of those bodies need individuals equipped with the attitudes, thinking and behaviours to realise those creative solutions, not to be happy with second best, and to be willing to challenge the 'that's how we've always done it' and '1001 reasons why not' brigades.

> **The one unchangeable certainty is**
> **that nothing is unchangeable or certain.**
> John F. Kennedy

The modern family is also very different from 50 years ago. The make-up of the modern family is different, with a far lower proportion of what was previously considered typical - Mum, Dad and 2.2 children, a car and a dog! When I had my son, a good friend came to visit me in hospital and said, *'With a daughter and a son, all you need now is a Volvo and a dog'*. (I changed my car for a Mini Cooper! Totally impractical but about as far away as I could get from typical! And we have never had a dog for other reasons – my life was so demanding that the thought of another living being to look after was a bridge too far, and my daughter's allergy to dogs helped me resist my son's pleas for one!)

As it turned out, we didn't last very long as that typical family unit and became, instead, the equally typical 'broken home' (although I really don't like that phrase), with my children's father starting a new family.

Like many other adults and children, we have lived in a different way to the majority of society 50 years ago. However, following the fight to keep my marriage together, and the natural grieving process - the upset and trauma - when it failed, I have not allowed myself to see our little unit as a negative, and it certainly has not prevented my children from thriving. Blaming children's failure to thrive and society's ills on changes in what constitutes 'family' helps no-one. Instead, we need to be focused on prevention rather than cure, and to look at what we can do to raise thriving children, equipped to take their place in the world, irrespective of circumstances. We, as parents, need to take responsibility for enabling our children to thrive and be all they can be. We also need our public bodies, social support systems and education systems to be clearly focused on creating an environment that empowers, enables and equips children and young people to thrive and develop the core capabilities, attitudes, thinking and behaviours to achieve.

One thing that heartens me is that, more than any other time since I started this work, I see people of all ages open to developing their thinking and examining what it really takes to succeed. People also seem, more than ever before, to recognise the power of the mind, and to realise that knowledge and technical ability can only take us so far.   No matter what any of us want to achieve, the equipped2succeed framework of attributes described in this book is essential to determine and realise personal, social and economic success.

A man who acquires the ability to take full possession of his own mind may take possession of anything else to which he is justly entitled.
Dale Carnegie

The Agony of Wasted Potential

One thing that really frustrates me is wasted talent and wasted potential. I see it constantly and have always been driven, both in my career and personally, to do something about it.

There are too many children and young people who have unrealised potential: who are not enabled by their environment and those around them to be all they can be. Some may be in a negative environment, and some in a loving, yet controlling, environment where they are narrowed or limited by the weight of other's expectations. In either environment, young people can get stuck on a pathway they don't want. Young people can develop the attitudes, thinking and behaviours that stop them succeeding; that stop them setting goals and pursuing their dreams; that paralyse them with fear and stop them taking a chance or having a go.

Some potential is easier to recognise. For example, academic, sporting or artistic potential is often easy to recognise, yet we still have too many examples of potential going unrecognised by the young person themselves, their family, community or school. Entrepreneurial talent, or talents for the future – those with ideas and skills that will be of value in the next phase of our societal or economic development - are more challenging to recognise and nurture. We maintain a cycle of unfulfilled potential unless we enable young people to try things, explore what they might be good at and find their passion; then provide an environment that enables them to flourish. Of course, passion comes into the equation, too. You can have all the genetic pre-disposition in the world to do something, but if that's not your passion, you are unlikely to do the work – the practice and learning - to pursue it and reap the rewards that brings (unless, of course, you have the sort of driven parents that tennis stars Andre Agassi and the Williams sisters had!).

This may be a good point to define what I mean by 'talent'. Having had numerous debates with friends and colleagues about the 'myth of talent' after reading Matthew Sayid's brilliant book, *Bounce: The Myth of Talent and the Power of Practice*, I mean by 'talent' a genetic pre-disposition for something. Many people have a genetic pre-disposition for something but don't 'do the work' to turn that into success, and there are those with less genetic pre-disposition who 'do the work' and succeed. 'Doing the work' means applying everything in this book - systematically developing yourself to be the best.

DOING THE WORK - Overcoming the paralysis of fear and unlocking potential.

Another key driver for me is that there are too many young people who have talent and passion, but who are frightened to pursue it: don't know how, or don't learn how, to unlock their power and potential. Those who never realise that 90% of success in anything is what happens between our ears, and that there are all sorts of things we need to do to make the most of our talents and passions – success doesn't just happen, and waiting to get lucky doesn't do it. It is not always the most talented that achieve the most, but those who have all the other attributes essential for success: those who decide what they want, decide what they're prepared to pay to achieve their goals, have a growth mindset, and go to work in relentless pursuit of their goals. That includes developing the attitudes and thinking essential for success.

All the knowledge, experience, hard work, practice, qualifications etc are only part of young people achieving and succeeding – being all they can be. To really achieve holistic success, they need to take control of their attitudes, thinking and behaviours and develop the generic capabilities and competencies essential for success in any field of endeavour and in life.

Many people think successful people are just lucky, just more talented, more driven or have special gifts etc. It is true that successful people in all fields of endeavour have something special, but that's not luck, it's the attitudes, thinking and behaviours described in this book. An article in Vogue Australia November 2011, *The Myth of Overnight Success* by Sarina Lewis, reinforces that, apart from a genetic pre-disposition for ballet, the young people succeeding in the elite environment of Australian ballet have got there through relentlessly 'doing the work' in all sorts of ways over many years. And that's the same in any other elite environment in the arts, business, engineering, sports, technology etc.

Opportunity is missed by most people because it is
dressed in overalls and looks like work.
Thomas Edison

If you read about successful people in any field, many overcome all sorts of obstacles and adversity and all demonstrate the characteristics described in this book. Many develop them by osmosis – learning from their environment, learning the lessons from negative and positive experiences, and from people who've achieved in their field. But these characteristics can also be learned and systematically developed. All it takes is the will to learn, grow and improve, the confidence to honestly self-reflect, and the discipline to continuously take the necessary action. I have seen tremendous achievements once young people have a goal, realise what they need to do to achieve it, and are given the tools and environment to develop.

Getting Away from the Excuse for Being Less than We Can Be

'That's just the way I am.'
'That's just the way he is.'
'That's just the way she is.'

Many people don't systematically critically reflect, or reflect and are too critical of themselves, or have an inflated view of themselves, and either think they can't change or don't want to change. We are not generally taught the power of positive self-reflection to grow and improve. Many people accept what others tell them about themselves and accept *'That's just the way I am'*. The teacher says, *'You'll not get any more than a C'*, and the young person fulfills that prophecy. Many people accept children and young people as, *'That's just the way he is'* or *'That's just the way she is'*. We all have personality traits, but much of the way we are is learned and can be unlearned. We can all change. We can all achieve. But we need the awareness, knowledge and tools to do so. Most of us have not been systematically taught to develop the attitudes, thinking and behaviours described in this book, or have had the opportunity to absorb them by cultural osmosis. The sooner we all recognise and enable our children and young people to develop these core attributes, the sooner they will be equipped to create and build their own positive futures in an ever-changing world.

Defining Success

Now, what do I mean by 'success'? That is explored in more detail in the *What is Success?* chapter, but in general terms, it is about achieving positive personal, social and economic goals and helping those around us to achieve their goals. Success is about achieving and making a contribution.

The key thing is to holistically make the most of life in all areas, and that comes from feeling we're living the positive life we're meant to lead, and determining our own positive future.

> *Success is NOT what you think it is...*
> *it is what you believe it is...*
> *and most never believe.*
> Doug Firebaugh

During the journey of creating the equipped2succeed framework and materials, it's become clear to me that it is within us all to choose our own future if we are empowered, enabled and equipped with the essential attitudes, thinking and behaviours to do so.

> *The quality of a successful person is to flow and not to freeze.*
> Ralph W. Emerson

I hope you enjoy reading **How Can We Equip our Children to Succeed?** and I truly hope it helps with the most important role we have, raising our children and young people to be all they can be. And finally – please remember that we all make mistakes in our parenting: caring for and teaching our children. The important thing is to acknowledge, apologise and move on:

> *Aim for success, not perfection. Never give up your right to be*
> *wrong, because then you will lose the ability to*
> *learn new things and move forward with your life.*
> *Remember that fear always lurks behind perfectionism.*
> *Confronting your fears and allowing yourself the right to be*
> *human can, paradoxically, make you a far happier and more*
> *productive person.*
> Dr. David M. Burns

Chapter One

Some Essential Stuff

In this chapter, I want to have a look at some essential 'stuff'. I use the word 'stuff' to mean the 'stuff of life': the fundamental core of things.

So, what do I mean by 'essential stuff'?

In order to enable and equip our children or the young people in our care, as the adult and parent in the relationship, (see *1) there are some attitudes, thinking and behaviours that are essential for us to reflect on, consistently practice, and constantly review. Let me start with some definitions of attitude, thinking and behaviour.

 Definitions

attitude:
- A feeling or opinion about something or someone, or a way of behaving that is caused by this;
- A settled way of thinking or feeling; typically reflected in a person's behaviour. A state of mind or a feeling;
- A position of the body or manner of carrying oneself; implying an action or mental state.

Phrases we commonly use regarding negative attitude:
'S/He has a very poor attitude towards authority.'
'S/He seems to have undergone a change in attitude recently, and has become much more unco-operative.'
'I don't like your attitude.'

'That boy / girl has a real attitude problem' (= behaves in a way that makes it difficult for other people to have a relationship with him / her or work with him / her).

It's often very difficult to change people's attitudes, and it's our attitudes that have enormous influence over our thinking, behaviour and performance. It's therefore vital that we positively enable our children to develop attitudes that equip them to succeed.

thinking
- The act or practice of one who thinks; thought.
- A way of reasoning: judgement:
  Characterized by thought or thoughtfulness;
- When you use your mind to consider something:
- Someone's ideas or opinions.

behaviour
- The way that someone behaves - the manner of behaving or conducting oneself.
- Actions and reactions in different circumstances.

We commonly use the word 'behaviour' in a negative context.
Phrases we often use:
    'Her/His behaviour is out of control.'
    'His/Her behaviour is so challenging.'
    'Her/His behaviour is often appalling.'
    'His/Her behaviour is very difficult.'
    'S/He is notorious for her/his bullying behavior.'
    'Her/His behaviour is inappropriate.'

Empowering, Enabling, Equipping - Essential 'Stuff'

If we are to empower, enable and equip our children with the attitudes, thinking and behaviours essential for success in all areas of life, there are a few things I view as part of the bedrock of our relationship with our children from which we can nurture them to thrive and succeed as they grow. The following essentials are a given when I talk about anything else in this book.

Accept we are human
and get things wrong

BALANCE AND JUDGEMENT

RECOGNISING INDIVIDUALITY AND UNIQUENESS

LOVE – THE UNCONDITIONAL, NO PRICE VARIETY

Do what we say we're going to do, when we say we're going to do it

Justifying ourselves
- being accountable
to our children

Openness

Challenge and Support
- getting that in balance

CHILDREN ARE LITTLE PEOPLE AND DESERVE THE SAME COURTESY AND REGARD WE GIVE TO OUR PEERS

UNCONDITIONAL POSITIVE REGARD

Model the attitudes, thinking and
behaviour we seek to develop
in our children

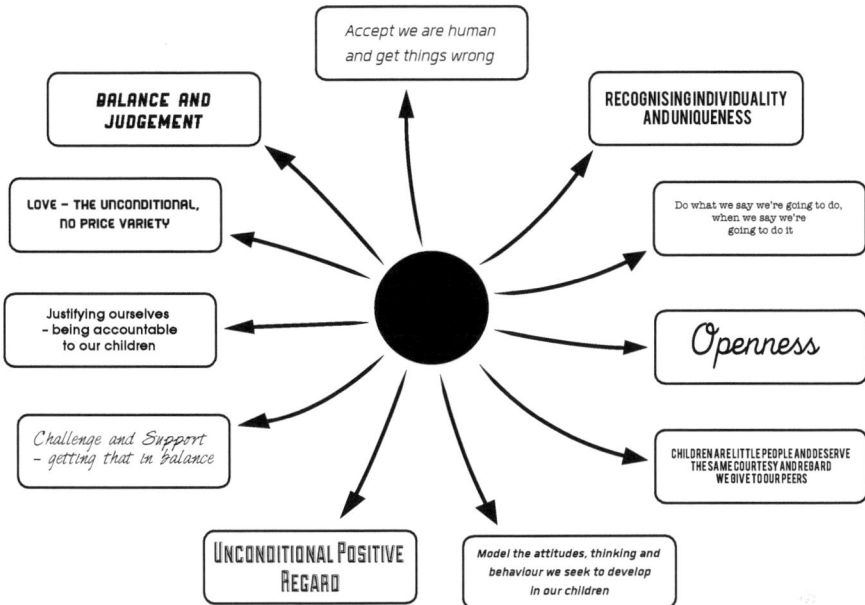

So what do I mean by all these?

Love – The Unconditional, No Price Variety;

Definition:

> The affinity experienced between people who are naturally able and willing to tune into one another's emotional, intellectual and physical states - and respond to them in a nurturing and stimulating way.

In short, we must ensure that our behaviour doesn't leave our children feeling that we'll only love them if they do certain things. Our love should always be unconditional and we should make it clear to our children that we will always love them, no matter what. This sort of love does not measure; it just gives. That doesn't mean we allow them to do what they want; that would certainly be irresponsible parenting. We just need to make sure that we challenge what they do, say and think, rather than them as people. What we're really saying is, 'I love you. However, that's unacceptable', or 'I love you. However, you could improve your performance by being a bit more organised with your study'. We have a totally different emotional relationship with our children than with anyone else, and need to be mindful of this when we're dealing with challenges.

When Harriet's father and I separated and divorced, she was very hurt, upset and angry. This came out in all sorts of ways over subsequent years, but at one point, when she was 12, we had a period of time with her seemingly focusing all her hurt and anger on me. She would be fine with everyone else, including being all sweetness and light with her dad. It reached a point one night, after George was in bed and I was, yet again, reduced to tears, when I asked her, 'Why are you constantly giving me all this grief?' That evening has stayed with me because of her immediate response, 'I know I can say whatever I like to you and you'll always be the same'. I know that when children and young people are emotionally troubled they tend to 'act out' where and with whom they feel most secure, so my response was, 'That is one of the best compliments you can pay me but I really have had enough!' It was a watershed moment, from which we found ways for Harriet to vent her hurt and anger in more appropriate ways, and build a more positive path forwards. I maintain that I had the potentially challenging teen years in a concentrated spell. The point is that Harriet was aware of my unconditional love, which allowed her to show her pain with me in a way that she rarely did with anyone else and, as a parent, you want to be that person for your children.

When working with the parents of sporting youngsters, I always emphasise that they have a different emotional relationship with their child than the coach, and therefore need to think very carefully about the feedback they give. I was doing a workshop with parents of boys in a football academy some years ago, and was emphasising the importance of finding something positive to say about your child's performance, even if they've had a poor match.

One mum said that as she brought her boy to practice 2 or 3 times a week, and went all over the country to watch him play, she had a right to say what she wanted. Before I could answer, a man on the front row stood up and faced the group. He said he was in a football academy as a teenager, and could still recall the sick feeling in his stomach when he got into the car after a poor match, waiting for his dad's critique. He went on to say that he would never do that to his son.

In *Chicken Soup for the Soul*, Jack Cranfield and Mark Victor Hansen share a true story that exemplifies the power of love. A mother lifts a car that her sons are trapped under to save their lives. There is no way that the woman was strong enough to lift the car under normal circumstances, but her mother's love gave her extraordinary strength when they were in danger.

Love is the most powerful emotion, and has tremendous power to enable us to achieve and experience good things; and it is the most powerful factor in us being able to nurture our children.

According to Virginia Satir:
> *We need 4 hugs a day for survival.*
> *We need 8 hugs a day for maintenance.*
> *We need 12 hugs a day for growth.*

However, those hugs need to be backed by **substance**: being there to provide care, strength and empowerment as well as hugs.

Unconditional Positive Regard

Unconditional positive regard is linked to unconditional love, but I feel it's worth mentioning separately. It is always crucial to demonstrate with our children, in our language and behaviour, unconditional positive regard. It is important in building our children's confidence and self-regard, whilst developing acceptable, appropriate behaviour. That doesn't mean that we don't challenge inappropriate attitudes, thinking and behaviour in our children, but we make sure our children are clear it's their behaviour we object to, not them. It's vital we separate the person from the behaviour.

For me, a concrete example of this is using the words 'good' and 'bad' in relation to behaviour. Both words are heavy with judgement. Would we ever seriously use the words 'good boy' or 'good girl' with our peers? No. That's because our peers would view it as patronizing and judgemental. The only time those words tend to seriously be used in adult relationships are in controlling, unhealthy relationships that are definitely not mutually affirming. However, somehow we think it's OK to use that language, with all the loaded judgement it implies, with our children! Using those phrases definitely implies we are judging our children as people. Secondly, they imply that our children's behaviour is about pleasing us rather than establishing behaviour that is more widely appropriate and acceptable.

When we are challenging our children, we need to separate the behaviour from the child and give our reasons. I always find asking questions is a good way of enabling children to realise that what they're saying or doing is inappropriate. It's also a good way of putting them in someone else's shoes, which is a good lesson in empathy.

When challenging inappropriate language' we may say things like:
'Where have you learnt that?'
'What do you think it means?'
'How do you think that makes people feel?'

And finally:

'Please don't use that language because I find it unacceptable and so do most of society. It may be used in the playground, but not in our, or anyone else's, home. People find it offensive and hurtful.' I realise this coaching approach can be a longer method of dealing with things when we're all time pressured, but I assure you, it pays off.

Recognise Individuality and Uniqueness

A recurring theme in this book is recognising and treating our children as individuals, and not treating them the same. They are unique individuals and need to be nurtured in a way appropriate to their needs. Of course, we need to be fair and not show bias in what we give or do for our children, but all that is balanced by what is appropriate to support and challenge them to be their best. I have personally experienced too many examples of parents being rigid about treating their children the same, when they needed to treat them quite differently to ensure they thrived equally; there are a few examples of this later in the book. We must not compare them unfavourably, rather acknowledge that we all have strengths and weaknesses and that one strength is not more valuable than the other. We must celebrate what each of our children is good at, and enable them to positively acknowledge the things they aren't good at. We must celebrate difference without attaching judgement to that.

For example, Harriet is fantastic when it comes to science and technology. She made the most amazing boat with a motor in school when she was 9. Her teacher waxed lyrical about her technological ability and, from a very young age, you could trust her to make an excellent piece of furniture from a flat-pack kit. Scientific data and analysis in her field fascinates and excites her and is one of the reasons she got a first class degree. English, on the other hand, is and always has been a challenge for her. You would not trust George with a flat-pack: absolutely no interest and you would be waiting a very long time for something approximating the picture on the box! However, one of George's great strengths is his linguistic ability. If you wanted someone to speak in public, or produce a piece of writing in a witty, intelligent style, he's your man. He's read avidly from a young age and has always enjoyed words, finding English a breeze at school. One of the few assignments he did in his brief foray with A-Levels was a piece for A-Level English in the style of Bill Bryson. It was quite brilliant. He also wrote and delivered a very appropriate, eloquent and moving eulogy at his Grandad's funeral at the age of 19.

Harriet needed a certain level of English to succeed in education, but also needed to feel it was not the most important thing in life. Sometimes, our education system places too much emphasis on the importance of the spelling test! I needed to boost her confidence by emphasising the things that she was good at and helping her address challenges in literacy, sufficient to get her to a level where she could focus on her interest in the science of sport. George used his linguistic ability to sail through much of compulsory school with little effort, and I accepted that he was not interested in academia or making things! He has been focused on continuously improving his performance in his field of endeavour from a very young age, and my role has been to empower, enable and equip him to do that, rather than expect him to follow a traditional educational route for someone with his academic ability.

The point is that we challenge and support our children in different ways according to their needs. We accept differences in our children: celebrate what they're good at and accept what challenges them without judgement. Challenge them to improve in areas that are vital to their future performance and success in life and their chosen fields of endeavour, like the attitudes, thinking and behaviours described in this book and those things specific to their field. In the *Learn All the Time* chapter, there is a lot more about being a learner, and in the *Developing Technical Ability* chapter, I explore the importance of developing out-of-the-ordinary expertise in their chosen field.

Balance and Judgement

One of the biggest challenges we have as parents is maintaining appropriate balance and judgement. However, we need to consistently exercise balance and judgement if we're to effectively empower, enable and equip our children to be all the can be. In this, I feel it's vital to constantly reflect and review: be learning parents, learning from our children, our peers, circumstances, from what goes well and what doesn't go so well. When I think of balance, I think of a pendulum. The pendulum always swings one way and then the other. If it stayed at either side or central all the time it wouldn't be helping us grow as people. The swing only helps us achieve balance if we are clear about what we're trying to achieve, so below are some examples of two ends of the pendulum spectrum.

Taking responsibility

enabling and allowing our children to take responsibility	V	abdicating our responsibility
making our children take too much responsibility	V	'nannying'; taking control, making decisions and doing everything for them

We need to gradually empower our children to take responsibility, whilst recognising that this does not mean abdicating our responsibility. We have a vital role, in providing the right environment and blend of guidance, coaching, modelling, challenge, support and nurturing to ensure our children are enabled and equipped to take responsibility.

Advocating for our children

advocating for our children	V	making excuses for them

Our children need to be able to rely on us to be there for them when they need us, but the moment we start making excuses for behaviour that does not enable them to succeed, we are failing them. I have sat in too many parents' evenings as a teacher and experienced parents belittling their child in front of me, or making excuses for their children, and too many parents evenings as a parent where I've needed to advocate for Harriet and George (and challenge George as well!). On that point, I always insisted Harriet and George came to parents' evenings with their father and I. As you'll read below, I believe openness is important.

Framework of acceptable behaviour

having a clear framework	V	not being rigid for the sake of it

I talk elsewhere in the book about rules; basically, children need to know where they are – know that if something is unacceptable on Monday, it is unacceptable on Tuesday, Wednesday, Thursday, Friday, Saturday and Sunday. They also need to see that things are reasonable, and rigidity for no good purpose just teaches them to be rigid (for no good reason), or means they waste too much energy waging war on your rigidity.

Negotiating around the line

being prepared to negotiate   V   knowing where the line is

Children learn so much from adults negotiating with them, but unless they do that within some sort of framework of values and acceptable behaviour, they are at sea far too early in life.

One of the most important judgements and balancing acts we need to make as parents - one of the most challenging - is knowing when to accept something in our child's attitude and behaviour and when to challenge, mould or seek to change it in some way. I do not believe it's acceptable to use 'S/he's just like that' or 'S/he's only young' as an excuse for unacceptable behaviour. I do not believe children should be stifled, but I do think it's our duty as their parents to challenge and support them from a very young age to think and behave in a way that will help their future progress, and which is socially, ethically and morally acceptable. That doesn't always mean being compliant!

Being prepared to listen to our children's views, question them to help them articulate their views better, challenge thinking and debate things is vital if we are to raise our children to think effectively for themselves. The major judgement I have of myself as a parent is not how my children behave when I'm there, but how they behave when I'm not there: how they think things through; how they organise themselves and their thinking; how they rise to challenges; how they motivate themselves; how they persist and are resilient without my presence. I judge myself on how they think for themselves and behave in a way that helps them realise their goals whilst being mindful of the needs of others.

Values
Values are like fingerprints. Nobody's are the same, but you leave 'em all over everything you do.
Elvis Presley

Values - the ideals, customs, institutions etc for which we have an effective regard. These values may be positive, as cleanliness, freedom, or education, or negative, as cruelty, crime, or blasphemy.

Principles - a personal or specific basis of conduct; according to personal rules for right conduct; as a matter of moral principle.

How do we help our children to develop positive, ethical, robust values and lead a principled life?

Values are important because they are the foundation upon which we make important decisions in our lives: with whom we are friends, how we treat people, how we view the world etc. Our attitudes, thinking and behaviour, our aspirations and expectations, are all shaped in some way or other by our values. They are established and develop as we grow, and those we are closest to in our early lives have a major impact.

They are the things that are important to us, the essence of what we believe in. Values can come in all shapes and sizes – *love, calmness, faith, personal growth, making a difference, courage, honesty, confidence, financial security, financial independence, self-determination, friendship, making a contribution, determination, integrity, respect for others' heritage, culture and individuality, caring* – the list goes on.

We all need to decide what values or principles are most important for us to provide a positive framework for our children. For most of us, this framework is not a specific, conscious decision that we write down when they are born, but rather an unwritten set of values that emerges and develops as they grow. Here are a few values that I view as important:

- Valuing and being 'there' for family and friends.
- Treating others with respect and valuing others.
- Challenging inequality and prejudice.
- Integrity.
- Viewing the world in awe and wonder and taking delight in experiences.

- Doing the things you choose to do to the best of your ability, and always seeking to improve.
- Focusing your time and energy on things that are important to you, such as family, friends and pursuing your goals, and being pragmatic about the things you need to do – such as school subjects you don't enjoy and chores.
- Being open-minded.
- Being the change you want to see in yourself – your success is down to you and no one else (to paraphrase Mahatma Gandhi's *Be the change you want to see in the world*).
- Contributing.
- Being open and honest (but not at the expense of hurting people).
- Believing that you can be, do or have anything if you're prepared to do the work.

I think there are some key elements to establishing values that enable us to determine our own positive future within society, and to contribute in meaningful ways in our community, be that our family community, the local community, our community of interest, wider community, or specific field of endeavour. The following is a starting point for you in re-defining your values and considering the values you seek to develop in your children.

- The qualities you think are important in people - those you want to develop in yourself and your children, the sort of person you want to be, and the qualities you admire in other people:

  ....
  ....
  ....
  ....

- The things you think it's important to achieve for yourself and for others:

  ....
  ....
  ....
  ....

- The things you believe in:

  ....
  ....
  ....
  ....

- The things that are important to you:

  ....
  ....
  ....
  ....

Knowing the Difference between Right and Wrong

I need to mention the whole right and wrong debate, as many people will have that as their most important value. I have been very influenced in my view on this by a play I studied at A-Level, *Major Barbara* by George Bernard Shaw. Andrew Undershaft is talking to his estranged son, Stephen:

'Stephen: I know the difference between right and wrong.

Andrew: [*hugely amused*] You don't say so! What! No capacity for business, no knowledge of law, no sympathy with art, no pretension of philosophy; only a simple knowledge of the secret that has puzzled all the philosophers, baffled all the lawyers, muddled all the men of business, and ruined most of the artists: the secret of right and wrong. Why man, you're a genius, a master of masters, a god! At twenty-four, too!'

What he is saying is that the difference between right and wrong is a matter of interpretation, as is what we believe to be acceptable and unacceptable behaviour. Some follow the commandments of their religion, most of which are basic 'rights and wrongs' that we all accept. However, we have seen, in history and currently, where a particular interpretation of religious doctrine has led to persecution, violence and loss of basic human rights. There are some basic human rights that, for me, are a given, but can be summed up as caring for each other and doing nothing to harm others, unless it is to stop to ourselves and others being harmed.

Obviously, what is most important to me is valuing and empowering our children and doing everything we can to ensure all children have basic human rights; to be safe, have enough to eat, education and self-determination. This, of course, is also the case for adults, but children are more reliant on us to advocate and 'fight' for them.

Caring for our family and friends and being there for them when they need us is important in a civilised society, but we always need to balance our capacity to do that with earning a living. Earning my own living has always been very important to me, and a principle that I have endeavoured to pass on to my children. Beyond that, there are many things that are a matter of context and, in terms of the way we treat others, are summed up by treating everyone we meet with respect and value, and challenging attitudes and behaviour that does not respect and value others.

There are many things in this box of knowing right from wrong that some would view as open to interpretation. I come at this from the perspective of the daughter of a mother who certainly believes she knows the difference between right and wrong, and a father who is prepared to debate.

Do What You Say You're Going To Do, When You Say You're Going To Do It!

We all know how vital this is in relationships with peers, partners, colleagues, customers etc. It is even more important with our children. I remember, as a child, my parents saying we might 'go for a ride later'. That meant a ride round the Peak District in Derbyshire, and possibly stopping at a pub and having a glass of pop and packet of crisps in the playground or in the car. (My mother would never dream of going into the pub and leaving us outside. In fact, I can't remember her ever going into a pub.) Now, for a gregarious child living in a small village where the social highlight was Sunday School or Church on Sunday, this sort of outing was significant. I can still feel the disappointment if it didn't happen. There are always times we need to change plans, and that's a part of life we need to ensure our children are prepared for.

However, we need to give the same sort of priority to doing what we say we're going to do with our children as we do in our working and social life with our peers. I still remember how disappointed Harriet was when we didn't go to see *Titanic* at the cinema when I had promised her that she and I would go together. And she still remembers! I console myself with the fact that she wouldn't have remembered this one thing if letting her down had been a common theme in her upbringing.

Challenge and Support – Getting That In Balance

This is one of the most challenging things, but it's vital when we're seeking to empower, enable and equip our children that we constantly seek to balance our challenge and support to help them grow in their ability to realise their potential. Generally, we learn most of the attributes in the equipped2succeed framework from experiential learning rather than teaching, as such. That means giving our children opportunities to learn them and consistently re-enforce them in our behaviour. We cannot teach someone to take responsibility without giving them opportunities to take responsibility. That means challenging and supporting our children to take responsibility for themselves, and ensuring that we behave responsibly. We cannot teach positive thinking without consistently challenging and supporting our children to use positive language and have a positive attitude, and modelling positivity ourselves.

Accept We are Human and Get Things Wrong

The important thing is to acknowledge when we fail (without beating ourselves up about it), apologise and move on. That takes courage and confidence. Some people wrongly see apologising as a weakness, especially adults with children. On the contrary, it shows tremendous strength to say sorry, and children and young people appreciate it so much as they are generally unused to adults admitting their mistakes and apologising. Being prepared to admit when you're wrong and apologise is very valuable in building and maintaining good relationships, and authentic apology without shame is a valuable lesson for our children. However, it is definitely one of those things that we need to model.

It's also important for our children to see that people are human and can get things wrong, as they will face that throughout life in themselves and others. It's vital that they don't see getting things wrong as failure and let it undermine their confidence and self-regard, but rather see it as a learning opportunity. And we need to model that, too!

There is also a whole world of difference between being constantly apologetic - which indicates low self-regard - and / or thinking that, as long as we apologise it's OK to keep messing up. I mean a genuine apology: having the confidence to acknowledge, apologise and move on when we make a mistake, and doing everything we can not to make that same mistake again. We need to be learners and try to ensure that we don't keep making the same mistakes, as that then renders our apology of little value.

Getting things wrong once or twice is forgivable.
Repeatedly getting the same things wrong makes our apologies worthless and teaches our children two things.

> Firstly, that it's OK to behave inappropriately as long as we say sorry afterwards.
> Secondly, that it's OK not to learn.

Neither of these are helpful for our children.
I'm just like that is usually an excuse for inappropriate, unhelpful behaviour and habits that we choose not to do anything about.

Model the Attitudes, Thinking and Behaviours we Seek to Develop in Our Children.

Yes – we need to do it too!

What we really want is for our children to take on board our positive traits and not our negative ones. However, it doesn't work like that until they get older and, hopefully, start to be more discerning in what behaviours they choose to emulate.

Openness

I believe it's important to have an open, honest relationship with our children where we can discuss anything. I abhor hypocrisy and 'sweeping things under the carpet' that may be controversial. Our children are only able to deal with things, their feelings and challenges in life, if they can openly acknowledge them: and they feel much more supported if they can openly discuss them. This isn't easy for many people, and all three of us have found open, honest feedback - or sharing our feelings - challenging on occasions. However, being able to articulate and discuss our feelings is crucial if we're going to form positive relationships, be assertive and effectively make the most of our experiences in life, even when that's painful.

Children deserve the same courtesy and regard we give to our peers

I have always been angered at the lack of respect for children, and some general thinking that we don't need to behave as well with little people as we do with adults. The sort of rudeness I have seen from adults towards children, in many and varied environments - from supermarkets to schools - has always astounded me. All too often we behave with children in a way that we wouldn't dream of behaving with our peers. This ranges from smacking children who are 'naughty' in a supermarket when they are just being naturally curious or are bored and haven't yet learned how to manage themselves appropriately, to belittling them publically in the name of 'discipline'. Telling our children to say 'thank you' in a loud, obvious way (often when they've already said thank you) is more about us showing others that we're doing our job than teaching our children. Is it not ludicrous and illogical to hit a child who has hit another child to teach them not to hit? Of course we need to challenge inappropriate behaviour, but we need to teach our children to behave acceptably and appropriately by teaching, coaching and modelling the behaviour we seek to develop. Does hitting children do this?

I have seen many incidents that have escalated when an adult is rude to a young person; the young person takes offence and is rude back, so the adult then takes offence and the whole thing escalates. We are the adults and we need to be mindful that children and young people are learning, and they need to learn from us: reflecting the behaviour they experience in their behaviour, and reflecting the way they are treated in the way they treat others.

We need to model the behaviour we want to see in our children, and there is no more succinct or powerful way of putting that than in this poem:

Children Learn What They Live
Dorothy Law Nolte

If children live with criticism, they learn to condemn.
If children live with hostility, they learn to fight.
If children live with fear, they learn to be apprehensive.
If children live with pity, they learn to feel sorry for themselves.
If children live with ridicule, they learn to feel shy.
If children live with jealousy, they learn to feel envy.
If children live with shame, they learn to feel guilty.
If children live with encouragement, they learn confidence.
If children live with tolerance, they learn patience.
If children live with praise, they learn appreciation.
If children live with acceptance, they learn to love.
If children live with approval, they learn to like themselves.
If children live with recognition, they learn it is good to have a goal.
If children live with sharing, they learn generosity.
If children live with honesty, they learn truthfulness.
If children live with fairness, they learn justice.
If children live with kindness and consideration, they learn respect.
If children live with security, they learn to have faith in themselves and in those about them.
If children live with friendliness, they learn the world is a nice place in which to live.

Let's enable our children to live what they learn in the positive, empowering environment we create for them.

*1 I use the expression, 'adult in the relationship', as too often I hear parents, teachers and coaches behaving as a child. In fact, we can all act as children on occasions, especially in emotionally charged situations. By that I mean those sorts of irrational outbursts reminiscent of the toddler who can't get his or her own way, wrapped up in our own issues and unable to step back and look at things rationally. This behaviour can include not listening or really hearing what our children say.

Chapter Two

What is Success?

Everyone has inside him/herself a piece of good news!
The good news is that you really don't know how
great you can be, how much you can love, what
you can accomplish, and what your potential is!
Anne Frank

This chapter is about what it *is* to succeed, rather than what it takes to succeed.

It's a big question, and one too few of us ask ourselves and systematically answer. We talk about success. We write about success. Success is often linked with celebrity, academic grades, winning, how far we get up the career ladder and money. All of those are valid in their own way, but it's vital that we define what success means to us in a holistic way, in all areas of our life. So, what do we really mean by success? Success must have specific criteria or we wouldn't be able to acknowledge people and their achievements, and ourselves and our achievements, as successful. And what do we envisage as success for our children and those young people we care for?

There are some general 'criteria' you can use as a starting point for your own reflection and debate with others about aspects of success. I hope this is also a starting point for thinking about how we may enable our children to develop their own success criteria, guided by the values they will develop as they grow.

My 'wheel of life' success criteria includes:

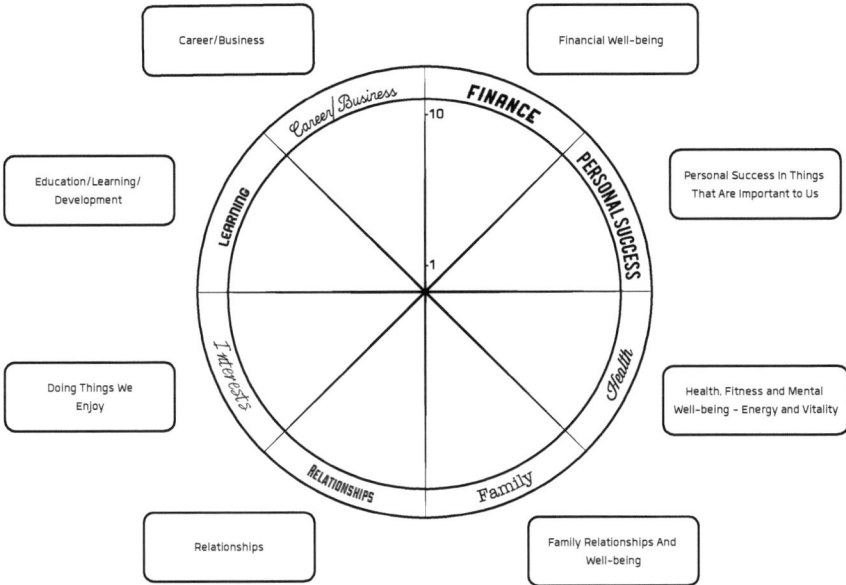

This is where you start to reflect on your success criteria.

The Wheel of Life – What Does Success Mean To YOU?

Financial Well-being

Enough money to live the life you choose? But is it that straight forward? (I may add - enough money 'that you have earned from your own endeavour'?) Certainly, for me, having 'financial literacy' comes into this, which is explored in the *Develop Technical Ability* chapter. (If we think this isn't important – we need to think of our perspective. I've met many people in the workshops I've led who say money isn't important. They are usually comfortably off, financially, and often have secure jobs!

You only need not to be able to feed your family or buy school clothes, or take your children on a visit or a holiday, or have experienced big financial failure(s), to reinforce the importance of financial well-being!) Of course, what financial well-being looks like is different for us all, and below I want you to consider what it means for you.

....

....

....

....

Family Relationships and Well-being

For me, this includes, for adults and children, being safe and secure, being nurtured, feeling loved and cared for, feeling love and care for our family, getting on well with our close family, being able to be open and honest. What does this mean for you?

....

....

....

....

Personal Success

This includes feeling that you're living the life you're meant to live – being, doing, having what is important to you. Continuously developing yourself. Contributing to your family, your community and beyond in meaningful ways. How do you perceive personal success?

....

....

....

....

Health and Mental Well-being – Fitness, Energy and Vitality

This is an area that I feel needs consistent focus and reflection, as most of us want to be healthy and fit, but sometimes that is sacrificed when other demands take over. In terms of diet, I think few of us have much excuse for not eating healthily, given the plethora of advice that's around.

Certainly, for me, balancing work and caring for my children and enabling them to pursue their interests has meant my fitness regime has not been ideal. Sometimes, I should have been stricter about taking some time out of something for my exercise regime, especially when managing the negative effects of stress. This is why I link health with mental well-being. I am constantly seeking the right diet, exercise regime and balance for me to ensure I have the health, energy and vitality to do everything I want to do for me and my family. Having our health and energy and feeling vital is a crucial part of enabling us to pursue our goals and enabling us to do everything we can to empower, enable and equip our children to pursue theirs. So, where are you with health, fitness and mental well-being?

....
....
....
....

Relationships

For me, this includes knowing myself, being able to manage myself effectively with others and all that entails, including standing up for myself and what I feel is important. It means being able to 'tune-in' to others and respond appropriately in personal, social and professional circumstances. It also includes feeling valued and valuing others. What are your success criteria when it comes to relationships?

....
....
....
....

Education / Learning / Development

I love learning! Having a growth mind-set, achieving, learning and training in my specialist areas is part of the continuous improvement that I value so highly. Formal and informal learning, training and study enable us to go on and earn our living doing work we enjoy, work we are passionate about, achieving in our chosen fields of endeavour, so we feel we're where we're meant to be.

....

....
....
....

We can add specific academic and career success criteria in our fields of endeavour.

NB. Qualifications success – I believe that we need to help our children focus and gain the qualifications and grades they need for their chosen pathway. The crucial thing is to make sure that young people are pursuing RELEVANT qualifications, those in areas they want to do and are interested in and / or are essential for them to achieve their future goals and possibly industry standard qualifications as well as academic qualifications.

Career / Business

Economic, personal and family well-being often come together when we're in a career, business or endeavour which brings the personal rewards that contribute to our happiness and well-being, and the financial rewards that enable us to support our family. I'm living one of my professional and personal goals and passions in writing this book. What are your career / business success criteria?

....
....
....
....

Pursuing Interests

We all have things that are important to us; that we enjoy for their own sake or as part of our personal ambition. These can develop and change with age and experience. I didn't like writing when I was younger, as I didn't think I was any good at it - my spelling was poor and it took me a long time to translate my thinking into writing. I was also a doer! Finding my passion and pursuing it has lead to me wanting to write and loving writing. Does this come in the interest or career section? Both, with me! I have an eclectic mix of interests beyond work, the major ones being sports – watching and playing. It's important that we pursue our interests and show our children the joy of being involved in something with like-minded people. What do you love to do?

....
....
....
....

For those who succeed in their field of endeavor there is almost always a cross-over from their interests to the way they earn a living, and their personal passions turn into career and business interests, for example:

Musical success – selling enough tracks and enough tickets to be recognised - able to earn a living from music - achieve financial success and artistic freedom.

Sporting success – winning medals, trophies, representing club, city, county, country - able to earn a living from sport.

We move to specific, individual success criteria in the *Set Goals* chapter, because general success criteria, desires or goals don't work on their own in terms of realising the results we're seeking. We have to be very specific about what we want to achieve and systematically align our actions to achieve those results.

We could no doubt debate this for hours, and I have done with lots of people, but the bottom line is that each individual needs to decide what success means to them. And we need to empower, enable and equip our children and young people to define what success means for them. Once you know what you want to achieve:

The will to win, the desire to succeed, the urge to reach your full potential... these are the keys that will unlock the door to personal excellence.
Confucious

How do we enable our children and young people to define success for themselves and develop the aspirations to succeed?

Some young people know what they want to do with their lives and others don't. In my view, as the adult in this relationship, as parents, carers, teachers, youth workers etc, we have a duty to guide and coach, but not to control children and young people's dreams and aspirations. We have a duty to enable young people to develop a robust value system that includes valuing themselves, their thoughts, their interests and their talents. Our individual value system and our view of the world is influenced by the people around us: our environment and our experiences. For young people, this is predominantly their family and extended family, friends, school and communities of interest in which they are involved, whether that be sports, arts, church groups etc.

As children grow up, they are influenced more and more by the world outside their home, and by their friends, friends' parents, teachers, and others they meet and interact with in the outside world. Young children learn from their parents, and they are influenced by their genetic makeup, which influences their personality type, e.g. shy, outgoing, smart, athletic, or neurotic (Harris, 2002).

Peer influence on behaviour gradually becomes more dominant as our children grow. Harris (1998, 2002) and Rowe (1994) maintained that peer groups have an even stronger influence than that of parents, although that extreme position has been refuted by other researchers (Berk, 2005). It is therefore up to us to help our children develop positive values that will guide them through life when they are young, and consistently reinforce those 'like a broken record' as they grow.

> ***Men (and women) are born to succeed not fail.***
> Henry David Thoreau

How do we know where we are now and establish our success baseline? How do we measure success?

How do we measure success? There are different measurements in different contexts – home, learning, interests, career and business. Which measures will you apply in your success criteria?

There are many *wheels of life* in personal development books. They are a simple tool for us to check where we think we are, how we feel about our current reality, and to start to define success for ourselves in the main areas of our life.

There are a few age appropriate *Wheel of Life* templates on the equipped2succeed section of my website that are a good starting point for reflection for ourselves and with our children.

 ACTION

Defining Success

Before we can start working with our children and young people on what success means to them, we need to be clear about what it means to us. You've hopefully started that earlier in this chapter, but here are some more prompts and ideas to enable you to focus on what success means to you:

- Work out a definition of success for yourself – write it in large, colourful print to go somewhere where you will see it daily, such as inside your wardrobe door.

- Use a *Wheel of Life* template – the one on my website or one with your own headings, and decide where you are now and where you want to get to in all areas that are important to you.

- Use appropriate *Wheel of Life* style questions to help your children determine their success criteria. Make sure your questions are very open to allow your children's imagination to flow. Their ideas may be focused and they may pursue them from a young age or they may change frequently. It's our role to help them frame their thinking, not impose ours, beyond 'achieving nothing is not an option', of course.

- Identify a few successful people – some people that everyone knows of and some local people, and list the characteristics that you think have made them successful.

- Identify a successful person in the field you're interested in and find out about them and their attitudes, thinking and behaviours that have enabled them to succeed.

- Identify books, articles, video clips etc that are inspiring about successful people to build up a library of success.

- Encourage your children to read, research online, watch programmes and videos of people who have succeeded in an area in which they are interested.

The difference between a successful person and others is not a lack of strength, not a lack of knowledge, but rather a lack of will.
Vincent Lombardi

Chapter Three

ACTION - DOING THE WORK

Life's not about expecting, hoping and wishing,
it's about doing, being and becoming.
It's about the choices you've just made, and
the ones you're about to make,
it's about the things you choose to say - today.
It's about what you're gonna do after you finish reading this.
Mike Dooley

We all respond differently to the things we read. I really hope that you find something of value in this book, and I hope that you are able to take something away to support you in your role as a parent. But, as with anything we learn, it's only of value if we use it. Developing new ways of thinking about things, responding differently to situations and creating new habits, takes time and practice. The adage 'use it or lose it' comes to mind. Throughout each chapter, I pose questions designed to help the reader reflect on the equipped2succeed framework - as individuals and as parents. In addition, at the end of each chapter, there is a brief ACTION section with some suggestions and tools for reflection.

The main purpose of focusing on action and doing the work is to emphasise that, no matter what else we give our children, it is essential that we enable them to understand that you get out of something what you put in to it: to enable our children to develop an out-of-the-ordinary work ethic. In reading an interview with Julia Roberts (when talking about her latest film, *August: Osage County*), I was interested in her observation about Meryl Streep, '.... *I've never seen anybody work harder than she does. She doesn't just snap her fingers and be a genius, she really is the hardest working*

45

girl in the room, and I was so grateful to see that up close'.

Whatever we want to achieve, there are few short cuts and there is no replacement for dedicated, focused work.

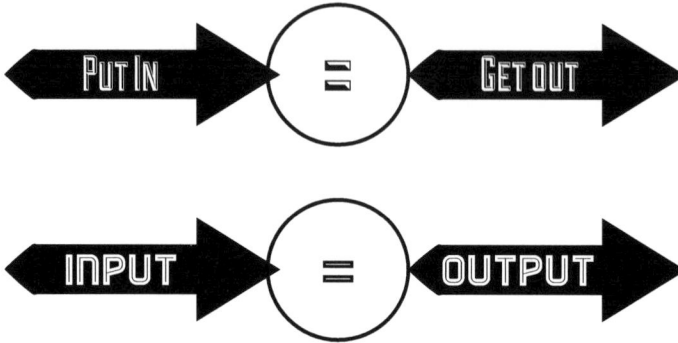

PUT IN = GET OUT

INPUT = OUTPUT

My experience of working with young people is that it is very important to develop their understanding of this equation - you get out what you put in - from a young age. Once our children reach their teenage years it is progressively more difficult for them to learn this and embed it within their attitudes, thinking and behaviour. A good example is the importance of breakfast: you need to put fuel in your tank if you want to perform at your best, whether that's at school, in sports, etc. Harriet clearly demonstrated her understanding of the equation in her approach to examinations from GCSE onwards. She looked at the criteria of what she needed to do to get the grade she wanted and did just enough to achieve that. This not only ensured that she achieved the grades that she wanted, it also meant that she maintained balance, keeping up her sports and other activities alongside study. George has consistently demonstrated this in his work ethic in sport, where he's consistently been first to arrive at training and the last to leave, and has done whatever it takes to continuously improve.

And where I excel is ridiculous, sickening, work ethic.
You know, while the other guy's sleeping? I'm working.
Will Smith

Reflection

One of the suggestions in most ACTION sections at the end of each chapter is to keep some sort of reflective diary.

It is always valuable to reflect, on our own and with others. Writing something down, however brief, helps us structure our reflection and have focused discussions with others. I realise this may be a challenge with our children and we have to be creative to find ways to engage them in reflective activities. One of the ways we can enable our children to reflect is appropriate questioning in a coaching style, such as:

'How are you feeling about ....?'

'How do you think that went?'

'What did you learn from that?'

'How can you apply what you've learned in other things or in the future?'

Timing and balance is all-important. We need to 'tune in' to our children's emotional state and know when to ask questions, when to just be quiet whilst they process challenges for themselves, and when to offer supportive words. We also know when deflection is avoiding an issue and they need a few challenging questions as a prompt to addressing challenges. Challenging to the right degree, at the right time, is challenging, and something we need to reflect on to keep improving our ability to enable and equip our children to develop the attitudes, thinking and behaviours in the equipped2succeed framework.

The work for us as parents is to model that behaviour. Our children need to experience us growing, developing and working in a focused, deliberate way for what's important to us, and what we want to achieve. This applies equally to our behaviour with our children, actively listening to them, even when we're busy, ensuring we focus on the positive with them, even when we're tired and stressed. Our children need to see us striving to improve in whatever way necessary in order to develop the work ethic and 'no excuse' culture for success.

To help the reader get to the bits in which they are most interested, these icons are used in each chapter:

Definitions

Underpinning knowledge or information

Action

From the heart – personal experience

In order to help you use and follow up what's in this book, there is an equipped2succeed downloads section on my website with:

- Activities and refection tools.
- Tools on the equipped2succeed section of my website that provide further information about certain topics.
- Bibliography of books and articles for further reading.
- Links to interesting on-line information, presentations and short films.

Go to **beverleyburton.com** and
click on the equipped2succeed downloads tab.

It had long since come to my attention that people of accomplishment rarely sat back and let things happen to them. They went out and happened to things.
Leonardo da Vinci

Chapter Four

What Are the Attitudes, Thinking and Behaviours of Successful People?

Developing the equipped2succeed Framework

The work behind this book has been developed over many years, informing and informed by work with young people and adults in a wide variety of contexts. I have always been passionate about developing whole people and even as a new teacher I went way beyond teaching subjects to find ways to raise aspirations and develop young people's thinking, attitudes and behaviours to believe in themselves and aim high. I chose *no limits* as the name for the company I had as a counter balance to the endemic culture of people putting limitations on themselves and those around them – in families, classrooms, sports, communities, work, public and private organisations – everywhere.

Fascinated by what it takes to succeed in any field of endeavour, I have studied people who achieve success, both in their specialist fields and holistically; informing the workshops and programmes that I have created. This has also informed the journey of raising my own children. As parents, the equipped2succed framework is all about identifying and developing the areas that are essential if we are to truly equip our children to lead happy, fulfilled personal, social and working lives.

Although I'm continuously learning, I have read enough, seen enough and experienced enough to know that success in anything demands that people develop certain characteristics or attributes.

take
responsibility

take responsibility for your
thoughts - actions - future

be passionate

find your passions, attach
powerful emotions to your goals
– be enthusiastic

DEVELOP
TECHNICAL ABILITY

DO THE WORK
10,000 hours rule
Practice C.A.N.I.

be persistent

work hard - stay resilient in the
face of adversity - stay **focused
on achieving your goals**

equipped
succeed 2

framework

MANAGE
RELATIONSHIPS

develop the skills to **manage
yourself effectively and get on
well with people**

manage stress

achieve peak performance
maximise positive stress
minimise anxiety

BE POSITIVE

remain relentlessly positive in thinking, language and behaviour

believe in yourself

build your self-regard & self-belief – **believe in yourself and what you can achieve**

The attitudes, thinking and behaviours it takes to succeed .... in anything!

achieve

succeed

be all you can be

© Developed by Beverley Burton

SET GOALS

CREATE YOUR OWN FUTURE
set goals – plan your steps to achieve them

DEVELOP YOUR WINNING BRAIN

use your brain power
unlock your potential and develop a winning mentality

MAXIMISE ENERGY

nrg = DEAR
Diet + Exercise + Attitude + Rest

always learn

be a learner
(learn from everything) expand your comfort zones

Some people are born with the attributes in the equipped2succeed framework and hone them, some learn them along the way, but they are common to success in any field of endeavour. Everything in this book has been informed by, and developed from, practice. Delivering workshops to help participants of all ages understand and develop the attributes in this book has simultaneously enabled me to refine my thinking and 'translate' concepts into something more accessible and useable, and to create the contextual links essential for making things relevant and real for people. This book has not been written from the findings of extensive academic research on my part. Academic research has value and has informed my thinking and what I share in this book. But science and its findings need to be mixed with the stuff of life. I have learned to value my experience, intuition and passion, and when I come across something I need to know more about, I ask, read and find out. There are references to many people and books that have helped my journey of discovery, and I thank each and every one.

My passion for learning has always been there, by all accounts from when I was very young – asking far too many questions for the comfort of the adults around me. I don't just mean academic learning – although I have always valued that – but experiential, coincidental learning that we generally don't value sufficiently. I want us all to be learning individuals within learning families, communities and organisations so that we can grow without artificial barriers. The equipped2succeed framework and this book is about how we can improve our capacity to enable our children to fulfil their potential.

I'm sure you will read this and think about other characteristics you would have included. For example, determination isn't a separate chapter because I believe determination and focus come from having goals that we are passionate about. Successful people are not determined per se, but determined in the things that are their focus and priorities.   All of the attributes in the equipped2succeed framework are inter-linked and inter-dependent: forming a development model that supports us to continuously improve.

Chapter Five

Take Responsibility

 Definitions

take:
- to get into one's hold or possession by voluntary action;
- to hold, grasp, grip.

responsibility:
- the state or fact of being responsible, answerable, or accountable for something within one's power, control, or management, an instance of being responsible;
- a particular burden of obligation upon one who is responsible;
- a person or thing for which one is responsible;
- reliability or dependability.

Take Responsibility – Thoughts, Actions, Future

The best place to find helping hands is at the end of your own arms.
Confucious

Those people who achieve success in any form take 100% responsibility for the things they can control in their lives – their thoughts, their actions, their goals and their future.

It is not what happens to us, but rather how we **respond** to circumstances that makes the difference. Those people who take responsibility do not allow circumstances to define them and do not use negative events or influences as an excuse for not realising their potential. Taking responsibility is the difference between those who set goals and achieve them, and those who don't.

Successful individuals:

- *take responsibility for their thoughts*

- *take responsibility for their attitudes and feelings*

- *take responsibility for their actions*

- *think 'choose to', rather than 'have to'*

- *accept responsibility for their own performance and results – positive or negative – in all areas of life - in study, in work, career, business, the quality of relationships, finance, health and well-being, fitness, income, sports etc.*

- *acknowledge and praise the contribution others make to their performance*

- *use positive and negative experiences for their own learning and growth*

> Enabling our children to take responsibility
> does not mean not accepting,
> 'he / she's just like that',
> but equipping them to take responsibility

To be successful, we need to refrain from blaming and complaining and assume total responsibility for our lives. We have to stop making excuses and take responsibility for successes and failures. People who take responsibility for what they can control create success. Those who have a habit of making excuses and do not take responsibility for what they can control rarely achieve their potential.

We need to empower, enable and equip our children
to take responsibility for their thoughts, their actions and
creating their own positive future.

Our Role As Parents

As parents, it is an essential part of our role to equip our children to take responsibility for themselves in adult life: gradually increasing the level of responsibility we expect of them as they grow. Sometimes, this is hard work - continuously needing to enforce and re-enforce expectations. Sometimes, it is so much easier to do it ourselves than get our children to take responsibility and do whatever it is that's expected of them. For example, from a relatively young age I have only washed the clothes that are in the linen bin: not trailing round bedrooms, scooping up discarded clothes. This was a two-sided commitment; if clothes were in the linen bin, my children expected them to be washed for when they needed them. I also stopped ironing their clothes, for the most part, from when they went to secondary school. By the time they were both 16, I expected them to take responsibility for ensuring any clothes they needed for a certain time were washed and ready. My children knew this was different to many of their friends, but they also recognised that I needed them to step up and take responsibility if I was going to provide for them, financially and in every other way, eg ensuring I managed my work to get them to activities, training, athletics meets, football and cricket matches.

In broader terms, I have endeavoured to empower, enable and equip my children to take responsibility: to think for themselves and be independent. I realise this can be uncomfortable for some parents, as we can't, on the one hand, create an environment that promotes independence, self-reliance and responsibility and, on the other, control what our children do. In this, I do not mean abdicating our role as parents to create a framework of expected behaviour and values, but allowing our children to make choices and feel in control of their own futures. All too often, I have seen the negative effects of parents 'nannying' their children, far beyond the necessity of safety, and I believe it is vital that we enable and equip our children to take responsibility.

I understand that it can feel good for our children to 'need' us, especially when they are becoming more independent, but we need to recognise that that is fulfilling *our need*, not theirs.

I believe our children need us more as teenagers - even late teens - than they do when they're babies, but our role as they become young adults is to coach, guide and be there for them rather than making decisions, controlling and doing it for them. Again, balance is important. Encouraging and enabling our children to take responsibility does not mean abdicating our responsibility as parents.

Rules or no Rules?

I've never been big on hard and fast rules. Children need a clear framework of values and principles, and they definitely need to know 'where the line is' in terms of acceptable and appropriate behaviour in different situations. However, rules are like boxes you need to fit into. Some people - little people and adults - dislike boxes, some people learn to like boxes, and some naturally like boxes. Some people feel confined by boxes and just want to push, punch and rail their way out of them. Rules leave little room for negotiation.

In my view, rules are very appropriate for safety situations and things that are fundamentally linked to values and moral codes of behaviour. You can set boundaries and frameworks, within which children feel secure and learn how the world and people work, without specific rules. I believe, as parents, carers and teachers, we sometimes use rules partly because we feel we should, and partly because it makes our lives easier to have blanket rules. When you are responsible for hundreds of young people in a school situation, some rules are appropriate for an orderly environment, fairness, ease of interpretation. It's the same in sport, where fairness and ease of interpretation are vital.

At home, I think negotiation and taking each situation on its merits according to the context, developmental age of our children etc is a much more valuable learning experience. Spending time negotiating rather than enforcing rules or punishing for contravening rules is better preparation for taking responsibility in a life that is rarely governed by hard and fast rules. I remember an important learning point for me on the whole rules thing. I was asked to say a few words at a Primary Head Teacher's retirement, and after the formalities, we were chatting about children - my daughter was 3 and his children were in their early 30's. He said he'd recently asked his sons why they thought he and his wife had not had the same sorts of hassles when the boys were teenagers as many of their peers had had with their children. The boys came back with a very simple answer, 'You never gave us anything to rebel against'. That struck a chord with me, and has stayed with me.

Now, my children will tell you they would have preferred some set rules rather than what they sometimes saw as the tedium of negotiation. My daughter, in particular, went through a phase of positively seeking something to rebel against and thought it was very unfair of me not to oblige. You see, if we come to an agreement about something, there's some sort of ownership or buy-in that makes it much harder for us not to comply. There were some things that weren't allowed, but there was always a discussion – sometimes on-going – about the relative merits and reasons for whatever stance I took on something. Just as intrinsic motivation is much more powerful than extrinsic motivation, understanding the values and rationale behind decisions is more enabling, moving forward, for our children to take responsibility.

There was little discussion about having TVs in their rooms. I didn't allow it, but I didn't say it like that; I just didn't enable it to happen and talked about the importance of us spending time together, having shared experiences, even watching TV and chatting about what we'd watched. The negotiation we had about what to watch was an important lesson in social intelligence and compromise. It also meant I didn't need to vet what they were watching. Harriet's view is that we watched far too much sport, but George and I have good memories of watching and chatting about cricket together. Equally, George was introduced to TV he would not have watched had it not been for Harriet's and my influence. He has certainly grown up with more understanding of the female perspective than some of his peers.

One of the perennials we face as parents is what time we expect our children home once they start going out. This has been a gradual process with both my children. I have not had set rules about what time to get in. Each time there was a discussion and negotiation, according to the circumstances. My daughter started going into town before the big clampdown on under-age drinking and the ID-only culture (of which I whole-heartedly approve). But there were lots of reasons to come home at a reasonable hour apart from me setting a time, and we constantly had those 'chats'. Both my children had goals, and they knew what they had to pay, in time and effort, to achieve those goals, so we come back to choices and consequences discussions. For Harriet, this meant not being too tired for school or study or her athletics, as she understood the better she did at school, the more choices she'd have and the more likely she was to be able to do what she wanted in the future. For George, it meant giving his all to training and matches to improve, advance to the next level of performance and achieve his goals.

It's also a valuable lesson to accept some rules with which we may not agree because there are much more valuable uses of our energy. For example, Harriet attended a school with a very strict uniform policy. I am one of the few parents and educationalists who is yet to be convinced about the real benefits of uniform, and Harriet knows this. However, I was always very insistent that she strictly abide by the school's uniform code. She had chosen to attend that particular school and I had supported that. We knew the uniform code and one of the conditions of attendance was to abide by that code. I explained to her that challenging it was a waste of energy and a diversion from what was really important in her education.

Choices and Consequences

Every choice you make has an end result.
Zig Ziglar

I believe a big part of our role as parents is to teach our children about **choices and consequences**. That means making sure our children have choices.

My children sometimes didn't like it, and would much rather I had told them what to do. Enabling our children to become responsible adults also means allowing them to make mistakes. Having choice and taking the consequences for that choice are crucial aspects of feeling empowered, being able to control what happens to us, and being in control of our life. Making our own mistakes rather than blaming our parents for a choice they've made for us is a very important lesson, and vital if we are to become responsible adults. It's also important that we guide our children's choices and avoid allowing them to keep repeating the same mistakes. I have seen too many parents use the line, 'That's …….. (name). S/he's just like that', rather than coaching and challenging their children to learn, improve and behave in a way that's more likely to bring positive results and enable them to achieve their goals.

Enabling Harriet and George to Take Responsibility and Understand Choices and Consequences

Life is not the way it's supposed to be.
It's the way it is.
The way you cope with it is what makes the difference.
Virginia Satir

We all seek to support our children to do their best in all their endeavours: in education, in their interests outside school and in valuing and contributing to family. What follows are a few examples of where I have endeavoured to:

- develop my children as individuals (and therefore,

sometimes, in different ways) to take responsibility and understand choices and consequences;
- equipped them to understand choices and consequences;
- empowered them to make choices;
- accepted their choices;
- enabled and supported them to take responsibility.

From an early age, my son was a bit of a golden boy at school; academically able, exceptionally able at English, exceptionally good at ball sports, socially intelligent – getting on with boys and girls alike from a young age - physically strong etc. You get the picture. Both my children went to a small inner city primary school, which was a microcosm of society, both ethnically and socially. This was a positive choice, and one from which they gained tremendous social intelligence. However, when you're at a small primary school you can soon become a very big fish in a small pond. I think this can have tremendous merits in terms of developing positive self-esteem, but you need challenges if you are going to build up the resilience and persistence you need to succeed in life.

One of George's challenges was his organisational skills. I therefore decided that a way to challenge him was to make him responsible for remembering his PE kit and swimming kit on the right days, which I implemented from Year 2, aged 7. Most mothers, in my experience, are quite afraid to do this because schools do have a tendency to judge parents when younger children don't have the right kit for school. However, I told his teacher, Mrs Davies, what I was doing and why, and she understood. He forgot his swimming kit a few times and took the consequences, but he soon learned that he'd rather swim than, 'Do work', as he put it. He never forgot his PE kit. I think his strategy was to take it every day, just in case. You see, that was important to him.

I didn't dream of taking this approach with Harriet. For one thing, she was vehemently independent from a young age and didn't need challenge in this way. Harriet always had what she needed for school and her activities. She would also have been hurt by the challenging approach I adopted with George. Harriet had other challenges at school, such as being on the dyslexic spectrum and finding the weekly spelling tests, amongst other aspects of English, very challenging. (One of the things that brought home to me how much we value being good at English, or linguistic intelligence, far more than other forms of intelligence in our culture and education system was the impact of Harriet and George being intelligent in different ways.)

Getting back to taking responsibility for kit, I have never packed football bags, athletics bags or cricket bags and have definitely not cleaned athletics track spikes or football and cricket boots. Harriet wanted to pursue athletics and George wanted to play football and cricket, and my view was that they needed to take responsibility for every aspect they could of that. I took parental responsibility for ensuring they were empowered and enabled to pursue their passions. I also ensured they were challenged and coached to gradually take more and more responsibility for themselves in that pursuit.

When George was playing representative age-group cricket for Nottinghamshire, they were, quite rightly, very strict on players having everything they needed, and I know many parents who packed their son's cricket bags, or at least checked that they had everything. (The consequence if you didn't have everything was that you may be 12th man; that is, you didn't get to bat or bowl but took drinks on and were a substitute fielder.) How is that helping our children to take responsibility? Yes, the negative consequences are considerable if you get it wrong, but that's what learning about choices and consequences is all about. However, just applying it in the small stuff, rather than when it takes on greater significance, is not adequate to equip our children to fully take responsibility for their thinking, behaviour and, ultimately, their future success in whatever they pursue.

Where I have been the same with both my children, in terms of taking responsibility, is with contributing at home. I think it's important that we expect our children to contribute at home. For one thing, feeling needed is a contributory factor to boosting self-esteem. It's also an important lesson in life that we need to contribute to whatever community we are part of, and that starts at home. I also think it's important to expect our children to contribute, no matter what other demands they have on their time. Eating, washing, tidying, cleaning etc is part of life and needs to continue whatever other demands we have, homework, exams, sports, drama productions etc. That is the reality of adult life, and it is our duty to ensure that our children are taught to handle conflicting demands on their time.

> ***Hold yourself responsible for a higher standard***
> ***than anyone else expects of you.***
> Henry Ward Beecher

Secondary School

Harriet and George attended the same primary school but different secondary schools because they made different choices. We lived in a city with a number of choices and they attended the schools they chose to attend. Of course, these were guided choices, but they knew lots about local schools from friends. Harriet looked at 3 schools and chose one, and George refused to look at any other than the one he decided he was going to. Both had the option of taking the entrance examination for the local private school, and they would have been eligible for a scholarship, given the primary school they attended: for different reasons neither wanted to do this.

Harriet went to secondary school, not knowing anyone and catching two buses to get there although it was less than 3 miles away. She enjoyed some of her time there, and achieved very well, both academically and in sport. However, she was bullied, but vehemently didn't want me to interfere having decided that handling it herself was the best option. Harriet observed that life got worse for those students who brought their parents in or told teachers. The discussions we did have were about how she might handle it, and it certainly made her an even stronger young woman. She went on to a Sixth Form College for A-Levels and loved that in every way, and is still close friends with people she met there. Harriet took a gap year after A-Levels; she really had had enough of study for a while. She worked in various jobs, travelled round Australia, and started University the following year, eager to study again. Harriet went all the way with education and is still taking further qualifications in her field, linked to what she's really interested in.

George went to an even closer Academy, one of the schools established to improve educational standards in the inner city.

It suited him. He viewed it that, as school was compulsory until he was 16, he would enjoy it. He enjoyed it socially and his best friends are still from school. He loved the football, captaining the team all the way through, and they won every competition at some point. He did what was required academically – just! Used to serving young people who were not necessarily living in an environment to prioritise homework, the school had a long school day and endeavoured to ensure that students did all the work they absolutely needed to do at school, and that suited George. His focus was elsewhere, and the school recognised and accommodated that for the most part. George went on to Sixth Form College to study A-Levels for a time, and that certainly didn't suit him. The debates and reading interesting literature in English suited him, as did the sport. Doing assignments in his own time didn't.

George left Sixth Form College after a term to focus on what he really wanted to do: cricket. Most of my peers couldn't believe I'd allowed him to leave. The most frequent comment was, 'But what's his back-up plan?' Firstly, I couldn't encourage my children to pursue their dreams and then halt that at some point when it got a bit risky. Secondly, my view was that if he felt he needed a back-up plan at 17, he'd failed before he'd really started. You have to believe and give it 100% to achieve big goals. Thirdly, a traditional academic route didn't suit him. He is intellectually able, especially when it comes to the English language, an avid reader, a great communicator, and socially very able. What he decides to pursue outside sport is not likely to be dependent on academic qualifications, but more likely to be aligned with his social intelligence and developing his entrepreneurial capabilities. He has always worked very hard at pursuing his goals and not used his energy on things that do not contribute to this. Academic study is something he will only pursue if it is very specifically aligned to his goals. George understood what Stephen Covey means here from a young age:

> **The main thing is to keep the main thing the main thing.**
> Stephen Covey

Allowing my children so much choice may be viewed as a risky strategy, but I believe they both gained a tremendous amount from attending the schools they did in their development as people and attained well, proportionate to the effort they put in. That is, Harriet got 12.5 higher grade GCSEs, an unnecessary number, and George got 8 higher grade GCSEs, enough to gain entrance to the next phase of education, A-Levels, which is what GCSEs are about – a passport to the next phase. (George did do a little study for GCSE Physical Education – having done very poorly in one mock examination, competition with his sister took over and he did what he needed to get an A* like her!)

Choosing Options

Many parents are very involved in their children's choices when they can start to choose courses at about the age of 14 in the UK. My children chose their options. We discussed it. I asked them questions about their choices and they chose. The main principles that I regard as important at that stage of education are to do what you enjoy and what you are good at. Harriet was exceptionally good at art but didn't enjoy it as much as other options. The enjoyment quotient won.

Getting the Grades

What I did with both Harriet and George was to coach them to set goals for their GCSE courses before they started. I asked them to decide what grades they would get in each subject: not what the teachers thought they could get or should get, but the grades they set for themselves. They used these as their goals, and I used them at parents' evening to advocate for them when they'd decided they were getting a C in a subject the teacher thought they could get an A in. Harriet did 12.5 GCSEs (more than anyone needs). She decided which subjects she wanted to get As in, and she couldn't do that in every subject and maintain her sports commitments outside school. Having clear goals was very useful when her German teacher said she could get an A with just a bit more work, when Harriet had decided she'd aim for a C in German. Every teacher said that, of course, only seeing their subject and not the whole of her workload. Her final results were exactly in line with the goals she'd set herself two years previously.

This same process also helped when George and his IT teacher saw things slightly differently. He also got the grades he chose, except in Business Studies. He had chosen that thinking it would have far more to do with real business and entrepreneurship. Regurgitating case studies from the internet was not his idea of business. As I reminded him when I was trying in vain encourage him to do an assignment, the clue was in the title!

Outside School

Harriet had part-time work most of the time from 15 onwards, through GCSEs, during A-Levels and whilst at University. Some of her peers were not allowed to work, as their parents thought it might interfere with their studies. She also maintained her athletics training throughout. I knew that was a very important release for her, as well as understanding the well-researched value of exercise and fitness on utilising the power of the brain. In addition, she also worked throughout every summer holiday. These things, and the industry qualifications she gained alongside her degree, meant she walked out of University into a number of contracts she'd negotiated for herself in her field. Academic qualifications are only part of what you need to succeed, even in the field of Sports Science, which is very dependent on having the right academic qualifications. George trained, attended coaching and played sport outside school, two or three times a week and at weekends, to become the best sportsman he could be. He is still on that journey.

In Summary

For our children to feel they can influence what happens to them, they need to feel they have choices: are responsible and increasingly able to take control of their future. They also definitely need to be raised to take responsibility, and have the confidence to take responsibility for their own performance in anything they do, whether that's tidying up after themselves, handling challenging situations with peers, studying for examinations, earning their own money, performing in sport, planning their internship or gap year, or progressing in their chosen career.

Responsibility rather than excuses!

Let us not seek to fix blame for the past; let us accept responsibility for the future.
John F. Kennedy

Coaching rather than Controlling

One of the ways I have enabled my children to take more responsibility for themselves is by coaching rather than telling or sorting things for them. See *The Basics of a Coaching Approach for Parents and Carers* on the section of my website.

Self-Determination

Above all else, it is our responsibility as parents to empower, enable and equip our children to determine their own positive future. The power of self-determination is the best gift we can give our children, and that means being independent and taking responsibility.

To the question of your life, you are the only answer.
To the problems of your life, you are the only solution.
Jo Coudert

According to educators H. Stephen Glenn and Jane Nelsen, authors of *Raising Self-Reliant Children in a Self-Indulgent World: Seven Building Blocks for Developing Capable Young People,* there are seven significant factors that are central for children to become confident, successful, self-determining young people, and these require us as parents, carers and educators to enable our children to take responsibility.

Characteristics of Thriving Children:

'I am capable.'

'I contribute in meaningful ways and I am genuinely needed.'

'I can influence what happens to me.'

'My feelings are important, and I trust myself to learn from my mistakes. I have self-control and self-discipline.'

'I can make friends. I know how to speak out, listen, co-operate, share and negotiate for what I want.'

'I can be counted on, and I tell the truth. Things don't always go my way, but I can adapt when I need to.'

'I try to solve my own problems, but I know that if I need help, I'll ask for it.'

Learning about taking responsibility, and choices and consequences, from a young age is one of the reasons Harriet planned, with minimum guidance from me, exactly what course she wanted to do at University, and made sure she got the grades to do it, took a gap year before University and, at 24, bought her own flat. It is also part of the reason George, when he failed to be selected for county age-group cricket at U11's, U12's, and U13's just kept saying, 'What do I need to do to get in next year?' until he succeeded and, as a teenager, took himself off to bed early the night before a cricket match without any prompting from me.

Too often, we want to keep control and dependency, especially when we define ourselves in terms of being responsible for others. We all want to be needed, but nannying and controlling can hamper self-determination:
our children pursuing the life they are meant to lead and the happiness that goes with that.

Becoming self-determining individuals (and knowing and feeling that we are) is a vital ingredient for holistic success. The bottom line is that we can only take responsibility for ourselves – our thoughts and behaviour. Inorder to empower, enable and equip our children to become responsible, self-reliant and self-determining individuals, we gradually need to consciously have less and less control over our children's attitudes and behaviour.

We need to equip them to take responsibility for creating, developing and maintaining their journey in life. It's also important to remember that it's not so much what happens to us in life, but how we handle it. To enable our children to make the most of opportunities and overcome challenges, we need to raise them to be willing to 'step up to the plate' and take responsibility for their own future.

Affirmations

- I am taking responsibility for creating the future of my dreams.
- I am relishing being responsible for my thoughts, actions and future.
- I am responsible for what I think, say and do.
- I am responsible for making a contribution.

Don't sit down and wait for the opportunities to come;
you have to get up and make them.
Madame C. J. Walker

ACTION

There's an interesting interview with Will Smith on You Tube, where he talks about the importance of understanding that rights and responsibilities are two sides of the same coin and how important it was to him to be taught, at a young age, to take responsibility for himself. It's called *Will Smith, The Secret of Success*. It's well worth watching.

Below are a few ideas to enable and equip our children to take more responsibility. Above all, we need to reinforce the positive:

Notice When Our Children Take Responsibility

Praise Our Children When They Take Responsibility

Reflective questions:

How are you empowering, enabling and equipping your children to take responsibility for themselves: to become self-determining young people and adults? At home? In school? In pursuing their interests? In setting their goals?

Think of times in the last few weeks when you have blamed someone for a problem or something that has gone wrong, when you know it was your fault. What message is that giving to your children about taking responsibility?

Think about the times you have made excuses for your children's behaviour. How could you have handled that differently, without belittling them in front of others?

Consciously take responsibility for your actions and thoughts – no-one has control over what you think but you, and it's important for you to demonstrate to your children that you acknowledge that. Practice distinguishing between yours and others' responsibilities – it is just as important not to take responsibility for things over which you have no control.

Think about how you may coach your children to do this using a questioning approach. See, *The Basics of a Coaching Approach for Parents* on the equipped2succeed section of my website.

Things to try:

- Decide on one or two additional things that you're going to expect each of your children to start taking responsibility for. Increase responsibilities as they grow.

- When your children have taken responsibility for something, ask them some questions to embed their learning and reinforce that taking responsibility feels good.
  How did taking responsibility make you feel?
  How do others react when you take responsibility?
  How do you feel when someone else takes responsibility?

- Ask your children to say who are the most responsible people they know. Ask them about those people and give examples of other people they may know that have taken responsibility in some way. What are the behaviours that show those people are responsible? Then ask your children what sort of things they can do to model what those who take responsibility do. Ask what they could take more responsibility for at home, at school, in their interests.

- Ask your children to take on small projects and see them through to completion. Then slowly increase the amount of responsibility they take. The more we do, the more we can do, and the better we get.

- Eliminate the excuse culture and our children blaming others for things for which they are responsible. Start focusing your children on taking responsibility for the outcomes of what they do – positive and negative. That could simply be reinforcing and celebrating successes, or saying sorry for something they've done, and saying what they're going to do to prevent it happening again.

  It's vital that children don't live in a blame culture. Enabling our children to take responsibility means encouraging them to acknowledge when things have gone well and when things have not gone so well. It's essential that we don't make them feel bad when they get something wrong, but rather take responsibility, see it as a learning opportunity, and move on.

- Use your reflective diary to reflect on things where you notice your children taking more responsibility so you can step back and reflect on progress.

Do your children truly believe:

'I can influence what happens to me'?

Chapter Six

Develop Your Winning Brain

If you correct your mind, the rest of your life will fall into place.
Lao Tzu

 Definitions:

develop:
- to bring out the capabilities or possibilities of; bring to a more advanced or effective state;
- to cause to grow or expand.

winning:
- the act of a person who wins;
- friendly and charming; as in *winning smile*

brain:
- the organ inside the head that controls and co-ordinates mental and physical actions; thought, memory, feelings, and activity;
- the part of the central nervous system that controls and co-ordinates mental and physical actions;
- used to refer to intelligence; as in *use your brain.*

Teachers, coaches, parents - in fact, all those of us who have tried to parent, guide, teach or coach young people – have, at some stage, used the phrase 'use your brain' or 'use your head'. However, how many of us explain how to do that? We commonly mean - think about it', and 'do it the way I've told you, the way I see it'. But we all think differently, and in order for us to 'use our heads' to maximize our potential and achieve our goals, it's helpful to understand more about how our brain works. Using our brainpower and developing the ability to effectively manage our mind are essential to learning and succeeding in any field of endeavour.

Although underpinned by science and research, this chapter is not an academic thesis on the latest research into the brain and the mind. It is designed to share some general information and insights to help us understand how better to use our mind effectively to develop the other 11 characteristics in the equipped2succeed framework. Most importantly, this chapter is designed to help us empower, enable and equip our children with some basics about their brain and mind that will help them achieve in learning and life. It is my firm belief that:

You get out what you put in.

In nothing, has this more truth than with your mind.

Successful individuals manage their mind effectively; instinctively, and from learning. For example, an athlete who's very focused and disciplined in training and naturally performs at their best in less important competitions, may need to learn to manage their stress or performance anxiety to perform at their best on the big occasions: when it matters most. This is also the case for young people in examinations, or for any of us in interviews, speaking in public, or pitching for contracts. All successful people realise that using the power of the mind is essential for success. They relax, visualise and mentally rehearse their chosen future, whether that's scoring that all-important goal, solving that science or engineering challenge, pulling off that amazing performance, finding a business solution, or sailing around the world.

Those who reach the pinnacle in their chosen field understand the power of the mind to find creative solutions and are capable of seeing things in different ways: making important connections between apparently unlinked things. We can learn from the people who have studied the brain and the mind, and those successful individuals who have shared how they have used and developed the power of the mind to realise their goals. This chapter is about developing our thinking for success: taking control of our thinking and enabling our children to take control of their thinking.

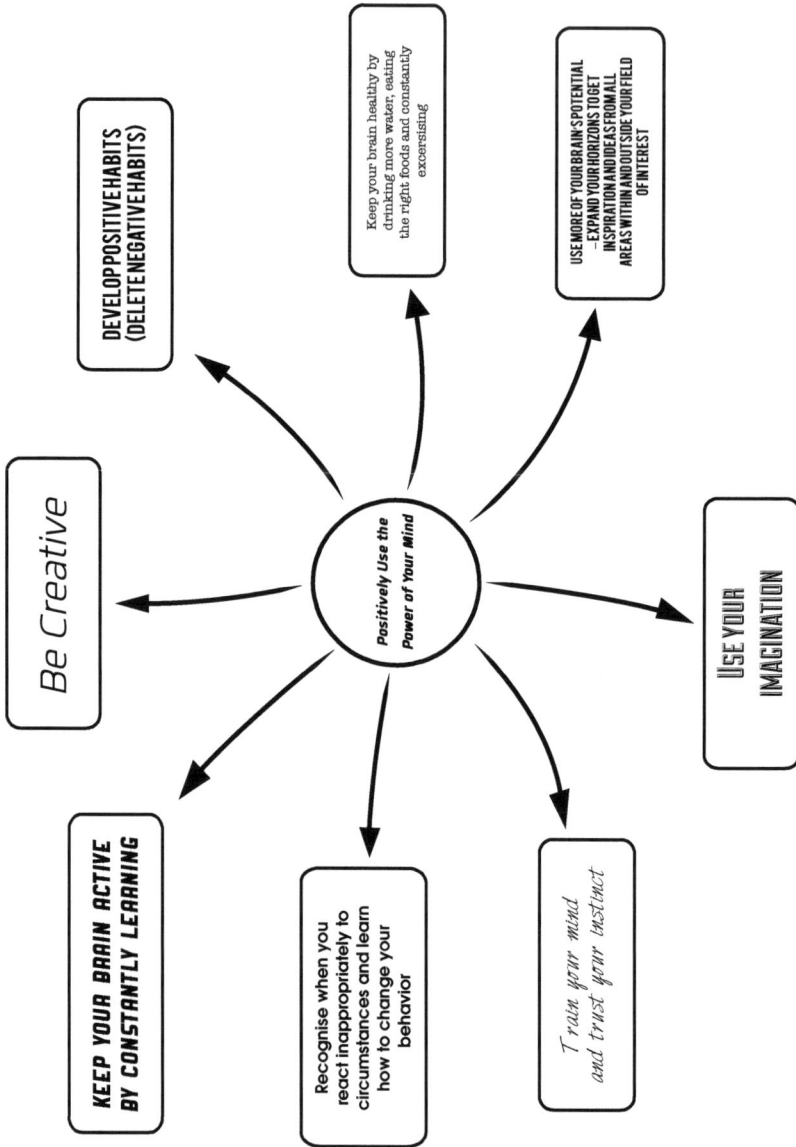

DEVELOP POSITIVE HABITS (DELETE NEGATIVE HABITS)

Keep your brain healthy by drinking more water, eating the right foods and constantly excersising

USE MORE OF YOUR BRAIN'S POTENTIAL – EXPAND YOUR HORIZONS TO GET INSPIRATION AND IDEAS FROM ALL AREAS WITHIN AND OUTSIDE YOUR FIELD OF INTEREST

Be Creative

Positively Use the Power of Your Mind

USE YOUR IMAGINATION

KEEP YOUR BRAIN ACTIVE BY CONSTANTLY LEARNING

Recognise when you react inappropriately to circumstances and learn how to change your behavior

Train your mind and trust your instinct

In order to achieve the holistic success we seek, it is essential to develop our mind in all the ways identified above. We need to develop a winning mentality – with all that entails. This phrase is often used in sport, but the relentless drive, determination and focus required to succeed in sport is just as essential in our other endeavours. Successful people have a growth mindset, expanding their mind and thinking and seeking continuous improvement. Mindset is a simple idea identified by world-renowned Stanford University psychologist Carol Dweck in decades of research on achievement and success. According to her teaching, a growth mindset creates motivation and productivity in the worlds of business, education and sports.

At this point, it may be worth being clear about differentiating between the brain and the mind:

🕮 Definitions:

brain:
- the organ inside the head that controls and co-ordinates mental and physical actions; thought, memory, feelings, and activity.

mind:
- the part of a person that makes it possible for him or her to think, feel emotions, and understand things:
- used to describe the mental processes that go on in the brain.

The comprehensive nature and diversity of use of the word mind clearly indicates its unique and powerful significance for us.

Our brain controls our body, all our physical processes, and everything we physically do – from growing our hair to breathing, from walking to dancing, from building a model to kicking a ball. Our mind holds all our experiences and the sum total of what we've learnt. Our thoughts grow in our mind where we hold all our beliefs. These determine our confidence, our self-belief, how we can conquer our fears, how persistent we are, and how we respond to situations, etc.

Change your thoughts and you change your world.
Norman Vincent Peale

We can use the power of our mind to succeed in achieving what we want in life, or allow our thinking to limit us. That applies equally to realising our educational potential, developing fulfilling personal relationships, reaching the pinnacle of our chosen career path or making a positive difference in our community or society.

Brain and Mind Basics

A man is what he thinks about all day long.

Much of what we know about the brain has been discovered in the past 30 years or so, and our knowledge is expanding all the time: increasing our capacity to understand and to more effectively use this master organ of the body. The brain takes in all information relating to the body's external and internal environments, and produces the appropriate responses. It is composed of several parts that process what we think; how we feel; where we move; what we see, hear, and taste; and all other bodily functions. We are going to take a brief look at main sections and functions of the brain, as a basis for us understanding how we can more effectively use our brain and manage our thinking.

Neocortex

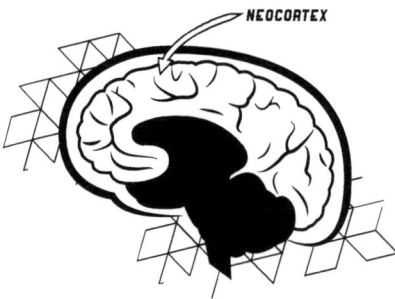

This is our own personal, individual, unique 'thinking cap' (yes, that same thinking cap we were told to put on when we were at school!). Knowing something about the power of the neocortex gives us an insight into the infinite possibilities we have within us all.

When we look at a human brain from the top or sides, almost everything we see is neocortex. It is the largest portion of the brain, comprising more than two-thirds of our brain mass, and is what distinguishes us from all other mammals. It's called 'neo' because it is, in evolution terms, a relatively recent invention of mammals and what enabled us to develop a new level of advanced behaviour. The brain has the same number of neurons as a galaxy has stars: 100 billion, and the majority of these are in the neocortex. Most of the neurons in the neocortex have between 1,000 and 10,000 synaptic connections with other neurons, enabling the most complex mental activity that we associate with being human. It enables us to make sense of the world and draw meaning from things. It is involved in higher functions, such as sensory perception, generation of motor commands, spatial reasoning, conscious thought, and in humans, social behaviour, language and high-level consciousness. It is what makes possible our judgments and our knowledge of good and evil. It is also the site from which our creativity emerges and home to our sense of self. The centre for intuition and critical analysis, it is in the neocortex where we have our ideas and inspirations, where we read and write, where we compose music or solve mathematical equations.

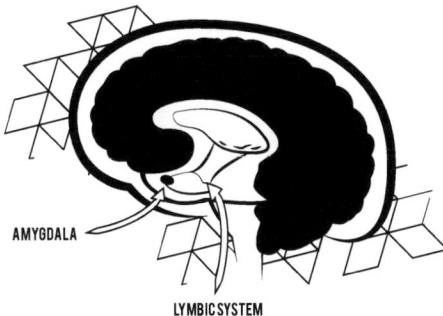

AMYGDALA

LYMBIC SYSTEM

The limbic system, or thalamus, is small but extremely powerful. Thalamus means 'inner room' in Greek, as it sits deep in the brain at the top of the brainstem. It controls emotions, long-term memory, and determines sleeping and eating patterns.

The limbic system is called the gateway to the cerebral cortex, as nearly all sensory inputs pass through it to the higher levels of the brain. In simple terms, it takes in information from our senses anddecides whether to send the messages to the neocortex or the cerebellum (reptilian brain). Part of its role is somewhat like a call centre, controlling where information goes next. At the centre of the limbic system is the amygdala. It is about the size of an almond and is known as the emotional centre of the brain as it plays a key role in the processing of emotions. It impacts how the brain creates emotional memories and responses. Research has shown that the amygdala is specifically linked to both fear responses and pleasure which, later in this chapter, you'll see is relevant in managing our emotional responses in situations where we experience real or perceived fear. It has also been found that the amygdala's volume positively correlates with the size and complexity of young peoples' and adults' social networks.

Much of the research points to the fact that our brain develops in the context of experience. Therefore, early social experiences are an important aspect of our children developing the neural circuits related to the experience of feeling or emotion and the related social skills. Factors such as positive and negative life events, and how they are handled by us as parents, and the quality of relationships, can be especially influential in the development of essential social skills. Most of us learn these social skills 'by osmosis' through exposure, mimicking and mirroring others. However, as with the development of other skills, our children develop these skills in different ways and at different rates and we need to undertake different levels of systematic reflection and coaching according to how easily our children learn from their social experiences.

Cerebellum

The cerebellum is sometimes referred to as the 'reptilian' as, in evolutionary terms, it is the oldest part of the brain.

Cerebellum

The cerebellum controls balance, co-ordinates movement and maintains muscle tone.

It is sometimes referred to as our 'survival brain', as when our brain perceives we're under threat, the cerebellum moves into automatic survival mode to protect us. When we're in danger and / or frightened, we go into our survival mode: Fight, Flight, Flock or Freeze. More on this later.

The Types and Functions of Neurons

Neurons are specialized brain cells that process information. Each brain cell has a central bit called the axon, and messages are sent out along the branches of the neuron, called dendrites. These messages are sent out electrically and chemically, forming networks and pathways. The nervous system consists of the central nervous system (the brain and spinal cord), the peripheral nervous system (the sensory and motor neurons), and the autonomic nervous system (which regulates body processes such as digestion and heart rate). All the divisions of the nervous system are based on the functions of neurons. Our nervous systems have four basic types of functional cells:

Sensory neurons: tell the rest of the brain about our external and internal environment. Sensory neurons are activated by information from our senses such as visible light, sound, heat, physical contact etc, or chemical signals, for example in the case of smell or taste, and transmit sensory information to the brain or spinal cord. They are responsible for converting various external stimuli that come from the environment into corresponding internal stimuli.

Motor (and other output) neurons: carry signals from the spinal cord to the muscles to produce movement, and other output neurons stimulate glands and organs.

Communication neurons: transmit signals from one brain area to another.

Computation neurons: The vast majority of our neurons are computation neurons. Computation neurons extract and process information coming in from the senses, compare that information to what's in our memory, and use the information to plan and execute behavior. Each of the several hundred brain regions contain distinct types of computational neurons that facilitate the function of that brain area.

What really distinguishes the nervous system from any other functioning group is the complexity of the neuronal interconnections. The human brain's 100 billion neurons each has a unique set of up to 10,000 synaptic connections, yielding about a quadrillion synapses or possible connections - a number so huge that most of us struggle to comprehend it! The number of possible distinct states of this system is virtually uncountable.

Developing the connections between these neurons enables us to learn things: physical skills, knowledge, attitudes and behaviour. How to walk, talk, ride a bike, throw a ball, play a game, dance steps, learn dance routines, solve puzzles, learn our own and other languages, solve scientific problems, cook, relate to others, develop socially acceptable behaviour, overcome fears – everything. Developing our neural pathways also enables us to move on in our thinking to the next level, just as you move to the next level in computer games by practising, trying new things and learning, gaining new insights to perform better and achieve our goals.

Right and Left Brain

Scientists have carried out an immense amount of research on the functions of the left and right hemispheres of our neocortex. They have discovered that each side of the brain concentrates on specific functions. The left side of the brain is the seat of language and processes in a logical and sequential order. The right side is more visual and processes intuitively, holistically and randomly. Brain research also confirms that neurons from both sides of the brain are involved in nearly every human activity.

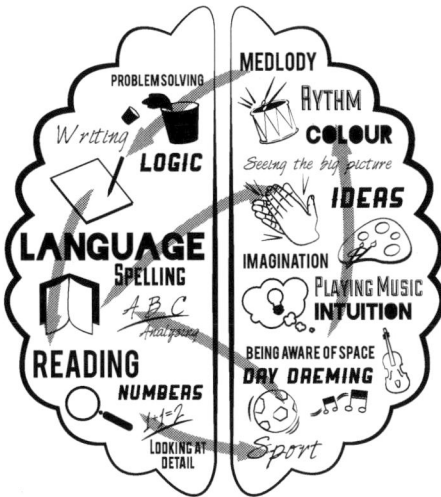

We are at our best in solving problems, being creative and finding solutions when we use the collective power of our brain to best effect. As we learn things, our brain makes up a series of connections or neural pathways. For example, learning your first chord on a guitar. This involves melody, rhythm and spatial awareness, but it also involves reading, sequence

The greatest, most creative footballers demonstrate using both sides of their brain all the time, seeing the big picture on the field, analysing, seeing that perfect pass and then accurately passing the ball. The best players use the power of their mind; visualising and mentally rehearsing or 'day-dreaming' (as some players describe their mental rehearsal process) scoring a goal, celebrating a goal or lifting a trophy.

Every goal I ever scored was with my head.
Thierry Henry

Those who succeed in all areas of life develop both sides of their brain. To effectively use both sides of our brain we need to not only 'train' both sides with study and skill development, but we also need to allow our mind to flow to solve problems, come up with solutions, and find ways to do things better.

All Our Learning and Behaviour Is Affected By Our Emotional State

Our brain performs best and enables us to learn skills and techniques when we are relaxed and focused. We need to be relaxed and thinking clearly for our brain to make the right connections between neurons, between the right and left sides of our s, for us to perform at our best in anything. If we are stressed or anxious, we don't perform at our best, whether that's learning something new, in examinations, in sport, getting on with other people, interviews, presentations, pitching for business etc. See the *Flow* section in the *Always Learning* chapter.

Memory

Everything we experience through our lives is stored in our brain: everything we smell, touch, see, hear etc. In fact, every sensation and piece of learning is stored in our brain. This is because we do not see with our eyes or hear with our ears. Our eyes only pick up light and our ears only pick up sound waves.

It is our brain's job to interpret the light that reflects on to the lens of our eyes and sound waves entering our brain. We all see, hear and interpret things differently. When our mind is interpreting information, it uses 2 types of memory: one is short-term and the other is long-term.

Short-term Memory
Our short-term memory consists of pieces of information from our senses - sight, hearing, smell, taste and touch - that our mind holds onto briefly. It may be referred to as our 'active memory'. Our short-term memory is like a processing unit, interpreting information for us. It takes information from our senses, sorts it, and once it has been interpreted stores this information in our long-term memory. Our short-term memory refers to how much information we can constantly pay attention to at any one time. It usually has a capacity of around 7 digits, regardless of age or level of education.

Long-term Memory
Our long-term memory is anything we remember that happened more than a few minutes ago. Long-term memories can last for just a few days, or for many years. Long-term memories aren't all of equal strength. Stronger memories enable you to recall an event, procedure or fact on demand, for example that the 2004 Olympics

were in Athens. Weaker memories often come to mind only through prompting or reminding. We may remember certain pieces of learning from school for years afterwards, things that have specific significance or that were taught in a particularly interesting way. Other things we seem to 'forget' the moment we leave school. What are stronger or weaker memories is very individual, according to the importance we place on things.

Long-term memory isn't static, either. We do not imprint a memory and leave it as if untouched. Instead, we often revise the memory over time—perhaps by merging it with another memory or incorporating what others tell us about the memory. As a result, our memories are not strictly constant, and are not always reliable. There are many different forms of long-term memories. The two major subdivisions are explicit memory and implicit memory.

Explicit memories are those that you consciously remember, such as an event in your life or a particular fact. Implicit memories are things that you do without thinking, like riding a bike - you once learned how, and you remembered how, but now you do it without conscious thought. We tend to remember and be able to recall things from our memories that are of greater importance to us: things we are particularly interested in, that have particular emotional associations, or that we learn in an interesting way.

The Impact of Memory

Some of the key conclusions that Dr. Wilder Penfield (a neurosurgeon from McGill University in Montreal) reached, after many years of research, are interesting for us to consider in relation to managing and focusing our mind:

- The human brain acts in many ways like a video recorder, vividly recording events. Whilst that event may not necessarily be easy to consciously retrieve by the individual, the event always exists in the brain.
- Both the event and the feelings experienced during that event are stored in the brain. The event and the feelings are locked together, and neither one can be recalled without the other.

- When an individual replays his or her experiences, he or she can replay them in such a vivid form that they experience again the same emotions felt during the actual experience, not only remembering how they felt, but feeling the same way again.

We are able to use our short and long-term memories simultaneously. When we replay certain events, we are able to experience the emotions associated with those events whilst also being able to talk objectively about them, just as Sally Gunnell does in recounting her 1992 Olympic final, later in this chapter. This has tremendous potential for us to embed learning and develop skills with systematic mental rehearsal. It is also helpful for us to understand the power of re-living positive and negative memories.

Conscious and Subconscious Mind The Basics

A man or woman who acquires the ability to take
full possession of his own mind
may take possession of anything else
to which he or she is justly entitled
Dale Carnegie

Our memories feed into our conscious and subconscious mind.

What is the Conscious Mind?

The conscious mind controls all the actions that we do intentionally, whilst being aware of what we're doing, or conscious; for example, when we decide to make any voluntary action, like picking up a glass. So, whenever we are aware of the thing we're doing, we are doing it with our conscious mind. The conscious mind can also be said to be the gate-keeper to the mind. If someone tries to present us with a belief that doesn't match our belief system, then our conscious mind will filter that belief. The same will happen when someone praises or criticizes us; we'll filter that with our reflection of what they are praising or criticising and bring our experience and self-belief to the forefront of our mind.

What is the Subconscious Mind?

The subconscious mind is the part of our mind responsible for all of our involuntary actions. Our breathing rate and heartbeats are controlled by our subconscious mind. Our emotions are also controlled by our subconscious mind. That's why we sometimes might feel afraid, anxious or down without wanting to experience such a feeling. Our subconscious mind is also the place where our beliefs and memories are stored. Affirmations, for example, are done on a conscious level and are always filtered by the subconscious mind if they don't match our belief system. The way we can change a limiting belief is to convince the conscious mind logically to accept it so that it can pass to the subconscious mind and reside there. Affirmations are a reminder to help this process.

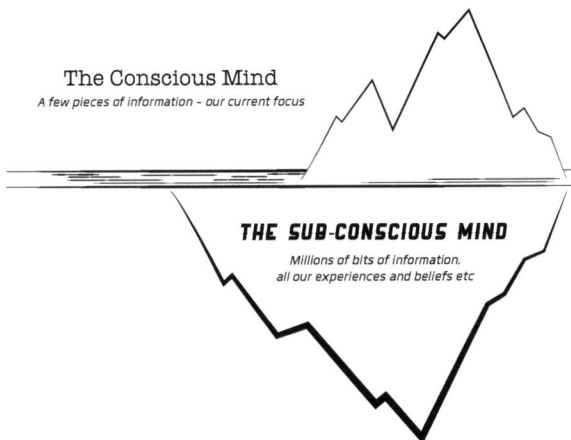

The Conscious Mind
A few pieces of information - our current focus

THE SUB-CONSCIOUS MIND
*Millions of bits of information,
all our experiences and beliefs etc*

Using the Conscious and the Subconscious Mind Together

*Life is a mirror and will reflect back to
the thinker what he thinks into it.*
Ernest Holmes

There is a simple exercise that we can do in order to understand the difference between the conscious and the subconscious mind. If we start to control our breathing rate as if we are going to systematically relax, whilst we are controlling our breath, our conscious mind is in charge. Once we stop controlling our breathing and let it flow naturally, our subconscious mind takes over and returns our breathing rate back to its norm. In one experiment I undertook whilst I was linked to a heart rate monitor, I saw how I could clearly lower my heart rate by controlling my breathing, consciously affecting two usually subconscious processes. One benefit of understanding how both can be used together is how emotions can be controlled. Since emotions are triggered by the subconscious mind, it's impossible to stop them. But knowing that the conscious mind processes thoughts, which are the primary trigger for emotions, we can learn to control our thoughts and, in turn, our emotions.

Just think about a couple of events or achievements in your life: things for which you are responsible.

1. Think of a particularly thrilling event, something about which you feel very proud and positive. Notice how you can recall the event in vivid detail. Notice how you are probably smiling as you do so. Notice your body language when thinking about it. Notice how you are feeling.

2. Now think about an event that you think was negative. Something you don't want to repeat. Notice how you can recall the event in vivid detail. Notice how you are probably uncomfortable and frowning as you do so. Notice your body language when thinking about it. Notice how you are feeling.

Now imagine the power of each recollection on our self-belief and ability to confidently pursue our goals. If we want to achieve our positive future, isn't it much more powerful to recall the positives from our past? Have a look at *Managing Our Memory Bank* on the equipped2succeed section of my website.

It is hard to fight an enemy who has
outposts in your head.
Sally Kempton

Reticular Activating System

At this point, it's worth mentioning the reticular activating system (RAS). In simple terms, the RAS helps us spot the things that are important to us. It helps us focus on the things we think about. Our brain wants to help us get what we're thinking about, so we start to attract or see whatever we're focusing on (whether that's positive or negative!). The RAS is the portal through which nearly all information enters the brain. The RAS filters incoming information and affects what you pay attention to and what is not going to get access to all three pounds of your brain. For survival's sake, our RAS responds to our name and anything that threatens our survival. It also helps us access the information that we need immediately. For example, if we're looking for a particular file on the computer, our RAS alerts our brain to search for the name of the file or focus on one word in the filename to help us find it. The RAS also responds to novelty. We notice anything new and different and therefore adding novelty, colour, humour and interest to our study or work can help us remember important information.

We can programme our thoughts each morning by focusing on what we want to achieve. There are thousands of pieces of information and potential stimuli around us all the time, and the RAS is the brain's way of helping us to focus on those things that are really important to us. It is therefore vital that we focus it on things we positively want to achieve rather than negative distractions: what we want rather than what we don't want:

- **Personal issues** If you're concerned about your child's behaviour, for example, devise a plan to deal with it. Make sure your plan includes appropriate behaviours, such as affirming and praise for things that your child has done well – no matter how small - and specific times that you can put your plan into action. Then put the issue on the back burner until you can act on it. This helps your brain to work on solutions and guards against a cycle of negativity and worry, which is only likely to make things worse.

- **Read over your long-term goals every day.**
- **Read your short-term goals every day.**
  This will help you spot those all-important opportunities that take you one step closer to achieving your goals.

This gets our brain focusing on what we want to achieve and prompts our RAS to spot opportunities to help us achieve them. Make sure that the last list you look at is your list of short-term goals; your RAS helps you keep them in mind. Even when you don't realise you're thinking about these goals, your brain knows that they're important and takes note of anything that might relate to them.

Fight – Flight – Flock – Freeze

Our brain's natural reaction to Fear – Anger – Stress

We all need to stay safe, be mindful of real survival situations, and intuitively react to protect ourselves. However, we are constantly interacting with the world, and every moment our brain is processing millions of information megabytes. The brain has a kind of shorthand to help it with this complicated task, and research shows that some aspects of the brain system have evolved to be hardwired to enable us to respond to physical threat and danger.

Fear is a fundamental aspect of **survival**. Our brain's most important function is to keep us alive. It does so by regulating our heart rate, body temperature, and a myriad of other physiological functions, whilst also constantly scanning the environment for possible threats and rewards. Researchers such as Dr. Joseph LeDoux, and other researchers mentioned in his book, *The Emotional Brain*, have made huge contributions to the study of fear and its affect on the mind/body systems. He says: *'All animals have* *to protect themselves from dangerous situations in order to survive, and there are only a limited number of strategies that animals can call upon to deal with danger'.*

However, our natural, intuitive survival response can often become confused with our perceptions of danger, or fear that is not linked to personal survival, and when this happens in examinations, interviews, important performances, or in relationships, it causes stress or anger that impede our performance or prevent us from handling things effectively.

Every thought you have contributes to
truth or illusion; either it extends truth or it multiplies illusions.
Nothing but your own thoughts can hamper your progress.
Anonymous.

A danger or threat, physical or emotional, real or perceived, is recognised in the amygdala, and rather than sending information to our neocortex for processing and considered thought, information is sent directly to the cerebellum, or 'reptilian brain', which produces our survival response. Great if we step out in front of a bus, not so good in a situation where we want to handle things calmly and perform at our best.

What Happens in Our Brain to Trigger Survival Mode?

Our survival instinct helps us stay alive by triggering neurological pathways in our brain, which enables us to react to danger without even having to think about it. Here is how it works: as we grow up, our brain 'labels' or encodes some stimuli (things we observed or experienced) as *'threats'* (e.g. food that tasted really bad) and others as *'rewards'* (e.g. food that we enjoyed). Just as the neural pathways we create when we learn something are stored in our neocortex, these neural pathways - or 'labels' - are stored in the amygdala. From then on, whenever we come across something encoded as either a 'threat' or a 'reward', the amygdala activates the limbic system to trigger an automated 'disengage' (refuse to eat something that smells bad) neurological response when facing a perceived threat, or an 'engage' (eat the ice-cream) response when facing a perceived reward. Similarly, our brain encodes facing an attacker or losing money as threats, whilst receiving money, water and a safe shelter as rewards.

Once our brain has decided there's a danger, it sends a flood of adrenaline, cortisol and dozens of other hormones that cause many changes in the body that include:

- heart rate and blood pressure increases;
- pupils dilate to take in as much light as possible;
- veins in skin constrict to send more blood to major muscle groups (responsible for the 'chill' sometimes associated with fear - less blood in the skin to keep it warm);
- blood-glucose levels increase;
- muscles tense up, energized by adrenaline and glucose (responsible for goose bumps - when tiny muscles attached to each hair on the surface of the skin tense up, the hairs are forced upright, pulling skin with them);
- smooth muscle (that is responsible for the contractility of muscle in hollow organs) relaxes in order to allow more oxygen into the lungs;
- a burst of increased immunity;
- lower sensitivity to pain;
- non-essential systems (like digestion and immune system) shut down to allow more energy for emergency functions;
- heightened memory functions;
- trouble focusing on small tasks (brain is directed to focus only on the big picture in order to determine where the threat is coming from);
- lungs take in more O2 and release more CO2;
- sweating increases to speed heat loss.

All of these physical responses are intended to help us survive in a dangerous situation by preparing us to predominantly either run for our life, or fight for our life. When our brain perceives a threat of any kind, it automatically responds in one of four modes. These are commonly known as **Fight, Flight, Flock, Freeze.** We don't usually choose these: we respond. Here are a couple of examples that illustrate the point before we explore them in more detail.

The Truck

If we're crossing the road with our children and a large truck comes round the corner, we don't want the information to go to our neo-cortex and for us to stand there thinking about it and deciding what best to do. We just go into the appropriate survival mode.

Should we fight the truck? Definitely not!

Should we freeze? Definitely not!

Should we flock, huddle together with our children? Definitely not!

Should we flee? Absolutely! We just need to run to the nearest side of the road to keep us safe.

The Wasp in the Classroom

When we were young, many of us can remember a wasp or some other stinging insect buzzing around our classroom. In this scenario, we're likely to see all four reactions:

A few children immediately want to fight it, grabbing anything they can to chase and try to kill the wasp.

There will be those who freeze, believing that if they stand completely still, the wasp won't sting them.

Some will flee, running out of the room to get away from the wasp.

Another little group will flock together, for no apparent reason other than they feel safer together, as if the wasp won't attack them in a group.

This is a modern day scenario of our ancient selves being faced with the threat from a wild animal. In fact, wild animals today can be seen acting in all these ways whilst faced with danger.

Fight

This is sometimes called defensive aggression. We feel in danger or threat and we start to fight. As we rarely need to tackle a predatory animal, there are few justifications for this in modern life. However, there are times when we might need the extraordinary bravery, strength and lower sensitivity to pain this gives us.

Lydia Angiyou was walking in the small northern Quebec Inuit village of Ivujivik in February 2006 when her nephew told her there was a wolf close by. When Angiyou looked behind her, she realized the animal was a 320-kilogram polar bear that had wandered into town and was only metres from Angiyou's son, Jessie, and her two nephews. The 43-year-old Angiyou started yelling and raced toward the polar bear as her son and nephews fled. However, having come face to face with the large animal, which had reared up on its hind legs, 5-foot-one-inch Angiyou started crying. 'He was really big. I tried to back up, and he smacked my forehead and shoulder with his paw.' The impact knocked Angiyou to the ground, and the bear hovered over her, striking her again under her nose. Fearing her face was going to be mauled, she lay down and started kicking, trying to keep the bear away. As the animal approached her again, Angiyou said she thought he was going to jump on her 'like he does to a seal.' 'I just fainted,' she said. When she recovered, the polar bear was right beside her. 'We were face to face,' she recounted. She then heard a gun shot. A villager who had been alerted by Angiyou's son fired a rifle into the air, hoping to scare the animal away. After several more shots, the bear went for the hunter holding the rifle and Angiyou stood up and fled as the villager shot the bear. She suffered only minor injuries during the confrontation. (As reported in the Montreal Gazette on 17th January 2008, when it was announced that Lydia Angiyou was to receive a *Medal for Bravery*.)

Lydia did this instinctively to save her son and nephews. She didn't stand and think about the consequences, and there are numerous other examples of extra-ordinary bravery and strength from individuals when their loved ones are in danger: when their survival instinct appears to give them extra-ordinary powers.

However, we don't always use our fight responses when we're in actual physical danger. Our 'fight' response can be real fighting when we are younger - someone upsets us and we don't have the emotional control to manage it, or command of language to articulate our feelings without resorting to physical aggression. When Harriet was very young she used to hit out if she couldn't make herself understood, until she learned the necessary emotional control and command of language to explain herself. In those who don't learn to manage their responses, this can persist into teens and even adult life, to be addressed (or not) by anger management courses. This response can also be seen physically in adults on the sports field when their aggression becomes uncontrolled. A notable example of this was David Beckham's reaction to a foul in the 1998 World Cup. He kicked out at Simeone in a loss to Argentina that saw England exit the tournament. He was pilloried and shamed in the British press, and did exceptionally well to put the incident behind him and go on to captain England.

Too often, our 'fight' response emerges from non-physical threats: when we feel under pressure in work, have financial pressures, or during challenging times in personal relationships. We can become 'stressed' or 'defensive', which manifests itself as verbal aggression, rather than rational, considered discussions. These cause issues in working and personal relationships, resulting in failure to resolve issues and challenges that may then go on to become persistent causes of stress. My stress levels were certainly a contributory factor in the breakdown of my marriage. I was working long hours in a particularly demanding role with unsocial hours - the opposite of family friendly - much of which was soaking up and trying to solve other people's problems. I had two young children, and when I wasn't at work I wanted to be with them. This meant that I was not systematically doing anything to manage my stress levels in terms of exercise etc. In fact, I knew little about how to do that. I just thought you coped. I then had a very steep learning curve! This is one reason why I believe in constant reflection to learn to handle things better: not to 'beat ourselves up', but to openly reflect and learn all the time to become more and more emotionally intelligent. The 2003 film *Anger Management* starring Jack Nicholson and Adam Sandler is a light-hearted look at this, with examples we can all relate to when we have let our fight mechanism control us, rather than us controlling it.

Flight

There are dangerous physical situations in which the safe course of action is to flee, or run away. We flee a tsunami, a typhoon, a sand storm, an earthquake, a volcanic eruption, or similar natural disasters. Our brain tells us to run away when faced with overwhelming physical danger, such as keeping ourselves away from a riot. In situations other than actual physical danger, flight is psychological rather than physical, and manifests itself in avoidance behavior: avoiding stating our views with someone who holds positional power over us, such as a teacher, boss or team coach; avoiding discussing topics we know will cause heated debate or confrontation with family or work colleagues; avoiding raising issues we may have with partners, friends, work colleagues.

All that avoiding the issue does is leave issues unresolved, and we end up living with situations about which we are unhappy or resentful. It can also stop us from asking for clarity about something we're unsure of, which can impact on our performance in education, at work, and in most other fields of endeavour. Avoidance can certainly sour relationships or keep them going at a superficial level in a mode of permanent compromise. Flight responses link to the passive behaviour described in the *Manage Relationships* chapter.

I have always thought it important to face things with my children, and to encourage them to face things rather than fleeing them: even those things that are uncomfortable and cause debate. My experience is that letting things go needs to be a deliberate response for a specific reason, rather than a default mode. If we let go too many things with our children when they're young, it becomes progressively more difficult to challenge behaviours that are unacceptable, or attitudes and behaviours that will hinder their progress, as they get older.

Flock
Traditionally, flock refers to the coming together of similarly threatened people, and then deciding on an appropriate type of response to the fear context or threat scenario, such as protesting against oppression. It can also describe the situation when teenagers, in particular, congregate in groups and flock together in order to reduce stress levels and feel safer. It can be a symptom of low self-regard and lack of confidence to need others around us. It can also be a sign of passivity to feel safer by 'going with the crowd'.

Freeze
Another response to real or perceived danger is to freeze, where the whole system becomes 'frozen'. In a physical sense, this comes

straight from the animal world, where it's designed to protect the animal from feeling pain during an attack, and if an animal is lucky, the predator might think it is already dead and leave it. There are examples of people 'freezing' in extreme danger or disaster situations, when the last thing they need to do is freeze. There are accounts of people appearing to be totally incapable of thought or action and needing to be just directed. For example, 'freezing' behaviour is sometimes cited in natural disasters, which causes evacuation delays, increases the danger, and further extends evacuation delays. In terms of perceived danger or fear, as opposed to real physical danger, we have all experienced the 'freeze' effects of our mind going blank in situations that are very important to us and that we view as critical. We can find situations and events stressful, which can cause performance anxiety. The situations that cause this vary according to the importance we place on them.

Some people may 'freeze' in examinations, whilst others are capable of performing at their best in examinations. For some, it may be performances, music and other arts performances, interviews, public speaking etc. Whatever the situation, we all need to find ways to perform at our best when it matters most to us, and overcome the debilitating affects of our natural 'auto-freeze' response.

It's important to note that this entire FIGHT, FLIGHT, FLOCK, FREEZE survival process is automated; in other words, our brain, or the neural pathways that are triggered, determine how we will respond without us consciously giving any real input.

It's therefore important that we change the neural pathways we've developed that produce responses which negatively impact on our performance.
Acknowledge our fear. Accept our fear.
Don't let our fear control us. Conquer our fear.

FEAR

The only thing we have to fear is fear itself.
Franklin D. Roosevelt

| **THINK** there is something wrong | ⟹ | Feel fearful and anxious | ⟹ | Experience symptoms of fear and anxiety |

Our survival reaction all comes down to our response to fear, whether real or perceived, and the anxiety that causes:

False
Expectations
Appearing
Real

The brain doesn't tend to recognise the difference between a real or an imaginary threat, e.g. running an imaginary argument or fight over in our mind causes stress, the sight of an exam paper or large household bill can cause stress, and we all know what happens when two people in 'reptilian' mode clash! In this mode, we don't find solutions. Firstly, we need to recognise times when we do 'go reptilian', train our mind to view things differently, and avoid the negative effects of worry and stress. We also need to tackle issues head-on and have the courage to search for solutions in the times when we are feeling frightened, stressed or pressured. See the *Managing Stress* chapter for more on this.

Pressure can have the same impact as fear in causing our brain to 'freeze'. If we're desperately trying to remember something, the more we 'pressure' ourselves to remember it, the more elusive it can become. If we just say to ourselves, 'It will come', firstly, we're giving our brain the expectation that we'll remember and, secondly, we're not adding pressure. Most of the time, the elusive information pops to the forefront of our mind. This tendency to freeze under pressure can be recognised in examinations, high profile performances in sports or the arts, interviews, business pitches etc.

The bottom line is that we're going to be frightened on occasions. If we want to succeed we have to be prepared to feel scared, acknowledge it and ignore it or deal with it. In her book *Daring Greatly: How The Courage To Be Vulnerable Transforms The Way We Live, Love, Parent And Lead,* Brené Brown talks about, instead of letting fear stop you, expect it to be there. Acknowledge it and, 'Say, 'I see you, I hear you, but I'll do this anyway'.' She goes on to say, 'It feels dangerous to show up, but it's not as terrifying as thinking, at the end of our lives, 'What if I had shown up? What would have been different?''

How Can We Use This Information to Improve Our Performance and Be Our Best?

Some men see things as they are and ask why.
Others dream things that never were and ask why not.
George Bernard Shaw

Learning and Performing at Our Best

Our mind is where we learn, from formal education to experiential learning, and we can massively improve our capacity to learn by using our mind more effectively. We can practise skills in our mind and it helps embed that learning in our neural pathways. This is not a replacement for learning and technical skill development, but a way of improving skills, knowledge and understanding. We can also practise situations in our mind to help us perform at our best on a day-to-day basis and for that all-important big occasion.

1. Improving Skills, Knowledge and Understanding

Learning new things and improving skills
As we see from considering the function of neurons, we learn by creating neural pathways in our brain. For skill development, we need conscious repetition and deliberate practice in order to create

those pathways. In terms of a physical skill, we need to work hard at repeating exactly the physical movement we want, whether that's a golf shot, using a computer keyboard, a sequence of dance steps, or playing a musical phrase in a piece of music. In any physical activity, we can only repeat it so many times before we become tired and any further repetition is counter productive, risking mistakes (creating the wrong neural pathways!) and chance of accidents and injury. This is where practising things in our mind comes in. If we've learnt what we need to do and know how that feels, we can practise repeatedly in our mind without the physical wear and tear and risk. We can improve our execution of skills by mentally rehearsing the physical movement in our mind. To perform at our best, we need to repeat physical skills precisely and accurately in our mind an perfect execution: deleting poor performance.

Driving on the 'wrong' side of the road!

My first holiday on my own with my children, then aged 11 and 7, was to Mallorca, somewhere new for us all. We landed at night and I'd hired a car so that we could get from the airport to where we were staying at a friend of a friend's house in Port de Soldeu, on the other side of the island. We loaded the car with our luggage and set off. Changing gear with my right hand was something new (it hadn't crossed my mind to get an automatic car!). To get the full picture, add to that: driving on the right, turning right into the right-hand lane and turning left into the right-hand lane; going round roundabouts anti-clockwise; and navigating in the dark with an inadequate map. Needless to say, it was a frightening driving experience! My children both got in the back every time we got in the car over the next few days and I took the car back on the third day!

So, how do you practise driving on the right in England, where we drive on the left? How do you practise driving a left-hand drive car when you don't have access to one? There's only one way, and that's in your mind. The following year, we went back to Mallorca and, again, I hired a car. Three weeks before we departed, I started 'training' myself drive on the right. Sitting up in bed at night, I relaxed, visualised and mentally rehearsed driving a left-hand drive car on the right-hand side of the road, using my experience from the previous year to systematically become competent to safely drive on the right.

When we got into the car at the airport, both children sat in the back (the experience of the previous year clearly still fresh in their mind!). The obvious fear they had acquired previously was replaced by a stunned silence as I drove without hesitation and fairly competently. I'm not saying I drove with the unconscious competence I do at home, but safely enough not to terrify us or other road users.

2. Improving our ability to perform well in specific situations, when it matters most and in achieving our goals

This can be:

- Preparing to go into a lesson. We have all had teachers with whom we don't gel. If we dread those lessons and mentally preview things being difficult, that's what we'll get. If we mentally rehearse smiling and saying hello to our teacher and focusing on what we can get out of the lessons, things will dramatically improve. This also works for those potentially challenging work meetings.

- Preparing for study or work. Thinking through what we want to achieve and how we're going to do it. Preparing our mind to perform well. Preparing for the discipline we need and deciding that we're going to positively look forward to doing what we need to do. Whether we decide we're going to enjoy it or whether we decide we're not going to enjoy it, we're right! We do everything so much better if we go into it with our mind prepared to do well.

- Withdrawing the right information from our mind when it matters most, even when we're under pressure and in competitive situations, e.g. exams, trials, interviews, big performances in any field. The last thing we need when we go into a pressure situation is for our mind to go into survival mode, which will result in all those bodily changes that induce 'freezing' rather than 'flowing'. This is as important as study, cramming and physically practising technical skills. If we know what we need to know to get the grade we want in an examination and don't practise performing at our best in that examination, we can risk our fear and survival mechanism 'freezing' our logical thinking and not allowing us to 'flow' and access the information we need.

- Using our imagination to rehearse situations, or to 'practise' performing in locations we may not have experienced before. Imagining walking into that interview or out on to that sports field, being in that performance space or examination room. Imagining achieving our dreams and goals and what it feels like.

We can help maintain and build our ability and BELIEF to perform at our best and achieve our goals by doing our own programming.

One of the most powerful accounts I have read of the power of the mind is in Sally Gunnell's book, *Be Your Best.* Sally recounts her preparation and performance at the 1992 Barcelona Olympics.

'Let me explain why I believe in the power of the mind so completely. Barcelona 1992: a world-class mind-game.
Ten months before the 1992 Olympics in Barcelona, my chances of winning a gold medal looked slim. I'd come fifth in the 1990 European Championships when everyone had me pegged as favourite. Now, they said I wasn't tough enough to win. They said I was the wrong build. Clearly, I was no sleek cheetah – I was short, with more tendency to go plump than develop big muscles – and it would have been so easy to accept their predictions.

Luckily, their negativity just made me think, 'Right! I'll show you!' Instead of quitting, I searched even harder for advice on preparation. I visited the 1968 Olympic champion of the 400m hurdles, David Hemery, to find out how he achieved his magnificent victory. He told me to visualize. 'Oh, I do that already, the night before a race,' I told him. 'I go through it all in my mind so I'm mentally prepared.' 'No I mean really visualize,' he said. 'Every day, several times a day, I want you to go through every aspect of the 400m hurdles Olympic final in your mind, from the instant the gun fires to the moment you cross the line. I want you to imagine every possible race. I want you to stand next to every possible competitor, with different athletes ahead at different stages. Only one thing must always be the same: you must always win.'

So I did. Every day, eight or 10 times a day, I went through that race in my mind. I did it while I ran; I did it lying down with my eyes shut. Sometimes the imaginary me made a mistake, so I'd see myself correcting it and carrying on. Sometimes I'd nearly get to the end and find I wasn't in front, so I had to rewind and play it again to make sure I was. I must have run that final more than 2000 times before I lined up for it on a warm evening in Barcelona.

I was so nervous I wanted to be anywhere else in the world but there. I left my coach in the warm-up area and then, for about 45 minutes, I sat in a room with the other competitors, all trying to psyche each other out. As we walked onto the track I could feel thousands of people watching us but I didn't look up. I just kept thinking to myself, 'Okay Sally, this is your chance. You really can win this. This is your moment.' We went to our starting blocks. There was more waiting around but I just wanted to get it over. A whistle blew, to warn us to get ready. My heart did a double beat and suddenly I had a strong feeling like I'd never had before. 'You're going to win this,' it said.

That was it. I don't remember anything of the race. I knew I'd crossed the line but had I really won? Or was this just another mental? I didn't know if I was going over it in my head or I'd actually done it for real. I had to keep saying to myself, 'You've done it! You're an Olympic champion!' I was in a magical cocoon and I couldn't take in everything, the stadium was a sea of British flags and people waving. When I saw my family and heard them say it, I finally knew it was true. I really had done it.

Seventy per cent of that race was won by my mind. From then on, I was totally sold on mental techniques and I continued to learn more about their potential. Visualization is not a magic potion you can only use once and never again, it's the ultimate 'use it or lose it'. The more you practise, the better it gets, as I found a year later, before the World Championships.'

We can apply the techniques Sally used to be our best in anything we want: education and training, physical activities, problem-solving, management and leadership roles, overcoming challenges and realising our goals.

3. Improving our ability to manage relationships

Systematic preparation also helps us with one of the most important aspects of our life, if not the most important aspect, that is the way we relate to others. Indeed, that is why an element of my equipped2succeed framework is focused on *Managing Relationships*. In family, personal, social and work situations we can continuously improve the way we handle our relationships with others. An important contribution to this can be mentally rehearsing scenarios and situations, going through them in our heads with various possible responses, and deciding how we will handle them. We can improve our handling of those everyday scenarios with our children and other family members, lowering the emotional temperature when there are differences, practising positive responses or practising keeping our protective force field or bubble in place when faced with things that irritate us from relatives who really aren't going to change!

4. Improving Our Ability to Respond to Challenges and Find Solutions

People like Leonardo da Vinci and Albert Einstein were masters of using the power of their mind to find creative solutions. Using the creative powers of our imagination and maintaining a positive, can-do, growth mindset can be the difference between rising to, or being overwhelmed by, challenges. We can think of those people who might help us, whether from history or currently, whether people we know or people we don't, and have an imaginary discussion in our mind to help us creatively solve problems. We can also use creative thinking techniques to improve our capacity to adapt, grow, be innovative and make the positive changes we need to make to overcome barriers and find solutions. There are some creative thinking tools that you can try and use with your children on the equipped2succeed section of my website.

5. Creating Positive Habits

> *We are what we repeatedly do.*
> *Excellence, therefore, is not an act but a habit.*
> Aristotle

Habits are behaviours that we repeatedly do. These are created in our neural pathways and we can help create and reinforce positive habits and delete negative habits by systematic, focused mental rehearsal. We need to physically create those habits by taking action and we can support that by mentally rehearsing maintaining those habits. It is said that it takes consistent practise over 21 consecutive days for most of us to develop a habit. That is the case with practising mental rehearsal and using positive thinking and language, just as it is with eating healthily or establishing an exercise regime. Of course, establishing new habits is easier for some than others. I think this depends on how engrained our old habits are, how open-minded we are and how well we have established our growth mindset.

Everything we do starts with a thought, and successful people generate the thoughts that keep their mind focused on the most important things and recognise the power of having space from tasks to effectively use their creative powers to help achieve their goals.

> *Basically, we are what we think we are and*
> *become what we think we will become.*

> *We are totally responsible for our thinking as adults and*
> *we have a responsibility to enable our children to take*
> *control of their thinking;*

*to think in a way that enables them to
succeed in life and their chosen endeavours.*

**Constantly reinforce with our children that we can
CHOOSE OUR THOUGHTS.**

*The greatest discovery of my generation is that human beings
can alter their lives by altering their attitudes of mind.*
William James

Creative Thinking Skills

Successful people understand themselves – how they think, how they learn, their strengths, and how they need to develop. They constantly challenge themselves to think innovatively or, to use a common management phrase, to think 'outside the box'. Creative Thinking Skills have never been more important. Nothing is certain apart from uncertainty. We have a wealth of information at our fingertips, but we need to be discerning in the use of that information. Our access to infinite amounts of information and digital stimuli supports individuals and teams to make tremendous advancements in all fields. However, it also means that individuals can feel inundated with information, and we all need to be discerning in the way we use that information to inform our development and our decision making. We also need to think creatively. Developing our capacity to think creatively helps us adapt and make the most of new situations, new information and new opportunities. Creative thinking makes a vital contribution to our capacity to succeed.

'Think outside the box' is commonly used in management speak to mean 'think creatively, unimpeded by orthodox or conventional constraints'. The value of developing young peoples' capacity to think creatively is demonstrated by the fact that there are currently a number of courses and qualifications on offer in schools and colleges that help young people develop their thinking and reasoning skills. These are very often taught at Post16, alongside A-Levels, when they may be of much more use than earlier in our children's educational life. These are mirrored by similar creative thinking courses used in business to maintain and develop the forward momentum essential to survive in a highly changeable, competitive economic environment.

We can help our children develop their capacity to think for themselves, spot opportunities and think creatively by encouraging them, from a very young age, to come up with their own solutions, both with puzzles and games, and also in real-life situations. We must also model being open to new ideas and encourage our children to think about things from different perspectives. Too much 'telling' doesn't develop thinkers. Whatever challenges our children face, it is always best to ask them for their ideas and suggestions when helping them find solutions. By insightful questioning, we can often bring our children to their own solutions. This boosts their self-regard and belief in their capacity to face challenges and find their own solutions.

Imagination is more important than knowledge
Albert Einstein

Creativity goes beyond knowledge recall and extends into knowledge creation. Using our imagination and creativity is crucial to 'create' the future we want, see the best path for us, adapt to and handle challenges. It is important to use our imagination and creativity with our knowledge and experience to perform at our best. In some circumstances, it can be more important! Sometimes, we can't see the way to do something better because we are weighed down by knowledge and experience of the way it's always been done. Sometimes, we have vast knowledge in a field and finding improvement comes from another field: education and business learning from sports; sports learning from physics, etc. Original ideas inevitably are created by conceptually blending subjects from different fields into something new, as was and is d by the greatest thinkers, one of the most notable being Leonardo da Vinci.

It's important to recognise, acknowledge and value our children's creativity and imagination. There is always a different way to do things. There's always a better way to do things. Whether it's academic study, music or sports, if we raise our children to value their ideas, they will find the best ways to achieve in what's important to them, including adapting teachers', coaches' and mentors' advice to suit them. They must be empowered to adapt accepted wisdom to suit their unique individuality or deference to accepted wisdom may hold them back. One of the ways our creativity is fuelled is by curiosity, and it's vital that we respond positively to our children's natural curiosity. We all know that the thousands of questions our children ask as they grow can be demanding, but we need to find ways to respond, and if we don't know the answer to their question, be honest and agree to help them find out. Making up fanciful stories in response to factual questions does not serve our children well, even when they're young. Being curious and developing our curiosity is an important aspect we glean from Leonardo da Vinci's thinking processes, and curiosity is one of the key elements in Michael Gelb's book, *How to Think Like Leonardo da Vinci: Liberating Creative Thinking And Innovation In The Workplace.*

In order to let our imagination and creativity flow, we need space. That can be environmental space, some people are at their most creative by the sea or looking over open land; some people when there's certain music playing; some people when it's quiet, etc. It can be 'head space', away from the myriad of demands we have around us.

Creativity is seeing what others see and
thinking what no one else has ever thought.
Albert Einstein

I'm at my most creative and productive whenever I'm away from the day-to-day stuff - ideas flow, writing flows, and solutions come. It doesn't necessarily mean being away by the sea (although I do like that option). It can be as simple as being in a café away from my office and home, where I can completely focus on what I'm working on. Things that don't involve me do not distract my mind. My RAS doesn't notice them. If someone comes into the café that I know, I notice, no matter how engrossed I am. It can also be just moving to another room or outdoor space. We are all different, and individually we need to find the conditions where we are at our most creative.

We think too small, like the frog at the bottom of the well.
He thinks the sky is only as big as the top of the well.
If he surfaced, he would have an entirely different view.
Mao Tse-Tung

People who use the power of their mind recognise the importance of

intuition   instinct   imagination

as well as facts, logic and analysis.

We need to trust ourselves - our belief, skill, instinct, knowledge and intuition - and go into things with belief in both ourselves, and the capacity of our mind, to make the right decisions.

If we allow pressure to 'freeze' our brain, or the way some put it, 'let the nerves get to us', our judgement goes. Keeping our brain in flow to access our accumulated knowledge and experience, as well as our intuition and imagination, is crucial, and we can only learn to do this by managing our mind: practising relaxation, visualisation and mental rehearsal to allow our mind to make the right connections when we need to make those all-important decisions.

Creativity can solve almost any problem. The creative act, the defeat of habit by originality, overcomes everything.
George Lois

Focus and Discipline

Focus and discipline serve us in whatever we want to achieve. They are natural partners with curiosity and creative flow, and an important part of us developing our persistence and resilience. What if Edison had given up after finding 9,999 ways a light bulb didn't work?

I have not failed. I've just found 10,000 ways that won't work.
Our greatest weakness lies in giving up. The most certain way
to succeed is always to try just one more time.
Thomas A. Edison

Developing our focus and discipline allows us to be creative, spot opportunities and coincidences, and recognise our infinite capabilities. This cannot be underestimated in developing our thinking for achievement. Learning something about our brain-power and training our mind, just as we train our bodies, will help us to think positively and achieve. Using our brain effectively, focusing our mind on the positive and always learning will lead to continuous improvement and success. All this requires focused, disciplined action on our part.

Think about when you first learned something, for example, riding a bike: how difficult it was, and how you kept practising and practising until your brain could tell your body how to do it well. You could then cycle without having to think about how to do it. So it is with everything – learning new skills, learning how to do things better, changing negative habits to positive habits, overcoming fear etc requires repeated, disciplined until they become a natural for us.

Developing Our Winning Mentality

Sven Goran Eriksson on footballer Mihajlovic:

> *He doesn't believe he can lose, and even if he does,*
> *it makes no impression on him.*
> *In every match he plays with exactly the same attitude:*
> *he's going to win.*

We have learned a lot about developing a winning mentality from sport, which has gone on to be applied in other fields, especially business and education. Sport is a field where constant improvement is essential: to gain our place on the team; to win trophies as individuals and teams; to retain funding at grass roots and elite levels; to obtain and maintain sponsorship; to gain and retain a contract as an individual etc. Sports Governing Bodies only get continued financial support if they can demonstrate improved outcomes. Some of the basics of a winning mentality are just as applicable in performing at your best in examinations in school as they are in performing at your best in the sports arena.

Definition of a Winner:

One's ability to maximise one's potential, even under pressure and in competitive situations.

Many people have ability, skill and knowledge that enable them to perform at their best in non-pressure situations. What's important to succeed in learning, business, sport, the arts, science, engineering and all other fields of endeavour is to perform at our best when it matters most: in that all-important examination, that crucial job interview, that pitch for funding to keep scientific research going, that important engineering breakthrough, and in those crucial performances. When it matters most, we need to be at our best. Training our mind is one of the ways we can ensure that happens.

'She / he's always in control' is a phrase often used about winners or high achievers in any context. Winners are able to control their emotional state when it matters most. They think correctly or clearly under pressure, not feeling fear. They therefore do not send their mind into survival mode or allow their mind to 'feel the pressure'. They **T.C.U.P.**

> Think
> Correctly (Clearly)
> Under
> Pressure

When under that pressure, we always have more time than we feel / think we have. Those who perform at elite levels sometimes talk about the feeling of time standing still when taking that crucial shot, making that important break-through, running that all-important race. We hear young people talk about having more time than they thought in examinations, when their minds are in flow and they are recalling all the information they need. In order to practice T.C.U.P. and perform at our best under pressure, we need to train our mind to flow rather than freeze when it matters most. Trust our skills, trust our knowledge, trust our experience, trust our ability to handle challenge and allow all our learning to flow to instinctively enable us to perform at our best.

⚡ Relaxation – Visualisation – Mental Rehearsal R – V – MR

Relaxation, Visualisation and Mental Rehearsal, which I abbreviate to R – V – MR, is the act of relaxing, visualising, mentally rehearsing and regarding what's in our mind as an objective reality. It is our own personal programming technique. Variations of this process are proven to work in sports, and are d, in their own unique way, by those who succeed in their chosen field of endeavour.

We can use this process for anything: helping our self-belief; discipline and focus in what we want to achieve each day and in the future; improving skills; improving every day life and relationships; performing under pressure; as well as for helping us to focus on our big goals. As our mind goes on working when we're asleep, one of the best times to embed learning, rehearse situations or see ourselves achieving our goals is just before we go to sleep. The vast power of our mind can then work on it overnight. This is an essential brain workout that helps us achieve the results we choose. It helps us take full control of our mind and choose our thoughts. That enables us to focus on where we want to be and what we want to happen rather than allowing negativity to limit us.

The relaxation, visualisation, mental rehearsal process can be used to improve every aspect of our well-being and performance: to relieve stress and tension and focus on improving our performance and achieving our goals.

equipped2succeed

Relaxation – Visualisation – Mental Rehearsal
e2s - R-V-MR - The process

Step 1

Relaxation *- enables our mind to be quiet and enables us to focus.*

Effective relaxation relieves stress, tension and anxiety. Relaxing enables us to clear our mind and allows us to be creative and to focus our thinking on what we want to achieve. Relaxation allows our brain to make the right connections to use our mind effectively to constantly improve our performance. Great thinkers, such as Leonardo da Vinci and Albert Einstein, are said to have recognised that they had some of their best ideas when they were so relaxed they were almost dozing. They therefore held a bunch of keys in their hands when they were sat beside the fire thinking so that if they fell asleep, the keys would fall, wake them, and they would be able to recall the ideas they were having in this relaxed state. Being relaxed helps us focus our mind on our desired outcomes – what we want to achieve. Learning to relax effectively enables us to train our mind in the same way we train our body. We can then use our mind to improve our skills, knowledge and performance through visualisation and mental rehearsal.

The basis of any relaxation is calming our breathing and relaxing our muscles. Being focused on our breathing, and consciously breathing in and out in a consistent rhythm, helps us to quiet our body and mind. We can relax our muscles by systematically tensing and relaxing our muscles throughout our bodies, starting with our head and moving all the way to our feet. Some of us can relax and quiet our mind easier than others. I still find any form of relaxation and meditation more challenging than some people. We also need to be conscious that it is very difficult to go through any form of systematic relaxation if we are full of stimulants, such as caffeine.

Step 2

Visualisation *– enables us to imagine in our mind what we want to achieve and how we want to perform.*

Visualisation enables us to go on a mental journey into our imagination, where we can vividly use the power of our thinking to see ourselves achieving what we want, achieving our individual peak performance. Image the scene in your mind – the classroom, the examination hall, the difficult discussion, the sports field, the board room, the stage, the interview, the relationship discussion, the training session - and see yourself in bright colour saying what you want to say, responding appropriately to others or performing at your peak in your chosen endeavour. We can watch our mental rehearsal happen – again and again – like action replays.

Step 3

Mental Rehearsal - *enables us to use our mind to practise our skills and performance.*

Through mental rehearsal, we can see, feel and hear ourselves achieving our goals. We can rehearse things in our mind, creating scenarios and achieving exactly what we want to achieve, practicing skills and reinforcing what we've learned, preparing for specific important and pressured situations. We can rewind and do it better: handling a discussion better; overcoming a good opponent; performing at our peak – preparing for education, training and all sorts of situations and performances – seeing ourselves achieving in whatever is important to us.

You can download music and a guided r-v-mr track, especially designed to aid this process, from a link on the equipped2succeed downloads section of my website. This link takes you to the free equipped2succeed r-v-mr tracks. The guided r-v-mr track talks you through the process to help you establish your own process. The music has been especially composed to help our brain relax, visualise and mentally rehearse.

Using relaxation, visualisation and mental rehearsal is important to train our mind for the everyday stuff of life, as well as to help us pursue our big goals.

I have used this technique from when I first started to learn how the brain works. I have especially used it to manage stress, see myself achieving my goals, manage relationships, bring about desired results in meetings, golf shots (although those who have seen me play may say I need lots more real and mental), as well as the practical example I described above, *Driving On the Wrong Side of the Road*. I have visualised and mentally rehearsed publishing this book for years. The focus and format was developed in my mind and was clear to me long before I started shaping all my material, which then became what you're now reading.

Harriet and George started to learn in detail about their brain and how it works when they were 12 and 8 respectively. George started using r-v-mr straight away for free kicks in football, with spectacular results. This proved to him that it worked, and he's used it ever since in pursuing his sporting dreams. Harriet has used it in all sorts of ways: for study, athletics, preparing for examinations, preparing for her driving test, and seeing herself buy her first home.

Use the power of your mind to perform at your best.

It is a common experience that a problem
difficult at night is resolved in the morning
after the committee of sleep has worked on it.
John Steinbeck

Looking After Our Brain

The brain represents three percent of the body's weight and uses 20 percent of the body's energy.

There is a lot we can do to look after our brain, our major physiological organ, and our mind, which is who we are as individuals. The majority of the energy consumed by the brain powers the rapid firing of the millions of neurons communicating with each other. The rest of its energy is used for controlling other activities - both unconscious activities, such as heart rate, and conscious ones, such as driving a car. At any given moment, not all of the brain's regions are concurrently firing. However, brain researchers using imaging technology have shown that, like the body's muscles, most are continually active over a 24-hour period.

Even in sleep, areas such as the frontal cortex, which controls things like higher-level thinking and self-awareness, are active. What is clear from all the research is that we need to look after our brain if we want it to perform at its best and get the most from our mind. The *Maximise Energy* chapter is relevant here, in that being D.E.A.R to ourselves, and looking after our Diet, Exercise, Attitude and Rest, helps us to maximise the potential of our mind.

Eating healthily – there are the basics of healthy eating, but particular brain foods that are recognised to help our brain's function include: whole grains – helping sustain energy for longer, oily fish, blueberries, blackcurrants, pumpkin seeds, tomatoes, broccoli, sage and nuts.

Drinking plenty of water - water is essential for our brain to work effectively and it's no coincidence that a headache is a sign of being dehydrated.

Exercising – our brain loves to move. Exercise helps get more essential oxygen to our brain, stimulates positive endorphins and our ability to think clearly. *Spark: The Revolutionary New Science of Exercise and the Brain* by John J. Ratey shows the amazing impact of exercise on the brain. Amongst other benefits for the mind, the book describes studies in American schools that demonstrate the value exercise has in the learning process, with exercise resulting in improved academic performance, alertness, attention and motivation.

We also need to use our mind! Use it or lose it! Our thinking improves the more we use, stimulate and expand our mind.

Iron rusts from disuse; water loses its purity from stagnation... even so does inaction sap the vigor of the mind.
Leonardo da Vinci

One of the best books for giving us a comprehensive overview of how the brain works, how best to make the most of our brain's potential and look after our brain, is Dr John Medina's *Brain rules – 12 principles for surviving and thriving at work, home and school.* There is a summary of his rules on his website: brainrules.net

Affirmations

- I am relishing using the amazing power of my mind.
- I am powerfully using my focus and positive thinking to pursue my goals.
- I am at my best using my brilliant brainpower to focus on my goals.
- I am enjoying the power of my creativity.

ACTION

Every day give yourself a good mental shampoo.
Dr. Sara Jordan

1. For 1 minute, write down all the things your brain is doing at this time (eg: controlling heart, lungs).
    Reflect on the enormous power your brain has to do all the things you don't even have to think about. Now imagine what your mind could do if you took control and systematically put into the world's greatest computer - your mind - things that will help you achieve your goals.

2. Think of the people who positively challenge your thinking (the people who want to help you achieve your goals – not those who put you down). In what ways do they challenge you to do better? What is positive about that? What is negative? Do you use them to give you a new perspective, expanding your thinking and understanding?

Remember that friction creates heat, and friction also creates new understanding and helps us develop if we positively harness it.

If you find some people too challenging at times, use R – V – MR to practise having a positive interaction with them where you gain new understanding and feel OK at the end.

3.   Practice using your imagination. Take yourself off to a place you know will be quiet and comfortable and consciously clear your mind for 30 minutes. You may have to start with 10 and build up slowly. You will be amazed how your thinking will improve, how you will have new perspectives and ideas regularly.

4.   Use the e2s r-v-mr tracks to:

- use your imagination;

- think positively;

- practise your skills;

- rehearse your day going exactly how you want it to go;

- rehearse a lesson or session;

- rehearse an important performance;

- manage relationships - get on with people;

- overcome fears;

- achieve your goals, the things that are really important to you – things you want to do, have, be.

Nothing but your own thoughts
can hamper your progress.
anon

Chapter Seven

Be Positive

 Definition

positive:

- explicitly stated, stipulated, or expressed;
- emphatic;
- confident in opinion or assertion; fully assured;
- emphasizing what is laudable, hopeful, or to the good; constructive: *a positive attitude toward the future;*
- not speculative or theoretical; practical: *a positive approach to the problem;*
- possessing an actual force, being, existence;
- constructive and sure, rather than sceptical;
- showing or expressing approval or agreement;
- full of hope and confidence, or giving cause for hope and confidence.

We Are What We Think We Are
and
Will Become What We Think We Will Become

I love the title of Emeli Sande's track, *Our Version of Events*, because that's exactly what we want our future to be, and what we want for our children: to be able to create their version of events. And surely we want our version of events to be positive? No matter what we do in life, a positive mindset, positive thinking, positive language and positive feelings bring better outcomes for us, and those around us. Much of this book is about the way we think and how that affects our potential, and our children's potential, to achieve. We attract into our lives the things we think about, whether they're positive or negative; so surely we want the positive version?

Our mindset influences everything we do
and we can choose our mindset.

This the last of human freedoms - to choose one's attitude in any given set of circumstances, to choose one's own way.
Viktor Frankl
Concentration Camp survivor and author of
Man's Search for Meaning.

We can choose the way we are in every situation, and approaching people, goals and tasks with a positive mindset has tremendous benefits in all areas of life.

Relationships – family, personal, professional, leisure and interests, as well as those people you come into contact with on a casual basis. No matter who we interact with, about what, being positive improves relationships and is better for everyone involved.

Whoever is happy will make others happy too.
Anne Frank

Goals – decide and articulate what you want, not what you don't want. Having specific goals and being positive and enthusiastic about achieving them will help us attract all the help we need.

Learning – we get much more from formal study and informal learning if we approach it with a positive, open mind-set – one that appreciates the joy of learning and the benefits for us.

Work – if we find the positive in our work, and are positive with others in work we will reap the rewards: with colleagues, with increased satisfaction and financial return.

Interests – whether our interests are sports, music, art, technology – we will have more fun, achieve much more and gain more satisfaction with a positive mind-set. If we can't be positive about our interests, perhaps we're pursuing the wrong ones. Let's avoid being that angry, energy sapper in the team!

Positive Mental Attitude – P.M.A.

Having a positive attitude and outlook is essential for success in any field. Research shows that elite athletes and successful business people alike all share a relentlessly positive mental attitude (PMA). For example, Colin Jackson, world champion hurdler and now successful athletics (track and field) commentator, when tested, was off the scale with his positive attitude. That's what helped him become an Olympic medallist, world champion, world record holder, and an exceptional competitor on *Strictly Come Dancing*.

Being positive: focusing our thinking on the positive things we want, rather than dwelling on the negative things we don't, is essential for success, both in specific endeavours and to achieve holistic success in living a happy, fulfilled life. By this, I mean enjoying every day, being grateful, relishing every experience, finding the positive in our experiences.

It's not our environment or what happens to us that determines our attitude, but rather how we respond to our situation.

Charles Swindoll sums it up very well:

The remarkable thing we have is a choice every day regarding the attitude we will embrace for that day.
We cannot change our past.
We cannot change the fact that people will act in a certain way.
We cannot change the inevitable.
The only thing we can do is play on the one string we have, and that is our attitude.

Some of the most successful people have experienced very hard times but maintained a positive mental attitude and succeeded in their field: business leaders, politicians, charity leaders, sports people, actors, musicians, people in every field of endeavour.

There are some key things to consider when seeking to improve and maintain a positive mind-set and positive feelings. For us, and our children, to think and be more positive, we need to maintain positive language. Our emotional state - our feelings - affect everything we are and everything we do. Therefore, the way we feel has a powerful impact on what happens and what we can achieve in all areas of our life.

Our mindset influences our emotional state and that of those around us. The way we think affects the way we feel, and vice versa, so if we are going to achieve and be happy, we need to ensure that positive emotions and feelings predominate in our thinking, which can be summarised as:

Enjoyment: happiness, joy, relief, contentment, bliss, delight, amusement, pride, sensual pleasure, thrill, rapture, gratification, satisfaction, euphoria;

Love: acceptance, friendliness, trust, kindness, affinity, devotion, adoration;

Surprise: astonishment, amazement, wonder.

Our feelings drive us and determine our momentum towards our goals. To continue the driving analogy, our feelings enable us to balance our life through the gears. We don't want to be stuck in reverse or neutral. However, if we drive in fifth gear all the time, we will burn out.

We are going to suffer sadness, anger and a whole host of negative emotions from time to time. We feel sadness when we suffer loss, but it's essential for our wellbeing that we accept it, without letting it overwhelm us for too long. We will feel angry about things from time to time. Firstly, we need to reflect and think whether or not it's something important enough for us to be angry about. All too often, I meet people who are angry too frequently about too many small things. Secondly, if it's something that means a lot to us, we must either do something about it then let it go, or, if we can't do anything about it, just let it go. Hanging on to negative emotions drains our energy: makes us anxious and blocks us from focusing all-important energy and feelings on the positive things in our lives.   It's challenging, but crucial, to find the positive and focus our attention on the positives in people, the positives in our lives, and the outcomes we want.

Moving Through Our Gears!

Reverse	"Woe is me." Negative feelings & language keep us in a negative cycle. Bored. Can't be bothered.
Neutral	Rest from the other gears! In danger of stalling! Don't know. Stuck. Unable to move forward. Telling ourselves we're getting nowhere. Lack of focus and direction.
1st	Moving forward slowly, on one thing at a time. Limited to focusing on one thing at once.
2nd	Picking up pace on achieving our goals.
3rd	Starting to implement plans in a more disciplined, determined way.
4th	Moving forward on all our goals in a systematic way.
5th	Full speed ahead on all our goals. Taking disciplined, focused action every day. Maintaining balance means we need to use neutral to ensure we rest enough, keeping our energy for the important things.

Being Positive – The Power Of Positive Language

There are three main aspects of language that we need to think about when improving our positive mind-set.

What We Say to Others - The Language We Use

Framing our language in the positive is vital. That means saying what you do want, not what you don't want.

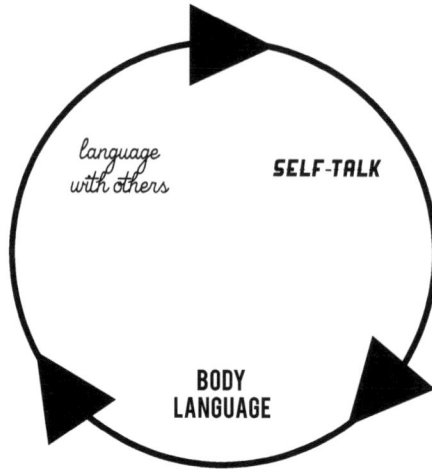

Finding the positive in situations and experiences. Here are some everyday examples in the home that we can hear ourselves saying with our children:

> **P:** Please put your dirty washing in the laundry bin.
> N. Don't leave your dirty washing on the floor.

> **P:** I need you to contribute more by ....
> N: You never help. I have to keep telling you all the time or I have to do everything myself.

> **P:** Keep your mouth closed when you're eating.
> N. Don't open your mouth whilst you're eating.

> **P:** Hold that thought. Wait until the other person has finished talking before you speak.
> N: Don't interrupt.

You'll notice that much of the issue is starting a phrase with 'don't'. Our brains don't really hear or register the 'don't', and therefore just hear the rest of the sentence as a command, and the behavior we're looking to modify continues. That's why we hear ourselves saying, 'I've told him / her over and over again not to do that'.

We just need to say what we do want, not what we don't.

There are times when we need to challenge our children's behaviour or attitude, and it's always best to do this within a version of the **Praise Sandwich.** Find a positive, say what you want them to improve, then end with a positive. This way we temper the criticism in a way that they can take it on board without it affecting their self-regard. There's more on the impact of our language on the self-regard of our children in the *Believe in Yourself* chapter.

What We Say to Ourselves - Our Self-Talk

> *If you think you can do a thing or think*
> *you can't do a thing, you're right.*
> Henry Ford

Self-talk refers to the ongoing internal conversation we hold with ourselves, which influences how we feel and behave. Self-talk is the most powerful of language in influencing our behaviour and what we achieve.

Negative self-talk is characterised by thinking such as:

'I can't.'

'I'm never going to get this done in time.'

'This test is going to be too difficult for me. I'm never going to pass.'

'I knew this would be a bad day as soon as I was late.' (You knew it, so it was so!)

Positive self-talk is characterised by thinking such as:

'I can.'

'I'll get this done in time. It will be a challenge, but I can do it.'

'This test will be challenging, but I know I'm good enough to pass. I will pass.'

'I knew I would make the time up after being late.' (You knew it, so it was so!)

The Power of Gratitude

> *The greatest discovery of any generation is that*
> *human beings can alter their lives by altering*
> *the attitudes of their minds.*
> Albert Schweitzer

One of the best ways of maintaining our positive self-talk is by practising gratitude. For me, this is powerfully described in Rhonda Byrne's inspiring film and books, *The Secret* and *The Power*. In brief, practising gratitude is reflecting on the things we are grateful for: family, health, friends, wealth, and abundance in our lives. By focusing on what we have, we put out positive thoughts of abundance and create those all-important good feelings that help us move on to achieve what we really want.

Body Language

We can change the way we think and feel by changing our body language, and this also has an enormous affect on the way we are received by people.

Why is body language so important?

Research undertaken at the University of Pennsylvania set out to determine to what extent a person's body language can affect the impression people form of him/her. The surprising result was that body language was found to be more responsible for the impression people form of you than your words. Here are some of the findings they came up with regarding the impression people form of you:

- 55% is based on your postures, body movements and gestures;
- 38% is based on the tone of your voice (tempo and frequency);
- only 7% is based on what you say.

This means that a total of 93% of the impression people form of you is determined by your **body language** (which includes both body gestures and voice tone), whilst only 7% is based on the words you speak.

Now, consider what impact your body language has on you and those around you. Think about how you feel when using positive and negative body language.

Positive body language is smooth, balanced, firm and open, characterised by:

> appropriate eye contact (dependent on culture);
> smiling;
> 'smiling' eyes;
> open posture;
> standing tall (without being intimidating);
> enthusiastic gestures;
> body language in tune with what you say;
> body language appropriate to the environment / situation.

> *A smile is a light in the window of the*
> *soul indicating that the heart is home.*
> Anonymous

Negative Body Language can take lots of forms, but most common are either submission or aggression:

> **Submissive** body language is characterised by:
> hunched inwards;
> head down;
> still;
> smiling with your mouth, but not your eyes.

> **Aggressive** body language is characterised by:
> disapproving facial expressions (frowning);
> sighing;
> invading personal space;
> large gestures.

I am very aware that my feelings are near the surface, and I have needed to work very hard to 'coat' criticism and disapproval in some way.

I have needed to learn to consciously frame issues in a way that focuses on challenging individuals to improve and positive outcomes rather than negative criticism that leaves people feeling negative I all sorts of ways. My negative body language was 'sighing', which is heavily weighted with disapproval. It makes people feel much worse than explaining clearly the issue and seeking to find a solution. I am on a continuous mission to address this, and would like to take this opportunity to apologise to anyone who has 'felt' my sigh, especially my children.

How We Receive What Others Say To Us

Just as it's important to be positive in what we say, it's equally important to receive what others say in a positive way. This doesn't mean agree with everything people say, but respond in an open, non-judgemental way.

Ensuring we receive what others say positively starts with listening actively.

Positive, active listening makes people feel we're interested and enables us to really hear what they say. It is vital for our children to feel they are listened to and heard by us.

Negative, disinterested listening makes people feel we're not interested, and we miss things and misunderstand what they are saying. I re-iterate: it is vital for our children to feel they are listened to and heard by us. Also, if we don't listen to them, what message are you sending to them about how important it is to listen?

There are times when we have other pressing priorities, and we really don't have the time to listen to a long story. In this case, we say that we are interested, but have 'x' (be specific rather than just saying busy – little people appreciate this just as much as adults) to do; and agree a time when we *can* listen. Of course, this is not so useful with little people who want to tell you NOW! But it's important for our children to learn that the world does not constantly revolve around them, as long as we do make time to listen more times than not.

How do you feel when someone is obviously not listening to, or hearing, what you say?

A few of other things to remember when considering how we can enable our children to think positively:

Mirroring – they will mirror us!

Modelling – they will follow the behaviour we model!

And the old Victorian adage, 'Do as I say, not as I do', doesn't work.

In all this, it is worth keeping in mind that even if you behave a certain way only 40% of the time, people will perceive you as behaving that way all of the time!

> *A positive attitude is like a fire: unless you continue to add fuel, it goes out.*
> Alexander Lockheart

Personal Energy

> *Be a fountain, not a drain.*
> Rex Hudler

At this point, it's worth mentioning how our positive or negative energy can affect others. We all have energy around us, and it is either positive or negative. Those of us who are more able to tune into other's feelings may feel the positive and negative energy of others more acutely. However, most of us have walked into a room and felt the negative tension or the positive warmth, the anger or the enthusiasm. What we need to be aiming for is to create positive energy and protect ourselves from negative energy.

We have all met people who are energy givers: who radiate positive energy and who make us feel better by spending time with them. We've also met those who are energy sappers: who drain our energy with their negativity if we don't protect ourselves. The term 'mood hoover' illustrates this very well.

Energy Givers and Energy Sappers

There are positive people who, by the sheer nature of their positive attitude and energy, give you energy. That doesn't mean people who are ingratiatingly nice, complement everything we do etc. Energy givers may be challenging but they do it from a positive standpoint of wanting us to be the best version of ourselves, achieve our dreams and goals, and know that some positive challenge is required to do that. Then there are the energy sappers, or 'mood hoovers'. They are negative, have a 'BUT' for every positive idea or solution we put forward and, if we allow them, soak up our positive energy and leave us drained. We need to remove the energy sappers from our circle or, if they are family, make sure our protective force field is intact and strong. My failure in this area has been that, by the nature of my 'can always improve' instinct and desire for people to be their best, I have too often tried to change those people around me. Many times, it would have been better to accept what I could not change and focus on protecting myself and on that over which I could actually have some positive influence.

So, if we need / want to associate with the energy sappers, as they are close family members or close childhood friends who, despite everything, we want to help, we need our protection mechanisms in place. Again, very successful people have these naturally and are generally better at not letting him or her 'get to them'. I believe that, naturally, they have a better in-built force field or protective 'bubble'. It has certainly taken me many years to develop mine, and I still have to very consciously pull it on or wrap it around me when the 'mood hoovers' are around.

Severiano 'Seve' Ballesteros, one of the greatest golfers the world has ever seen, talked about his 'bubble'. When he was young, his parents were rarely at his golf tournaments when most of the other boys' parents were there. He felt this, particularly when teeing off. He therefore developed his bubble, which he put around himself when he was making a shot, to shut out the outside world. We need to let all the positives in and let the negatives bounce off us. Sometimes, we do this the other way around: hear the negatives and not the praise, which damages our mood, our positive self-image, our self-regard and self-belief.

Use The Positive and Dispel The Negative.
Creating Our Own Protective Bubble or Protective Force-field.

My children say I live in my own 'bubble'.
I surround myself with positivity, positive people

(or, if they're not always positive, they very often are around me because they know I'll reframe things in the positive anyway). I am very highly tuned to people's positive or negative state, and as soon as they slip into negativity, my 'bubble' comes on and I endeavour to ensure all the negativity bounces off (not always successfully, but then I am human and sensitive to others!). I actively listen, I empathise, I endeavour to find the positives, I try to help them find solutions, but I don't allow their negative toxicity to drain me. I have taken on other's challenges many times over the years at an enormous cost to my own well-being. That doesn't mean I'm not critical. I am always looking for improvement and that means being critical, but when I criticise, I always endeavour to offer solutions. If I occasionally slip into negative criticism of something or someone, my children, friends and colleagues are genuinely shocked, and the look on their faces swiftly brings me back to myself. Isn't it great when our children reflect our thinking back to us and teach us the things we've taught them?

The bubble can be whatever image we want around us. It is just a visual representation of what we need to do in our mind when confronted by people who will sap our positive energy if we don't protect ourselves against it.

Just like anything else in life – with positive thinking,
you get out what you put in.

I am always optimistic and positive about what others can achieve. Having high, positive expectations of myself and those around me is essential to me as I have learned, from my own experience with my family and working with children and people of all ages, that most people live up to or down to the expectations of those around them. I am always seeking to find the positive in others, as well as challenging those around me to improve.

- **Say positive things to people and you get positives back, and vice versa.**
- **Adopt positive body language and you'll feel more positive and get positive responses from others, and vice versa.**
- **Receive what others say positively and actively listen, and people will respond positively to you and actively listen to you.**

The most important thing is what we say to ourselves; say positive things and we'll feel - and be - more positive to achieve what we want to be, do and have.

We therefore need to tell ourselves, and others, about what we want to happen rather than what we don't want to happen: frame everything we say, and think about, in the positive. Whatever we say and think about adds to its power, whether that is positive or negative, and we surely want to be always adding power to the positive.

Remember - our subconscious mind has a tendency to believe what we tell it! So we need to make sure we put in what we want to get out – positive language and positive thinking!

For example:
'I'm tired' – say it 10 times and, low and behold, you're feeling more tired. You shouldn't deny reality, but by replacing 'I'm tired' with 'I could have more energy' is positively telling yourself what you want rather than making yourself more tired.

'Do's' rather than 'Don'ts'

We need to tell others what we want and avoid saying what we don't want. This is especially important with our children, as we're modelling the behaviour we want them to adopt to give them the best chance of being all they can be.

Rather than 'Don't leave the dishes out', say 'Put the dishes away'. Rather than 'Don't speed', say 'Drive carefully'.
'I hate ....' Using the word 'hate' is very negative, and projecting extreme negativity affects us in a negative way. 'I could like .... better' has the same meaning with many things. When Harriet and George were young, the word hate was very strongly discouraged to say the least. I remember when George was young him starting to say about one of his class mates, 'I h......' and stopping himself and saying 'I could like ...... better'. It was initially very conscious and very laboured, and I'm sure had more to do with not wanting the positive language chat with me rather than any other reason. However, it has been an important contributory factor in helping to develop his positive mindset. If we are expressing our views about something vile, it's much better to say exactly what our objections are without using extreme negative emotions to express ourselves. If we dwell on negative emotions, we add to their power.

Please don't confuse positive with passive and easy. Positive people can be very challenging of themselves and those around them, but still be an energy giver. If positivity is combined with goals, ambition and competitiveness, positive people can be very demanding. The fact that they are positive can make them more demanding because they are not easy to criticise. It's far easier for people to put barriers up, and not engage with the moaner, the person who's very unfair, the person who's always finding fault: the energy sapper. This is much more difficult with the positive person, who challenges those around them to go that bit further, to do that bit better, and practice C.A.N.I. (constant and never ending improvement).

The optimist lives on the peninsula of infinite possibilities; the pessimist is stranded on the island of perpetual indecision.
William Ward

Positivity Health Warnings!

Internal Negativity - Why worry? What does worry achieve?

I like the way Ben Howard expresses that fear creates worry in his track *The Fear*: **'I've been worrying that we all live our lives in the confines of fear'.**

We can spend too much of our time fearing and worrying about what we don't want. As we attract what we think about, the more we worry about something, the more likely we are to realise the negative outcomes we fear. Simply dwelling on what we fear attracts it to us. How many times have we all said to ourselves something like, 'I knew today wouldn't go well', and we 'achieved' that self-fulfilling prophecy. We can so easily end up in a negative cycle, and surely we all want to live in a positive cycle?

Although my natural self is a positive, enthusiastic one, I have found myself, at times, in the negative worry cycle, and it's not a good place to be.

When I was an Area Education Officer, one of the Deputies repeatedly said to me, 'Beverley, worry is worthless baggage'. He had to say it quite a few times for it to become one of my mantras. What good does worry do? None. It doesn't solve anything. With all the negative emotions that go with it, worry just emotionally and physically drains us. That doesn't mean not taking responsibility. But taking responsibility is finding solutions to challenges, finding positive outcomes, and worry - by its very nature - is negatively dwelling on negative outcomes. So guess what? If that's what we do, that's what we get.

External Negativity

Keep your 'bubble' securely around you when faced with negativity from others. Don't let negativity penetrate when faced with those who catastrophise things: the 'cynical sods' and the '1001 reasons why not guys'.

Catastrophising Stuff

There are those who 'catastrophise' things: who often talk about challenges (which they call problems) and constantly re-frame them for different audiences, creating melodrama with their tone of voice and body language. Each time they repeat the issue it is re-enforced in their mind, and as they've told it lots, in different ways, to different people who often build on the negative aspects of the issue, the grooves of doom and gloom become well-formed and embedded in their brain. Sometimes, the magnitude of something that is quite minor grows as the heart-felt negative emotion attached to the challenge takes hold. Sometimes, the original story is someone else's, but by repeating it, the teller takes on the negativity within it.

Dwelling on the negative simply contributes to its power.
Shirley MacLaine

'Cynical Sods'

There are those who are cynical; they see the negative in every situation, always assume the worst, and tell everyone it won't work, whatever the 'it' is. You can spot them in groups in all walks of life. We cannot always avoid the cynics; they may be family members, individuals in our class or team, people we work with. However, they are definitely energy sappers, rather than energy givers, and it is vital that our bubble is reinforced against their toxic negativity.

We can become bitter or better as a result of our experiences.
Eric Butterworth

'1001 Reasons Why Not Brigade'

One of the recurring themes in this book is that successful people take action, are creative and find solutions. They DO THE WORK. They pursue their goals, train, learn what they need to learn, find the people who can help them etc. In contrast, we have all met those who do everything they can to avoid change and the effort that entails: who protect the status quo and do everything they can to stay within their ever-shrinking comfort zone. They will always give you 1001 reasons why not to do something. They often call themselves realists and brand others (very often me!) as idealists.

There are also those who live in a 'paralysis of analysis' that prevents them from having the courage take action and build the momentum to keep moving forward.

The pessimist sees difficulty in every opportunity.
The optimist sees the opportunity in every difficulty.
Winston Churchill

The Power Of Positive Thinking With Harriet And George

I have many examples of when I have used the power of positive thinking in achieving my goals, with my children, with young people in limiting, negative environments, and in some of my very challenging times. What I want to share are a few examples of how I have endeavoured to enable my children to develop a positive mental attitude. I have always endeavoured to be positive with my children: positive about what they're good at, rather than dwelling on things they are not so good at; positive about their achievements, celebrating success all the time; finding the positive from all situations. Negative situations often offer more opportunity for us to learn if we're prepared to reflect, review, reframe, change and grow.

This doesn't mean I haven't challenged my children to improve and take responsibility for their performance: at all times, and in everything. As I continuously emphasise in this book, our children are individual and unique, and as much as we want to equip them with positive values, we need to find the most appropriate ways for them, as individuals, to learn and develop those values. Treating everyone the same is the exact opposite of equal opportunities, and treating our children the same does not empower, enable and equip them as individuals to be all they can be.

The Strong-Willed Toddler

When my daughter, Harriet, was about 18 months old, she was dancing (really stamping, but we are talking about positively framing things, so we'll call it dancing!) on a low occasional table. I had said, numerous times, 'Harriet please get down from the table', saying it in various ways in different tones of voice, and sounding more like Joyce Grenfell by the second. Harriet's father, came into the room in the middle of my entirely unsuccessful efforts and said, 'Harriet, just come and look at this'. She immediately got down off the table and went to look at what he was pointing out! I was just trying to stop her doing something; he was offering her an alternative. And when she wasn't in defiant mode (not a mode in which to start trying to reason) it was then an appropriate time to explain clearly why dancing on the table is not allowed.

For a bit of light relief, and to no doubt hear a version of yourself at times with your children, experience the late Joyce Grenfell, one of the finest comedians of her generation, on You Tube. There are three in particular that make me smile and think, 'Is that really what I sounded like at times when my children were younger?' They are all based in a nursery school: *Nursery School 2 – Flowers*, *Free Activity* and *Going Home.*

Value What Our Children Are Good At
Accentuate The Positive

Boys Football and The Power Of Accentuating The Positive

Having stood on the touchline from when George started playing competitive football at the age of 6, I became progressively more concerned about the relentlessly negative language at the side of the pitch. Parents yelling at their children inane, negative comments in a tone of voice that meant the words were only part of the problem. 'What do you think you're doing?', 'You're standing still', were a couple of the most common comments, said with inherent disapproval in their voices. I would have liked one brave boy to have put his hand up, stopped the match, and rationally, loudly have said, 'What I'm doing is trying my hardest to play the best football I can and enjoy it.' I would often be a lone voice praising every boy and commenting on everything positive they did.

There were also examples of managers who moaned about boys and did not let them play because of 'their attitude'. These were the same managers who negatively yelled at boys throughout the match. My response to this 'sort your attitude out' kind of comment is always the same. We are the adults in the relationship with young people. We need to work with young people to ensure they know what we mean by an 'appropriate attitude' in any situation and model the attitude we want to see.

At George's request, when he was 12, we started our own football team, George, his father, and I. He played for Nottingham City School Boys, representative football, on Saturday, so we started a Sunday team. George is a natural leader and gathered together players he thought were good, most of whom couldn't get a game for the clubs they were at because they were either too timid, lacking in confidence, were not in the right 'clique', or had a 'bad attitude', and I trailed around Nottingham, filling my car with boys for training and matches. I did workshops on having a winning mentality (including positive attitude) for the boys as part of their training sessions, and workshops for their parents, though few attended.

Only positive language allowed was a big part of the ethos of this team. On the pitch, if players moaned at their teammates they were warned and then substituted. Moaning is negative and brings down the whole energy level and performance of individuals and the team. A brilliant striker, our best goal-scorer and one of the best in the league, who had played for a few clubs, was a classic example – he very quickly *got down on himself* and his teammates if things weren't going his way. I'd warn him a couple of times and then substitute him. He would stamp up and down the touchline for a while, shout or cry, and then we would wander round the pitch and chat about why it was important to stay positive, for your own performance and your team's performance. He soon learned to be more positive with his teammates, whether to stay on the pitch or to avoid 'chatting' to me. Unfortunately, things didn't go so well for him in school and he was excluded at 13, never to attend a mainstream school again. He really did need to be systematically enabled to develop the attitudes, thinking and behaviour in this book, rather than being on a negative roller coaster: a cycle of punishment and engaged in 'educational' activities of little real value.

The model on the touchline was positive, too. The advice to parents, although we didn't have many there, was to frame what you have to say in the positive: praise, say what you want the boys to do, avoid criticising etc. I led the touchline, cheering on with positive comments, and others followed.

Don't get me wrong, we weren't a 'nicey, nicey' team, giving everyone a go with an attitude that it doesn't matter if you win or lose as long as you participate. We went out to win. We had a team full of kids with ability who wanted to play football, some of whom wouldn't back down from a fight. This occasionally turned into too much physicality, but we usually managed it by re-enforcing 'let the ball do the talking'. This new team, with many boys who'd been unable to get a game or who had been very unhappy at other clubs, mostly won their matches. We were one of the most ethnically diverse teams in the league and came across prejudice, on occasion, mainly from adults - opposition management, parents and referees - but we quietened them by challenging racist comments politely, assertively and appropriately, and ultimately by winning.

Remaining Positive, Even In The Face Of Adversity Focusing On Positive Outcomes

Anyone can be positive when things are going well. What's important is to find that positive force within you, even when things are at their worst.

Like many people, the most negative time of my life was separation and divorce. I was angry, upset, and full of all those negative emotions you experience when you feel as if you were supposed to be married for life and then, suddenly, you're not.

I don't want to share the details of my separation and divorce here. That would not serve anyone involved, me, my children, my children's father or his wife and children. What I do want to say is that, after fighting for a year to save my marriage, I finally realised that, no matter how much I tried to change it was broken beyond repair, and I made a conscious decision to move on without malice and not put my 'baggage' onto my children. I had seen too many families torn apart, not by divorce, but by the aftermath of divorce. I decided that we had two fabulous children together and I needed to make our future relationship work for them and me. There is nothing more sapping of your vitality and spirit than carrying around negativity and bitterness. Don't get me wrong, I am by no means a 'hard' person: strong, yes, but not hard. On the contrary, my emotional state tends to be quite close to the surface. I even had a moment of sadness about my divorce lying on a beach in Melbourne with my children at Christmas, 2012 (the first Christmas Harriet, George and I had spent the whole time together for 15 years!). I was listening to Emeli Sande's Album, *Our Version of Events*, and when *Suitcase* came on, which is about a partner leaving, momentarily those feelings of loss returned.

The break-up of a relationship is sad. The break-up of a relationship that involves children is even sadder, as they can suffer as a result of something over which they have no control. But my view is that, as the adults in this, it is up to us to make it the best we can for our children. I have therefore maintained a cordial, friendly relationship with their father (in my view, a much better description than ex-husband), and I have done everything I can to ensure that Harriet and George maintain a good relationship with him. My daughter was 8 when he finally left, after a year of coming and going, and she was devastated. They had always been very close, and within a year she went from being number one girl in her dad's life to number three; and numbers one and two lived with him (his new partner and their baby daughter). My role was to ensure that Harriet and George were 'good', emotionally and in every other way. George was only four and so not nearly as affected. He can remember very little before the new norm we quickly established.

Just a few of the things I did in the early days to keep it positive and good for Harriet and George, and ultimately myself and their father:
- ensured that their dad consistently had time with Harriet and George;
- encouraged Harriet to stay with her dad after months of her refusing to do so - let her see I was OK with it, and

encouraged her to see it as fun;

- insisted that Harriet and George go to their dad's together, to start with, so that their sibling relationship stayed strong (George would have stayed way before Harriet, but that then may have created a further trauma for Harriet and a weakening of their relationship, which I have to say has always been, and still is, amazingly strong);

- did our divorce with a kit from W.H. Smith - I have seen far too much pain, anguish, expense and deterioration of relationships caused by involving lawyers;

- their dad and I communicated constantly - I always made a point of speaking to him about important things to do with Harriet and George, rather than his new partner and, subsequently, wife;

- did not criticise their dad to Harriet and George. I didn't hide my feelings - they saw quite a lot of me sad and crying - but I endeavoured not to criticise him, his new partner and family. I remember our first holiday on our own together, a few months after he had left, setting off to drive to Cornwall with tears streaming down my face saying, 'We'll be fine', 'We'll have a good time'. I was putting one foot in front of the other, which was what was required in the early days. We were fine and we did have a good time!

- asked everyone else not to criticise their dad in front of Harriet and George;

- maintained a very good relationship with his family, and still do have a great relationship with them. His father and I were particularly close and his passing in 2012 was a sad time for us all;

- encouraged Harriet and George to have a good relationship with their father's 'new' family. That has been rocky, at times, with Harriet and George behaving in ways that I didn't condone. However, I have always thought that was something for their father to manage in his home and really out of my control. On my part, I have always been firm not to criticise or be negative in any way, but to reframe and contextualise things they criticise. I can honestly say that has not always been easy, but I think positive relationships are so much better than negative ones, and surely what we want for our children are positive relationships?

All that set the tone for the future. Their father and I always went to parents' evenings at school together, ran a football team together, and have always communicated about the important things in Harriet and George's lives. We have had our differences, but at the end of the day, we have two fabulous children together that I have had the good fortune to share my life with over the past 25 years. The outcome is that both Harriet and George have a good relationship with us both, and their sister and brother from their father's second marriage.

I've Not Always Got It Right, But I Am A Learner

I have made mistakes – I have been, and can be, overly critical – seeing what has not been done rather than focusing on what has been done at home and at work. These mistakes have only brought home to me how important it is to remain relentlessly positive. Using a version of the 'Praise Sandwich' always achieves better results: praising what has been done before suggesting an improvement and then following up with praise.

What I have learned is the huge importance of maintaining a positive mental attitude is one of the most important factors if we are to live the life we choose. Enabling our children to be positive is one of the most important roles we have in empowering and equipping our children to be all they can be.

Laughter is the sun that drives winter from the human face.
Victor Hugo

Affirmations:
- I am grateful every day for the abundance in my life.
- I am feeling the benefits of being positive with myself, and others and I feel good.
- I am being positive about what I can achieve and am achieving more each day.

- I am using my 'bubble' to protect myself from negativity.
- I am feeling the tremendous benefits of being much more positive with my children and all those around me.

ACTION

Try the activities below and see what a difference being positive makes. These activities are designed for all ages, and you can adapt as appropriate to try with your children.

The following activities and tools are all available on the **equipped2succeed** downloads section of my website, beverleyburton.com

Positive Me

Positive Mental Attitude – The Rules

Positive Language Exercise

Positive Alphabet

Practising Gratitude

NB This chapter in no way attempts to deal with issues related to clinical depression or any other related mental health issues.

Chapter Eight

Be Passionate

There is no passion to be found playing small - in settling for a life that is less than the one you are capable of living.
Nelson Mandela

Definition

- passion
- strong and barely controllable emotion;
- a state or outburst of strong emotion;
- an intense desire or enthusiasm for something;
- a thing arousing great enthusiasm.

When Billy Elliot (in the film 'Billy Elliot') is asked in his audition what it feels like when he's dancing, he says:
'It's like electricity running through my body'.
That is passion.

The most successful people pursue things they are passionate about. They pursue things to which they attach powerful emotions. This helps maintain their drive and determination, even when the going gets tough. Their enthusiasm is obvious and infectious, helping attract that all-important support that everyone needs to succeed.

Passion is energy. Feel the power that comes from focusing on what excites you.
Oprah Winfrey

Most of us rarely define what we really want, or identify what we're really passionate about, let alone really believe that we can follow

142

our passions. Most of us have dreams and passions as children and young people, but we're often taught to be sensible and realistic, rather than to follow our passions.

Finding our passion is as important as finding out what we're good at. Genetic pre-disposition and technical ability are important to succeed in sports, dancing and many other areas of physical activity, as is a predisposition for mathematics and science if we want to pursue medicine or engineering. However, it is passion that sets apart those people who train and study harder and longer and give more time, focus and energy. In short, passion gives people the fire to go that extra mile to pursue excellence, rather than settling for mediocrity. There are many young people with less innate ability who achieve more because their passion gives them the drive to work harder and sacrifice more to achieve their goals. Many have achieved phenomenal success with passion, a phenomenal work ethic and a willingness to learn, rather than obvious technical ability or traditional study and career path. Look at the achievements of Richard Branson, Alan Sugar, Mary Kay Ash and Oprah Winfrey.

Nobel Prize Winners are epitomised by passion in their field, rather than traditional academic excellence being a common denominator, whether that is Aung San Suu Kyi, striving for democracy in Burma, or Physicist Richard Feynman. Many successful people in sport and the arts achieve far greater things than peers with more natural ability because of their unstoppable passion. Look at Sally Gunnell's journey to winning gold in the 400 metre hurdles at the Barcelona Olympics in 1992, against all the odds and all the predictions of more 'natural' athletes winning. Read more about Sally's passion and mental approach in the *Develop Your Winning Brain* chapter. We can all think of sports teams and dance groups who, with their passion and enthusiasm, have beaten an opposition that is technically better on paper.

Find joy in everything you choose to do.
Every job, relationship, home...
it's your responsibility to love it, or change it.
Chuck Palahniuk

Passion is not always what we do, but sometimes we do things to achieve our passion; we follow a path that brings the outcomes we want. Young people don't study for years to become a barrister because they love to study, but rather because of what they can achieve as a barrister. There are people who are passionate about business - the whole process and the rewards it brings. They are not necessarily passionate about the business they are in, but the art of doing business. Of course, combining both takes satisfaction in business achievements to another level. Anita Roddick combined her passion for natural products with a passion for ethical business to found *The Body Shop*. She demonstrated that you can make a profit and make a positive contribution to the community; you can trade on a global scale and support campaigns for human rights, whilst opening scores of shops a year. Reviewing the second edition of her book, *Business as Usual*, the Guardian said, 'There is no disputing Anita Roddick's passion and she has now poured her heart out to help those who want to follow in her footsteps'. Paul Smith has pursued business in his passion, tailored clothing with a twist, with shops in many major capital cities. He started by learning tailoring at night school in Nottingham and, in a recent documentary, he demonstrated that same passion and enthusiasm that got him started.

Fun is important in communication, and so is passion. I believe that communication is the most important tool of leadership and passion is the most important element of communication. It is passion, above all, that persuades. For all its modern emphasis on communication, so much of business forgets this crucial element.
Anita Roddick

There are elements of science that are beyond the understanding of many, but there are people who, with their enthusiasm for sharing their passion, bring it to life for us. These include Stephen Hawking, with one of the biggest-selling books on physics of all time, *A Brief History Of Time: From Big Bang To Black Holes* and Susan Greenfield, author of, *The Secret Life of the Brain*, who has done much to help us understand the field of neuroscience with her enthusiastic talks and writing about how the brain works. Richard Feynman, theoretical physicist and a Nobel Prize winner, throughout his career demonstrated his passion and enthusiasm for exploring the world around him. Now, thanks to the web, Richard Feynman's unique talents as a brilliant physicist and an inspiring communicator, are being rediscovered by a whole new audience. One of the biggest hits on YouTube is a new animated video, featuring Richard Feynman's words, which has gone viral. In the film, Feynman can be heard extolling the beauty and wonders of science contained within a simple flower. As well as the flower video, *THE FEYNMAN SERIES (part 1) – Beauty*, which, to date, has been watched nearly three quarters of a million times, there are many other videos featuring his ground-breaking theories which clearly demonstrate his enthusiasm and passion for his work.

So, Why Is Passion So Important?

Powerful, positive emotions give us self-motivation and infectious enthusiasm – the get up and go - to achieve our goals, and passion is one of the most powerful emotions. We will ultimately succeed in the goals we are passionate about.

> *Dreams are astoundingly important.*
> *They keep nagging you because you're supposed to fulfil them.*
> *When you sense you're special, you're not neurotic or grandiose. Something inside you is calling to you and you have to listen. When you love to do something; that means you have a gift for it...*
> *And when you're gifted at something, you have to do it.*
> Barbara Sher

Successful people attach powerful emotions to their goals, and if we want to equip our children to succeed in achieving their dreams and goals, we need to do all we can to empower and enable them to find and pursue their passions. Firstly, we need to allow them to pursue things in which they show an interest (rather than what we want them to be interested in). This may entail trying lots of different things to find those specific things that spark their interest. We then need to do whatever we can to enable our children to pursue those passions.

To Feel It   To Be Enthusiastic   To Be Focused

The road to success is fuelled by determination. For me, there's a simple equation which leads to determination:

$$goals + passion = determination$$

> determination - a decisive, unwavering movement
> towards reaching a set goal or end.

Being passionate and enthusiastic about what we do is a huge contributory factor to realising our goals. Passion and enthusiasm also help us to enthuse others, which increases our chances of success.

Enthusiasm Can Make Things 100% Better.

I have frequently been accused of being 'too enthusiastic', often by people who see their role as a job, or who have lost their passion, enthusiasm and energy for what they do. I don't think we can be too enthusiastic; it's a matter of focusing our enthusiasm. I have had a long journey to really focus my enthusiasm and there have been times when my enthusiasm has bubbled over in ways that may make people not want to get into lifts with me!

Fall in love with some activity, and do it! Nobody ever figures out what life is all about, and it doesn't matter. Explore the world. Nearly everything is really interesting if you go into it deeply enough. Work as hard and as much as you want to on the things you like to do the best. Don't think about what you want to be, but what you want to do. Keep up some kind of a minimum with other things so that society doesn't stop you from doing anything at all.
Richard P. Feynman

Harriet – Collecting Activities

When Harriet was young, I said she must try everything she wanted to try and then she'd find out what she liked, what she was good at, and what she wanted to stick at and pursue. This worked just fine for some years, but she stuck at almost everything she tried! Harriet was the opposite of the child who 'butterflies' between activities, picking them up and dropping them. She just kept collecting interests and activities that she didn't want to give up. As 'stickability' is important, I didn't want to pressure her to stop, but we reached a limit when I realised I was forever strapping her younger brother into the car seat...to take her to ballet, which she pursued aged 3 to 11, piano aged 5 to 12, swimming aged 3 to 9, gymnastics aged 6 to 9, to name some of the the main ones. That's not including sports, clubs and productions at primary school, and art classes that she did in school holidays. You get the picture.

From 10, Harriet played netball and still does, but during her teenage years athletics took over and she had to choose. Being a great fan of Jonathon Edwards (triple-jumper) from a young age when she was 11 Harriet asked if she could go to athletics. She proceeded to train up to 4 times a week, and compete during the season, until she went to University. She tried all sorts, but settled on sprinting, hurdles, long jump and triple jump. Harriet was, unlike most of her peers, always more interested in the training than competing. She loved all aspects of training: aerobic, strength and conditioning and technical training. Alongside pursuing PE to GCSE and A-Level, she gradually narrowed her interests to sports science and all aspects of training the body to perform at its best. Harriet got a first class degree in sports science whilst also gaining industry-standard gym instructor and personal training qualifications. She now trains others in this and, as I write this book, she has just completed her first *Tough Mudder*. Harriet is constantly pursuing her passion for this field, and we constantly hear the enthusiasm in her voice when talking about what she's discovered in her latest bit of learning, whether that's about nutrition or strength and conditioning coaching. All those hours in the car trailing round different training venues for different physical activities fed her enthusiasm, helped her find her passion, and informed her journey.

George – It Must Involve A Ball

George's journey was more simple and focused than Harriet's. It had to involve a ball. I gave George the same opportunities to pursue interests as Harriet. He did try a few things she was doing; gymnastics lasted a few months. George has never been the build for gymnastics, but he had a go and discovered that himself. He went to athletics (track and field) for a few weeks because he thought it would be good to throw things, but when youngsters first started they made them try all the different athletics disciplines and, after a while, he got into the car following a session and said that he wasn't going back. He'd spent the whole session running – not something he enjoyed. These were only ever brief side roads that George tried in the wake of his sister's interests. Most of his life has been a clear road focused on football and cricket. When I say his life, George was kicking and throwing a ball before he could walk, and he showed very little interest in any other play activities. His main passion was for football when he was younger and then cricket gradually took over.

A few months into studying A-Levels at Bilborough 6th Form College, George called me one lunch time to say: 'Mum, I need to tell you. I'm leaving Bilborough. It's just getting in the way.' They were expecting him to do assignments in his own time! What he meant was that it was getting in the way of totally focusing on what he was passionate about and really wanted to do, cricket. Many of my friends and lots of other people asked me why I was allowing him to give up his education. What was his back-up plan? My response was always the same: 'If you can't pursue your passions when you're 17, when can you? If he feels he needs a back-up plan now, he's failed before he's started.'

Passion and enthusiasm are essential to give us the focus and drive to DO THE WORK and be single minded in pursuit of our goals.

My Realisation!

I can remember exactly when the significance of passion was really brought home to me. After a particularly tough time in my life, challenging personally and in my career, I was considering leaving my field, education, and pursuing another area. I was at a cross roads, and was associating the stresses, strains and negativity I was feeling at the time with the education world in general, rather than just my role at that time. All I could think was that I needed to move away from something about which I cared so deeply. As part of some development work I was leading, outside my main role, I was at a conference in Edinburgh and all I remember about that conference is hearing Jack Black, of Mindstore, speak. He only spoke for a short time, but it was enough. He emphasised the importance of passion if we are to succeed and be where we're meant to be. I leaned over to the person I was with and said: 'Education and learning is the only work I'm passionate about'. I just needed to find where I could best pursue what I believed was important - improving the life chances of young people by enabling them to learn, realise their potential, and become the best they could be. In short: empowering, enabling and equipping our children to succeed. Like most key moments in our lives, I remember that moment as if it was yesterday, sitting in that hall and realising that I needed to follow my passion in education and not be defined by the job role I was in. That moment started the journey to this book.

If we know what we're passionate about and believe it's legitimate to pursue that passion, we start channelling it - doing all the things we need to do to achieve our dreams. Many children love things for a short time and then move on to other things. Some just hone their passion as they grow, challenging themselves more, whether that's in building complicated models and pursuing engineering, playing and then creating their own computer games, becoming more and more accomplished musicians etc. It's during teenage years that many young people sometimes struggle to maintain or find their passions if they're not already established. It's then that we need all our ingenuity as parents to just keep them pursuing things they enjoy, whilst continuing to give themselves maximum choice by achieving as much as they can in their education.

I am always expanding my understanding of the power of passion and. I am, therefore, eagerly anticipating renowned educationalist Sir Ken Robinson's forthcoming book that explores finding your passions and talents in great depth. *Finding Your Element - How to Discover Your Talents and Passions and Transform Your Life.*

Language and Body Language

Our language and body language communicate our passion. There are times when we need to do things that we may not be enthusiastic about: chores for our home, essential caring activities for our family, challenging training sessions and essential work towards our goals. Enthusiasm helps us to do all of those things more joyously and successfully, things such as study, examinations, basic work to earn the money to start our business or get the deposit for our first home, maintain our fitness regime, projects at work, work on our home etc. If we do everything with enthusiasm, it's far less like hard work. We are also more likely to get support from others if we do things with enthusiasm, eg teachers, coaches, work colleagues - all those who help us realise our potential. If we are in an interview, trialling for a team, seeking support for a project or venture, or in any other circumstance where we are in competition with others for a place, role or support, we are much more likely to succeed if we do it with passion and enthusiasm.

The passionate are the only advocates who always persuade.
The simplest man with passion will be more persuasive
than the most eloquent without.
Rene Descartes

We can change our mind-set by altering our language and body language, and vice versa.

Language We Associate With Enthusiasm And Passion:
Yes
I will
I am
I want

Vision
Strength
Absolutely
I'm sure
There's no doubt in my mind

Language we associate with a lack of enthusiasm and passion:

Maybe
We'll see
Not sure
I might if I can
That would be OK but.....
It's all right for her / him but ... (then comes the negative envy or excuse)
I'd do that if I could but .... (then comes the excuse!)
I'd like to do that but I can't see me............
(then comes the low aspiration and lack of self-belief
that become fear of failure and an excuse!)

Body language we associate with enthusiasm and passion:

Smiling
Energetic
Intense

Body language we associate with a lack of enthusiasm and passion:

Slow
Lethargic
Looking bored
'Going through the motions'

Building and Maintaining Passion and Enthusiasm

There are a few things we can do to really develop, maintain and use our passion and enthusiasm to help us realise our goals and ward off that doubting voice in our heads. We need to consciously enthuse, learn and celebrate success to maintain our motivation and to motivate others to help us pursue our goals. These are also things we can do with our children to help them develop their enthusiasm and passion for life and the things they want to achieve.

Find out More – Become an Expert – Become the Best.

To pursue our passions and succeed, we need to be enthusiastic and learn more about the things we are passionate about, e.g. business, sport, medicine, science, music, law, engineering dance etc. When our children show an interest in something, we can help them pursue it in all sorts of ways. Children have a great capacity to focus: to be completely absorbed in one thing to the exclusion of everything else, and sometimes we can underestimate the importance of that. Let them become absorbed. That's how Bill Gates became an expert in computers. And any successful person will tell you the importance of having that sort of focus. (However, there has to be some balance if we are to raise rounded individuals. Our children need to learn to get on with others, irrespective of their career path and for me, ensuring my children are emotionally literate, assertive and work well in teams has been a priority.)

Show Enthusiasm in Everything We Do

Liven up our smiles – not with that false, painted-on smile, but honest smiling with our eyes, as well as our mouth. Think about how you smile when you greet people. Show your appreciation through your smile. Communicate your passion, enthusiasm and energy through your body language. We all need to get on well with people – personally, socially, and in our work. Smiling, enthusing and taking an interest in others is an essential starting point. We also need the help of others to achieve our goals. It's really important that we teach our children to greet people with a smile, be open and positive, and take an interest in other people. Saying 'Hi' and then having your head stuck in some electronic mobile device, just doesn't do it! Enthusiasm is infectious and allowing and encouraging our children to be enthusiastic about what they do starts at a young age; we need to help maintain that enthusiasm in what they do as they grow. Again, we need to model the behavior we seek to develop and the foundation of this is LISTENING ENTHUSIASTICALLY to their account of something at nursery or school, to sharing some new thing they've learned. In fact, aiming at all times to listen enthusiastically, taking an interest in their interests, asking open questions about something they've done or are doing etc.

Broadcast Good News – Celebrate Success

Share good news with friends, family, and people you work with. This is not bragging or boasting – it's sharing positive, good news. Don't be like the energy sappers and tabloid newspapers – focused on the negative. Broadcasting good news activates you, makes you feel better, and makes others feel better, too. It's vital we celebrate our children's successes, the little ones and the bigger ones.

I have a passion and enthusiasm for life - for the small things, as well as the bigger things - and have endeavoured to ensure my children keep that awe and wonder which we all have when we're young to fuel their continued passion for life and pursuing their goals.

Affirmations:
- I am passionately enjoying what I do.
- I am passionate about achieving ……………..
- I am passionately learning everything I need to …….
- I am passionately making the most of opportunities.

ACTION

Persist

Advance

Serious / strong

Search for glory / recognition / significance / strive

Integrity

Optimism

Nothing interferes

To achieve your goal, your life may sound like a perfume counter — full of Passion and Obsession, leading to Joy. Do It!

It's therefore important to imagine ourselves experiencing the things we're passionate about, and bringing our imagination to life: seeing what we want to achieve in bright, vibrant technicolour - hearing it,smelling it, tasting it. Using all of our senses to bring our passion to life in our imagination.

To help bring things to life and fuel our imagination, it can be helpful to create a visual collage of what realising our passion looks like: images that help us clearly picture the desired outcomes of passion. We can do this as a poster or electronically, whichever works best for us.

Below are some prompts to help you reflect on your passions. You can use these yourself and, adapted appropriately for their age, with your children.

1. When do you feel passionate?
   How do you feel when you are passionate about something?
   What is it about those times or that activity that makes you feel like that?

2. What do you do that you feel passionate about?
   - daily
   - weekly
   - monthly
   - annually

3. It's important to set a goal to ensure we think about and DO the things we are passionate about more often - at least some part of every day, or, if it's something from which we want to earn our living, we need to wholeheartedly pursue our passion. Here is some food for thought that you can also adapt to use with your children:

If you are passionate about getting a 'good' job and earning 'good' money – (only you can define good for you!) find out about the sort of work you like; spend time imagining yourself in that role, read about that work, study, take courses and find opportunities to get experience in the sort of work you like.

If you are passionate about having your own business, spend time imagining yourself in business and find information, read about those who have started their own business, get advice – there's lots of free advice out there - develop your skills and find ways to get experience in the sort of business you would like.

If one of your passions is a particular sport or athletic pursuit, set a goal, join a club or join a better club, get a coach, talk to people in that sport, plan in time to practise, play, watch or read about those who have reached the pinnacle in your sport.

If one of your passions is films – set a goal and plan going to the cinema every week / two weeks / month to suit your circumstances – find out what's on, find someone who would like to go with you (don't drag along a reluctant friend as it will only spoil your enjoyment, and this is about **your** passions).

If your passion is to make a film – make one – it doesn't matter how amateur to start with. You will only learn properly about film making by doing it. 'You Tube' has made it easier to realise that any of us can make a film.

If you are passionate about travel – spend time imagining yourself in the places you want to travel to; find information and ways to visit, work in, experience the places you want to travel to.

> *Life is not a mystery to be contemplated.*
> *It is an adventure to be chartered.*
> *Create your destiny!*
> Kristen Goodsell

Those who clearly know what they want, are passionate about achieving that, and prepared to do what it takes, in energy, time and effort, are the exception rather than the rule and destined to succeed.

Chapter Nine

Set Goals

Consciously Create Our Own Positive Future and
Empower Our Children to Create
The Future of Their Dreams.

*The greater danger for most of us lies not in setting our aim too
high and falling short: but in setting our aim too low,
and achieving our mark.*

Definitions:

set:
- a specified place, position or time;
- arrange as required;
- put in the ground to grow.

goal:
- the object of a person's ambition or effort; an aim or desired result;
- the result or achievement toward which effort is directed; aim;
- the destination of a journey;
- an instance of sending the ball into the goal as a unit of scoring in a game – the purpose of the game.

All successful people dream and think big.

All successful people have goals.

All successful people believe they will achieve their goals.

All successful people plan and work purposefully, step by step, to realise their goals.

All successful people use their imagination to really see, feel and hear themselves achieving their dreams.

Champions aren't made in the gyms. Champions are made from something they have deep inside them –
a desire, a dream, a vision.
Muhammad Ali, Heavyweight Boxing Champion

We all have dreams, but how many of us believe our dreams are attainable? How many of us turn those dreams into goals and really see ourselves achieving them? Dreams that we convince ourselves are unobtainable are much safer than specific goals and action plans that we can measure ourselves against. Leaving them as dreams means we don't have to risk failure.

All successful people map their path to achieving their dreams – one step at a time – or take huge leaps of faith when an opportunity arises. There are those in every field who have enormous natural ability, instinct, and the winning mentality to succeed, and we can all learn from them. They DO THE WORK: systematically set goals, map out the steps, and deliberately put one foot in front of the other each day towards achieving their goals using every opportunity that arises. Goals give us deliberate, conscious focus on what we want to DO, HAVE, BE and enable us to spot opportunities to realise them.

Setting goals is all about deciding what we really want, and using our imagination and positive thinking to enable us to see, hear and feel ourselves realising our dreams and goals. As Muhammad Ali put it, 'create your own future history'. An important part of systematically setting goals is writing them down. We then need to start mapping the steps and take deliberate action every day. This enables us to attract and spot the right opportunities, and engage support from appropriate people to achieve our goals and create our own positive future.

One thing that's really important in setting goals is to **FOCUS ON WHAT WE WANT TO BE, HAVE, DO...**not on what we don't want.All too often, we're clear about what we *don't* want, but a bit hazy about what we really *do* want. To paraphrase Shirley McLaine, dwelling on what we don't want adds to its power. Likewise, **dwelling on what we *do* want adds to *its* power.**

We need to ensure we focus our thinking and energies
on what we really want!

Setting goals and taking action to achieve them helps us focus our thinking, time and energy on realising our own positive future.

I really wish I'd learned the power of setting goals earlier in life. Not the narrow targets you are set by other people at school or in work, but life goals. I realise I have naturally had goals from a very young age that have kept me focused. However, had I learned the process and techniques described in this chapter, I feel I could have wasted less time, achieved more in life and work, been myself more and had more fun.

There is a great deal of evidence in all human endeavour that demonstrates the power of setting goals. Don't get me wrong, setting goals is not the whole answer to achieving those big dreams; it's just the start, the guiding thread that keeps us focused on the path ahead and helps put set-backs into perspective. Specific, measurable goals keep us focused, help us make decisions, drive us forward in the right direction and enable us to maintain the passion, enthusiasm, energy, vitality and perseverance necessary to realise our dreams.

A person who aims at nothing is sure to hit it.
Anonymous

Successful people know where they want to get to, although they rarely know exactly *how* they are going to get there – the `how' comes. Most very successful people naturally dream and think big, and they use the power of their imagination to believe and see themselves achieving their dreams, keeping themselves focused on the 'prize', which is especially useful when the going gets tough. Everyone has doubt. Everyone has moments of, Can I really do this?' Having very clear goals, and seeing and feeling ourselves achieving them, helps us silence the negative 'chimp' in our head. Dr Steve Peters' brilliant book, *The Chimp Paradox*, expertly explains how we can stop ourselves from sabotaging our own success by taking control of our negative 'chimp'. With clear goals, plans and belief we can counter-balance negative thoughts and emotions and silence the doubting voice in our head: the voice that gives us excuses not to do things and persuades us that what we really want is not attainable.

So What Stops Us from Focusing On Our Dream and Setting Big Goals?

There are people who put their dreams in a little box and say, 'Yes, I've got dreams, of course I've got dreams.'
Then they put the box away and bring it out once in awhile to look in it, and yep, they're still there.
These are great dreams, but they never even get out of the box. It takes an uncommon amount of guts to put your dreams on the line, to hold them up and say, 'How good or how bad am I?' That's where courage comes in.'
Erma Louise Bombeck

Many of us are frightened to dream and think big, and we talk ourselves out of even daring to dream about what we really want. Our thinking is dominated by doubt, and many of us have been brought up in an environment that keeps our thinking small. How many times have you been told to 'be realistic', which has prevented you from doing something? We are too often overly influenced by the prevailing attitude and aspiration within our family and wider community. We are, all too often, limited in our dreams by the attitude 'people like us don't do things like that'.

If you accept the expectations of others, especially negative ones, then you will never change the outcome.
Michael Jordan

159

It has taken me years to have the courage and faith to write this book. I have always sought more credibility and experience to counter balance the doubt I have allowed others to put into my head. 'Being realistic' is the line given to us by those who are happy to keep the bar low, and it can mean that our dreams are not nurtured, but rather starved of the positive energy they need.

Be realistic is the most commonly travelled road to mediocrity.
Why would you be realistic? What's the point of being
realistic? It's unrealistic to walk into a room and flick a switch
and lights come on. That's unrealistic.
Fortunately Edison didn't think so.
Will Smith

Most of us are paralysed by thinking that we need to know 'how' before we start. However, what we need to do is start by defining exactly what we want to achieve – specifically what we want to do, have or be. What we need to do is to get started. Define what we really want to achieve and this will fuel our brains to go to work, generating ideas and spotting opportunities for us to create the path to our dreams.

It has been proven, time and time again, that people who set goals achieve success. Setting goals helps us to be clear about what we want: set priorities and create a clear plan. Consistently working with our goals enables us to obtain the results we seek. Successful people set goals and truly believe they are going to achieve them. They then focus their thinking, talents, energy and internal resources on succeeding in realising their goals.

Empowering Our Children Means, Being a Dream-Maker, not a Dream-Stealer

How can we enable our children to dream and think big: help them to realise that they have the power to determine their own positive future and enable them to avoid drifting into a life they don't want?

DREAM AND THINK BIG

*The reason most people never reach their goals is that they
don't define them, learn about them, or ever seriously consider
them as believable or achievable.
Winners can tell you where they are going,
what they plan to do along the way,
and who will be sharing the adventure with them.*
Denis Waitley

So why is it that we are not systematically taught the power of
setting goals and how to set them in school? I don't know, but I
really hope I can contribute to addressing that gap. Not the narrow
targets set by others - teachers, parents or, when we're older, in
work - but life goals. Children naturally have dreams and goals, but
all too often they are dampened by that dream-stealing phrase 'be
realistic'. Here are a few things that we can do to help our children
set and realise their goals:

- Be positive about the things our children want to do –
  children will want to do lots of things, and they'll change their
  minds, but it's important not to limit them with our pre-
  conceptions and judgements. Some of the things they
  choose will be the things they pursue. The most important
  thing is that our children have dreams.
- Have high expectations – in terms of expecting our children
  to aim high and pursue excellence in their endeavours.
- Encourage our children to try things in order to find what
  they have an interest in, and even a passion for. By 'opening
  windows' for our children, we help them see and experience
  things and find what they enjoy and think they could be good
  at. We thereby enable them to start having dreams and
  goals to pursue. Finding interests and passions also avoids
  that negative phrase, 'I'm bored'. I think boredom often
  comes from lack of stimulation or lack of challenge. Doing
  nothing should rarely be an option, and it's our role as adults
  in this relationship to challenge and support our children to

- find their interests, be interested in the world around them (and, by the way, as a result, be interesting people!).
- Think beyond our interests and norms – tune-in to their natural interests and help them pursue them.
- Encourage them to try new things and try things with them.
- Help our children think and go beyond what's around them.

At the wedding of my nephew, Nick, there was a marvellous moment when the bride and groom's mothers spoke. At one point Maggie Keough, Vivienne's mum, and Shelagh Bacon, Nick's mum, painted a very empowering picture with words:

'As parents, we open windows to the world for our children, to enable them to open their own windows'.

Some young people will have dreams and may clearly know what they want to do, what they want to pursue and where they're meant to be, from a very young age. They are focused and disciplined about working towards this. Others may not be able to put a name to what they want to do but show a determined interest, curiosity and passion and relentlessly develop skills that lead them to their field of endeavour. These young people go on to succeed in the arts, sports, the professions, business, and pioneer areas of science, engineering and technology etc. They are passionate about exploring, learning, practicing their interest and thereby develop expertise and excellence. They don't necessarily want to have a go at everything – they don't see the point, and that's fine.

Many young people don't really know what they want to do with their lives. Their passions change, either from changes in themselves, or as a result of the culture that prevails in their environment. Very often, our children need to be enabled and encouraged to explore different things and discover their passions and aptitudes. They generally know what they like and what they don't like, and we can find ways to nurture those interests, and find that all-important spark. As parents, carers and teachers, we often don't recognise the importance of interest, passion and aptitudes outside the things we measure in school. **Determination, persistence and perseverance come from having goals, aiming for something**

we really want. Enabling our children to find their interests and passions and define what they really want helps them to avoid doing qualifications or ending up in jobs by default that are not ideally suited to their interests or aptitudes. In order for young people to achieve their best, they obviously need to be encouraged to develop core linguistic and numerical skills and, beyond that, be able to explore disciplines to find their aptitudes and interests. They then need to be enabled, encouraged, challenged and supported to set goals and pursue the things they are good at.

Setting goals and doing what is necessary to achieve them is a habit, and the sooner we equip our children to develop that habit, the easier it is for them to embed the learning and maintain it. We can help them to set goals, things they want to achieve, from a very young age.

Setting Goals

Create a Vision

Take up one idea. Make that one idea your life - think of it, dream of it, live on that idea. Let the brain, muscles, nerves, every part of your body, be full of that idea, and just leave every other idea alone. This is the way to success.
Swami Vivekananda

The first step to creating our own future is to have a vision of the future we want and then set goals to achieve it.

Muhammad Ali is credited with using the phrase, 'Create your own future history'. That is, set goals, see, hear and feel ourselves achieving our goals, believe, and do the work. This enables us to focus on creating our own successful future. It also helps us to overcome challenges and barriers, and to remain persistent and resilient.

To create our vision and goals, we need time without agenda, schedule, 'to do' lists or commitments to allow our mind to use its infinite power. Our visions are unique to us: no one can see ours and we can't see anyone else's, even our partner's or children's. We can share our vision, and that's essential if we are to support, enable and empower each other to achieve our respective visions, but we can't own others' visions. As parents, it's essential that we are in tune with each other with regards to our vision of parenting in order to avoid inconsistency, which has negative consequences for children, as opposed to natural differences, which is healthy for them.

My Vision as a Parent

There are two things we should give our children:
one is roots and the other is wings
Hodding Carter

It started in the hospital room where Harriet was born on 4th July, 1988. She was a few days old and I lay there looking at her and wondering what she would be like when she was 5, 10,15 and so on. This led me to think about her appearing on Desert Island Discs when she was an adult. Desert Island Discs is a BBC Radio 4 programme where celebrities choose the 8 discs (tracks) they would take if marooned alone on a desert island. They invariably talk about the different phases of their life, including their childhood, and what their parents were like. I lay there imagining what Harriet would say about her childhood and her mother when she was on the programme. This vision has stayed with me, and has grown and developed over the years, as Harriet, George and I have learned together.

The vision that's guided me is hoping that Harriet and George would be able to say:

My mum:
- always believes in me

- helps me believe in myself
- cares
- listens to me and mostly hears what I say
- is open about everything
- has encouraged me to be open and talk about everything
- taught me the importance of always learning
- is positive and enthusiastic about what I'm doing
- encourages and enables me to pursue my dreams
- helps me take responsibility (well, insists I do!)
- is always there for me
- helps me develop my confidence
- tries to be relentlessly positive and encourages me to be positive and think positively (the word 'hate' is always deleted if it crops up at home)
- coaches me to be assertive and get on well with people in all situations (and handle the difficult ones)
- encourages me to do what I am passionate about
- taught me that you get out what you put in
- supports me to develop in everything I do
- guides, rather than controls, me
- advocated for me when things were difficult at school (but always asked first if I wanted her to, and mostly followed my wishes)
- always welcomes my friends
- has given me a sense of family and my roots
- negotiated – when it would have been much easier to just tell me
- encourages me to aim high
- encourages me to try new things – step out of my comfort zone
- challenges and supports me to always improve
- talks with, not down, to me – even when I don't understand, she just carries on talking as if I do and I have got used to asking questions until I do understand
- gets me talking about my feelings – I don't like it sometimes but I have got used to it, and it has given me the ability to articulate my feelings
- is fair

- helped me know 'where the line is', which meant I learned how to behave appropriately in different situations and learned to challenge appropriately
- apologises if she gets things wrong – and she does get things wrong!
- made sure I went to schools where I learned with people from all sorts of backgrounds
- doesn't judge me
- always gave me choices and is big on learning about choices and consequences - meaning that on the occasions when she said things were non-negotiable, we knew she meant it
- occasionally embarrasses me!
- loves me unconditionally

I could go on, but I think I've covered the main things that I believe are important and that have guided my behaviour as a parent.

Since those few days in the hospital, I have constantly reflected and learned: always trying to enable Harriet and George (born 16th September, 1992) to be all they can be. I set out to enable Harriet and George to be responsible, confident, caring, emotionally intelligent people successfully determining their own future. I have seen my role as a parent to be there for my children, supporting them to thrive in any environment and enabling them to find and nurture their talents and pursue their dreams.

What is your vision as a parent?
What do you want your children to say about your parenting?

George and Harriet have been very different with their visions and goals. Harriet had lots of interests and in education, took a path that gave her maximum choice, in terms of getting the grades, which gave her choice at each next stage, and gradually specialised in what she was really interested in. George has known from a very young age exactly that he wanted to play professional sport and has relentlessly pursued that.

Here are some of the questions you may ask yourself which will give you an insight into where you might take this with your children at crucial times in their educational and career decision-making:

1. What do you really enjoy doing?
2. What do you do that you're passionate about?
3. What are you particularly good at?
4. What's your field or specialism?
5. What's your particular niche within that speciality?
6. How does your passion and specialist field align?
7. How do you, or could you, earn your living pursuing your passion or specialism?
8. What are you doing to pursue your specialism?
9. What could you do to become an expert in an area of your specialist field?
10. What more could you do to pursue your specialism?

If I take Harriet as an example, these are the answers she would have given to those questions aged 15:

1. Sport.
2. Athletics and netball.
3. Athletics and netball.
4. Long-jump, triple-jump and hurdles.
5. Training in the gym and on the track.
6. I love the training and it helps me improve my performance in sport.
7. Get into sport in some way.
8. I train 4 times a week at Notts Athletics Club and I compete for them. I train for netball at school and captain the school netball team.
9. Take Physical Education and Biology at Advanced Level (she did GSCE PE and was just choosing her 4 A Level subjects).
10. Get my Level 1 Athletics Coaching Qualification as soon as I'm 16. (Harriet did the course the weekend after her 16th birthday).
    Help with coaching at the athletics club (this then led to working for the City Council helping with coaching in the summer and in fact managing the 'buddy' scheme to help children with special needs access sports coaching over the

summer when she was 18).
Go to University to study sport.
Learn more about training for sport.

Harriet graduated from Sheffield Hallam University with a First Class degree in Sports Science in 2010, whilst also gaining sports industry standard Gym Instructor and Personal Training qualifications during her final year. The week after she left University, Harriet started work in the sports industry, in a combination of short-term contracts and working as a personal trainer, and has progressed in the industry since then. The company she currently works for didn't exist when she was 15 and much of what she currently does, neither us nor the school knew anything about. If, therefore, we'd been focused on what she was going to do, rather than pursuing what she enjoyed and was really good at, I'd have been asking limiting questions and, more importantly, she'd have been asking limiting questions of herself. The pace of change is so rapid we can't envisage all the jobs there are and will be in the near future, let alone 10 years on, so helping our children align themselves with what they enjoy and are good at is an important part of empowering, enabling and equipping them to succeed.

If you can DREAM it, you can DO it.
All of our dreams can come true – if we have the
courage to pursue them.
Walt Disney

Your vision leads to specific goals. We then need to
continuously and consistently see, hear, and feel ourselves
realising our vision and goals.
The other ingredient, of course, is disciplined, deliberate
action – moving forward every day.

Translating Dreams into Specific Goals and Action Plans

Vision without action is merely a dream.
Action without vision just passes the time.
Vision with action can change the world.
Joel A. Baker

The process outlined below is all about translating what you want to do, your dreams and ideas, into your future reality. This is a systematic goal-setting process, with specific information about what you may do at each stage. It's a time-intensive process to start with, but like everything, the more you do it, the easier it becomes. You will make the process your own and adapt it to suit you and your children.

Goal-Setting Process

Summary of the Steps

Step 1   **Make an 'I want list' -**
         things you want to BE, HAVE, DO.

Step 2   **Choose a few things from your 'I want list' to**
         translate into specific GOALS and
         ACTION PLANS.

Step 3   **Create your goals.**

Step 4   **Create reminders of your GOALS.**

Step 5   **Create action plans for each of your GOALS.**

Step 6   **TAKE ACTION – keep moving forward towards**
         your goals.
         Stay in the now and take 1 step at a time.

Step 7 **BELIEVE**

Visualise and mentally rehearse. See, feel and hear yourself achieving your GOALS.

When you face set-backs, keep your eye on the prize…YOUR GOAL.

Step 8 **REVIEW > REVIEW > REVIEW**

Where do I want to be?

Where am I now?

What are the next steps?

Who can help me?

What am I going to do about it?

The process may seem 'long', as many young people might say (with great emphasis on the word), but the detail below is designed to enable you to understand the process, and the rationale behind it. Once we know what to do it becomes a simple process. The challenging bit is the discipline and focus of doing what we need to do each day. However, that becomes so much easier if our goals are aligned with our interests, passions, and what we're good at.

Step 1   Make an 'I want list' - Things you Want to BE, HAVE, DO.

I do this myself every time I do a goal-setting workshop, and there's always something new in what I write down that surfaces from my sub-conscious.

It helps to have some quiet, relaxing music on, without the distraction of lyrics. My favourite are some Ludovico Einaudi tracks. There are many suitable tracks on the *Islands Essential Einaudi* album, and are great for helping your mind get into creative flow.

Give yourself 15 minutes and make a list of everything you want to BE, HAVE, DO. Have a piece of paper with columns for each one, if it helps. There's sometimes a crossover between them, but that's OK. You're just trying to still your mind and focus on what you really want.

BE – the sort of person you want to be, e.g. an enabling mother, showing an interest in people, kind.

HAVE - the things you want to have, e.g. a mortgage-free house, a horse, a particular award or qualification.

DO – the things you want to do, e.g. be a writer, swim for a club, go to dance classes, learn an instrument, be a games designer, represent my county / country in ....?

Step 2   Choose a few things from your 'I want list' to translate into specific GOALS and ACTION PLANS.

Please make sure you have just a few goals and avoid overload – you can't focus on umpteen things at once, which I've discovered to my cost. Too often, I have spread myself too thinly, which has resulted in the frustration of only partly achieving my main goals. Most people recommend no more than 7 goals, and that might be a good start, with some smaller, short-term, easier, more obtainable ones, some which contribute to your big goals, and a couple of 'maintenance' goals. Maintenance goals are important so that, whilst we're pursuing our big goals, we don't lose sight of the importance of those things we need to do constantly and consistently, like spend quality time with our family.

Look at the Wheel of Life categories in the *What is Success?* chapter, which helps us decide our current and long-term priorities, which will be a combination of working towards bigger goals and maintenance goals. I recommend most people to think about creating and maintaining balance in their lives and choosing goals in different areas of life. However, sometimes it's relevant to focus on one. For example, for those who want to be elite athletes, or for those seeking to move on from challenging times personally, financially or in any other way, it is essential to focus on the main goal and then other things we want to DO, HAVE, BE will stem from that. For example, this morning I watched a news article on Australian TV about a 10year old girl who'd lost 30kilos in the last year. Her mother had decided to take things in hand and find a way for her daughter to lose weight. With some tenacity and perseverance, and trying all sorts of things, they had eventually walked 4 miles 3 times a week to achieve the weight loss. By focusing on that, other benefits had flowed - the bullying and teasing about weight had stopped, self-esteem had, in the mother's words, 'sky rocketed', the girl was now on sports teams etc and was generally enjoying life much more.

The other important factor is that we and our children may have big, long-term goals for which we need to create medium-term goals and current, specific goals and actions that are steps along the way to reaching those big goals.

An example that all parents can relate to is our children's progression through education. For example, when my daughter was doing her GCSEs, I encouraged her to focus on getting grades that gave her maximum choice about what she did at the next stage of her education. During the summer holidays, before she started studying for her GCSEs in the September, I asked her to decide what grades she would get in each subject and write them down. Not what the school said she should get but what she wanted to get to progress, and what she could achieve, given all the other things she did. She wrote them on a piece of paper, she folded and placed it in an envelope and we put it away. She also wrote each one on a small card, which she kept with her. When Harriet got her 12 GCSE results we compared them with the piece of paper and they were the grades she'd set, apart from one, which was higher and one, which was lower.

By Harriet deciding what she wanted to do it also enabled me to advocate for her when teachers were putting undue pressure on her. I remember a time at parent's evening when the German teacher was saying that Harriet could get an A if she just did a little more work. I was able to say: 'Harriet has decided that she's getting a C in German and I support her in that decision. She has other subjects that she's aiming to get an A in, and her athletics is important to her, at the local athletics club outside school.' Harriet was moved down a set in German, but that didn't adversely affect her confidence because she had decided what she wanted to do and knew she was on track.

This set a pattern for her deciding exactly what she wanted to achieve and realising her goals. Once Harriet decided that she definitely wanted to go to University, she focused on getting the A-Level grades she needed to go to the University of her choice, to do the degree of her choice, etc. After A-Levels, she was weary of study and took a year out before going to University, during which time she worked and travelled, using the money she had earned from working. This helped her in many ways; she gained valuable life and work experience and then went to university ready to study again (and much better prepared to combine partying and study).

I followed the same process with George for his GCSEs and he got the grades he set himself except in one subject. His goal-setting has been much more focused on his development as a sportsman: setting and re-setting goals, and being clear about, and very focused on, the next step in the journey.

Maintenance Goals – Establishing Positive Habits

Some goals are maintenance goals. They are things we want to develop as on-going positive habits such as a regular pattern of exercise, healthy diet, spending quality time doing something with our children etc. We may need to focus on these at a specific time, to create positive habits. Once we've established these habits, we pursue them as a day-to-day discipline and they no longer need to be a focus of our goals. For example, I had a goal many years ago to ensure that I had focused, quality time with Harriet and George, not just the things we all need to do on a day-to-day basis. I was working long hours, they were growing up and, contrary to popular opinion, I believe you need to devote more high-quality time with your children when they're older than when they're very young. Their needs are different when they get to the latter stages of primary school and as they enter their early teens. This is often a more challenging time, but that's when you need to do the work to ensure you reframe and reinforce the values you endeavoured to establish when they were younger.

This goal focused me and ensured that that bit of important, urgent work didn't take priority all the time. I ensured my children didn't miss things that were important to them: training, practices, matches etc. I could easily have found excuses to occasionally not take them - my work, their school work, being a lone parent - but that would have been abdicating my responsibility, and certainly out of sync with my vision. I would leave work to make sure they were there, and this also reinforced with them the importance of commitment. My car certainly knew its own way to the Harvey Haddon Athletics Stadium, Nottingham Netball Club, Notts County Centre of Excellence and Southwell Cricket Club, to name but a few venues! Of course, Harriet had made sure she'd had her pasta an hour and a half before training, so she was good to go when I got home – just in time to get to training. I only needed to set this goal once and the pattern became established, which meant I achieved my goal of enabling my children to pursue their dreams and passions and we spent a lot of time talking whilst we travelled. Talking in the car lends itself to chatting, and sometimes chatting about important stuff. It isn't as formal as sitting facing each other, or when your children (or you) can make an excuse to get away from the conversation.

Maintenance goals could include things like:
- Exercise Regime – finding a regime that suits you and doing it!
- Healthy diet.
- Consistently seeing friends.
- Consistently using positive language with our children.

Step 3 Create Your Goals

I have developed a number of goal-setting templates for different ages, and a selection are available as downloads on the equipped2succeed section of my website. The essential ingredients of setting a goal for me are:

GOAL - Be specific and make it measurable.

What's in it for me? - What are the specific benefits from achieving your goal? How will you feel?

What's in it for others? - I believe that every worthwhile goal has benefit for others. Whether that's simply a parent's pride and enjoyment at seeing their child accomplish something, or being able to financially support our family.

Vision - It's vital that you can see yourself achieving your goal, and know what it looks and feels like. Having a visual stimulus that encapsulates your goal helps you do this, eg a photo of the 'prize', a house, a business, a trophy or medal, a certificate, yourself smiling back at you with your goal realised. A young person I was delivering a workshop for in around 1999 was very sceptical about all of this, but said she'd give it a go. She set a picture of the exact model and colour of car she wanted as her screen saver, and within 6 months she had the car! (We've since become good friends and colleagues.)

Affirmations - An affirmation is a personal, positive thought or statement in the first person, present tense, affirming that your desired goal has been reached, or is within reach.

Create a few affirmations as if you've already achieved your goal and make sure they are dynamic and full of positive feelings, e.g.

'I am enjoying the thrill of training and competing in ....'
'I am loving the freedom and joy I feel in the water now I can swim.'
'I am excitedly reading my results which are ....'
'I am loving the stimulation of studying at my chosen university.'
'I am loving the feeling of being in our fabulous family home.'

Step 4 Create Reminders of Your GOALS

Create cue cards (credit card sized cards) with your Goal and Affirmation on. Carry your cue cards around with you as a permanent reminder.

Put your goals somewhere prominent where you can look at them every day – preferably just before you go to sleep, so that your subconscious can go to work on them whilst you sleep.

Step 5   Create Action Plans for Each of Your GOALS

Big dreams and goals can seem overwhelming until we break them down into bite-sized chunks, and move forward one step at a time (or, for those of us who find it impossible to work on one thing at once, a few steps at a time!)

On the equipped2succeed section of my website, there are sample action plan templates for adults, younger children and young people. You need to ensure that the format suits you, so tailor it accordingly without losing the essential elements.

What are the next steps you're going to take to achieve your goals? Our action plans should be dynamic. We need to be focused and disciplined when implementing our plans. However, we also need to be adaptable and respond appropriately to new situations and opportunities, adjusting and amending plans as we move forward and review each milestone.

Step 6   TAKE ACTION – Keep moving forward towards your goals. Stay in the now and take 1 step at a time.

DO THE WORK

STAY FOCUSED

STAY DISCIPLINED

SPOT OPPORTUNITIES AND TAKE THEM

Most people live and die with their music still un-played.
They never dare to try.
Mary Kay Ash

Step 7   BELIEVE

See, feel and hear yourself achieving your GOALS. When you face set backs, keep your eye on the prize...YOUR GOAL.

Visualise and Mentally Rehearse

Imagine yourself achieving your goals every day.

*I learn from the past but I dream of the future because that is
where I choose to spend the rest of my life.*
Humphrey Walters

Relaxation – Visualisation – Mental Rehearsal Process (R – V – MR)

By systematically relaxing, visualising and mentally rehearsing we improve our focus, self-belief and positive thinking to achieve our goals. We can also use our imagination to tap into our brainpower and find solutions to challenges. As you will have read in the *Develop Your Winning Brain* chapter, your subconscious mind doesn't know the difference between imagination and reality. Your subconscious mind believes what you tell it, positive or negative. So, focusing our mind on seeing ourselves achieving our dreams and goals helps us to achieve them. We can also use it to improve our skills and performance in anything we do. We attract what we think about, and using this process helps us spot the opportunities and people who will help us realise our goals.

Relax - Enable your mind to be quiet and focused – relaxation will relieve stress, tension and anxiety, allowing your brain to make the right connections to maximize your potential. Let your mind flow.

Creatively Visualise - In your mind, visualise how you want things to be – go on a mental journey, vividly using your imagination and the power of your thinking.

Mentally rehearse achieving your goals - Picture exactly what you want to BE, HAVE, DO; practice scenarios and situations in your head and watch them happen – again and again – like action replays, so you take control of your life with the power of your mind.

A full description of the relaxation – visualisation - mental rehearsal process is in the *Develop Your Winning Brain* chapter.

Step 8   REVIEW - REVIEW – REVIEW

Where do I want to be?
Where am I now?
What are the next steps?
Who can help me?
What am I going to do about it?

Use It or Lose It!

Give yourself something to work toward - constantly.
Mary Kay Ash

Like anything else, unless you systematically practice setting goals, taking action to achieve them and reviewing where you are, you'll lose momentum and it will become that much harder to achieve your goals. As well as big goals, decide what you want to achieve every day that will take you a few steps closer to achieving your goals.

Your goals may change, so recognise when your heart and belief isn't in something and take action to change direction.

Don't change just because the going gets tough – only when there's something else that you realise you are more passionate about and have more belief in.

Only those who will risk going too far can possibly find out how far they can go.'
T. S. Elliot

Affirmations
These are general affirmations that we need to make specific for our goals.

- I am enthusiastically becoming who I want to be.
- I am excitedly pursuing my dreams and goals.
- I am strong and disciplined to do all the things I need to do to achieve my goals.

- I am positively and passionately doing what I need to do to achieve my goals.

ACTION

NOW DO THE WORK - IT'S DOWN TO YOU

NO ONE ELSE CAN DO THIS FOR YOU
NO ONE ELSE WILL DO THIS FOR YOU.

AND

We Certainly Can't Do It For Our Children – We Can Only Empower, Enable and Equip Them To Do It For Themselves.

Goal-Setting tools on the equipped2succeed downloads section of my website:

Goal-setting Process

Make an 'I want' list

Goal-setting Guidance

Affirmations Guidance

Goal-setting Templates

Goal Action Plan Templates

e2s R – V – MR (Relaxation, Visualisation and Mental Rehearsal) Tracks

Follow the goal-setting process and tools, and use the relaxation, visualisation and mental rehearsal link to support you in achieving your goals and helping your children set and achieve their goals.

Chapter Ten

Always Learn

*Insanity: doing the same thing over and over again
and expecting different results.*
Albert Einstein

 Definitions:

learn:
- to acquire knowledge of, or skill in, by study, instruction, or experience;
- to become informed of or acquainted with; ascertain;
- to memorize;
- to gain (a habit, mannerism, etc) by experience, exposure to example, or the like; acquire;
- to start to understand how we must change the way we behave;
- to be told facts or information we did not know.

always:
- at all times; invariably;
- for all time; forever;
- at any time; in any event.

Why is it Important to Continuously Learn?

Successful people are always learning. They are open-minded and have a growth mind-set. They are hungry to learn. They expand their comfort zone. They are not the people always moaning about what's wrong. We've all met them; they know what's wrong with the country, the local football team, the town, friends, and rarely come up with solutions. If they do suggest a solution it is usually simplistic and/or negative. The moaners rarely learn, improve and grow.

Successful people are always seeking to grow: expand their understanding and learning; become experts in their field, and explore horizons beyond. They are hungry to learn, finding sources of learning and people with experience and expertise in their field from whom they can learn. If you talk to, listen to or read about anyone who is a leader in their field, they will always mention what they have learned from making the most of opportunities, from experience, and from those who have helped them.

Results! Why, man I have gotten a lot of results.
I know several thousand things that won't work.
I am not discouraged because every wrong attempt discarded
is another step forward.
Thomas Edison

In order for our children to succeed in personal, educational, social and work contexts (whatever that work is), they need to be motivated to learn and have a growth mindset. By learners, I mean those who reflect, learn and seek to improve. We owe it to our children to empower, enable and equip them to be learners, not only within the confines of formal education, but also to make the most of opportunities to broaden their horizons and thinking. This is especially important in areas that align with their interests and contribute towards them realising their goals.

 Develop a Growth Mindset

The person who views the world at fifty the same as he did at
twenty has wasted thirty years of his life.
Muhammad Ali

Mindset is a simple idea discovered by world-renowned Stanford University psychologist Carol Dweck in decades of research on achievement and success - a simple idea that makes all the difference. *In a growth mindset, people believe that their most basic abilities can be developed through dedication and hard work—brains and talent are just the starting point. This view creates a love of learning and a resilience that is essential for great accomplishment. Virtually all great people have had these qualities.* Mindsetonline.com

Successful people find and implement solutions: not just in the obvious fields of science, engineering, technology and business, but in all fields. Look at the way Sir David Brailsford has taken Great Britain from languishing somewhere near the bottom of world rankings, with two bronze medals at the 1996 Olympics, to one of the most successful cycling nations in the world. Team GB won fourteen cycling medals in Beijing in 2008 (eight gold, four silver and two bronze) and twelve at London 2012 with, again, 8 gold. His growth mindset is an essential element of his capacity to lead this phenomenal improvement: challenging the way things are done, identifying issues, finding solutions and implementing change.

C.A.N.I. – Continuous And Never-ending Improvement

To achieve success, we need to be open-minded and learn from everything - not just formal learning. We need to encourage and enable our children to learn from their experiences, from others, from their successes, and from their mistakes and failures. It is so powerful for children if we can enable them to view failure or mistakes as a learning opportunity rather than something about which to be ashamed.

Intelligence is the ability to adapt to change.
Steven Hawking

Models of Learning

To help our children to become learners, it's helpful to know something about the learning process. There are a few learning models that help us conceptualise the process of learning and help us focus on what's important, particularly when it comes to helping our children become learners. They also emphasise that it's not only about skills and knowledge.

Cycle of Self-Development

There are four distinct aspects in an individual's development, at any age:

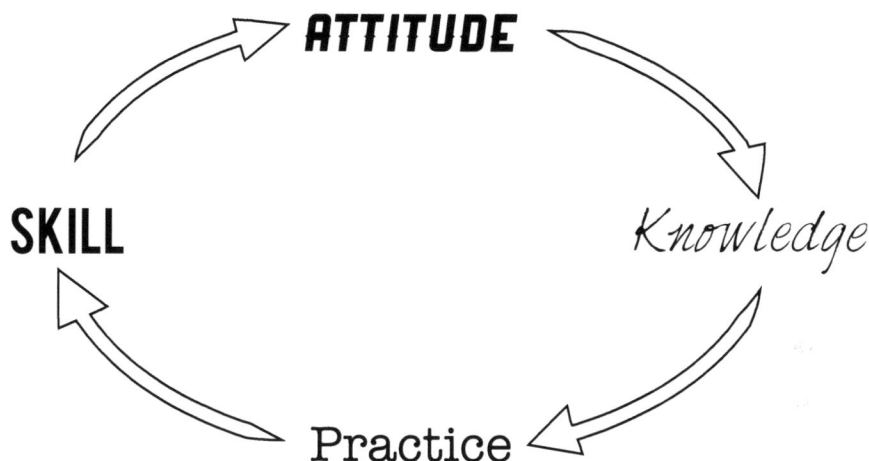

ATTITUDE

SKILL

Knowledge

Practice

Attitude

It was character that got us out of bed, commitment that moved us into action, and discipline that enabled us to follow through.
Zig Ziglar

The three essential elements of attitude in learning are **need to, want to and can do**. It's important to know and accept what we need to learn, then really want to learn. The other vital aspect is approaching learning with a can-do attitude. It is often said that our attitude determines our altitude in life and the *Be Positive* chapter reinforces this viewpoint.

Knowledge
It is vital to have a desire to seek knowledge. We gain knowledge in all sorts of ways: **formally,** in a school or college, or **informally**. Informal learning is all around us, all the time, if we take notice. This includes:

- listening to those around us - this is very powerful; indeed, we learn to speak by listening, mainly to our family;
- watching others, and the plethora of visual communication we have at our disposal;
- learning from other peoples' experiences and stories;
- modeling the behavior of those around us - this is where we need to be mindful as parents. It is not unusual for us to criticise aspects of our children's behavior that they have, in fact, learned from modeling us!

Practice

Practice is the **action** part of the process. We only embed learning and develop skills and behaviours with deliberate practice. We have to do the work. Whether that's learning to walk, talk, write, add, use mathematical models, sing, make something, fix something, use a computer, sell something or play sport, it's only by focused, deliberate practice that we become proficient and skilled.

Skill

As time passes, with practice, we become more and more skilled and reach unconscious competence: being able to do something without consciously thinking about it.

Attitude, knowledge, practice, skill provides the basis of a never-ending cycle of continuous improvement.

The K.A.S.H. Box

Another way of looking at learning is the K.A.S.H. Box.Some years ago, David Herdlinger reconstructed KSA (Knowlegde, Skill, Attitude) into a quadrant, adding Habits. This has become known as the **K.A.S.H. Box**. The purpose of this was to show that, more often than not, poor performance - whether organisationally or individually - is not an issue of knowledge and skills, but rather poor attitudes and habits.

Bringing habits in is interesting, as we all have them, but tend to only pick them up in others when they are negative. Positive habits are a crucial element of learning; in our attitude to learning, in the learning process and in ensuring that we embed the things we've learned that are useful to us.

Most people, educational institutions and organisations spend their energies, both in time and money, on developing the left half of the K.A.S.H Box.

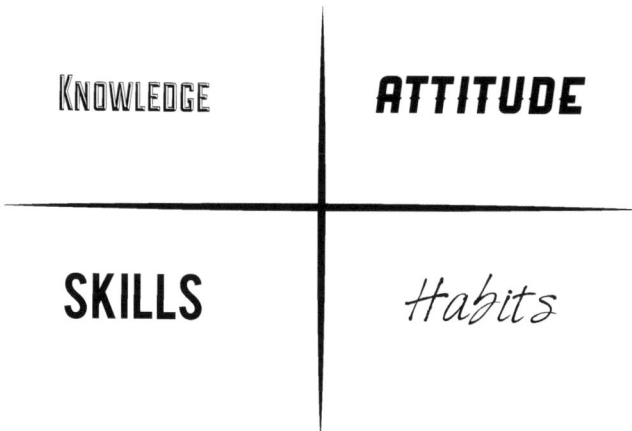

KNOWLEDGE	**ATTITUDE**
SKILLS	*Habits*

Much of the reason for poor performance in education, work, sports etc is as a result of not addressing the right half of the K.A.S.H. Box.

First we make our habits, then our habits make us.
Charles C Noble

Stages of Learning

The more that you read, the more things you will know.
The more that you learn, the more places you'll go.
Dr. Seuss

The following stages of learning are relevant in all the things we need to learn: to live and become the best we can be in our chosen fields. They are as relevant for learning to ride a bike as driving a car, for learning to write as learning to make that perfect shot.

Unconscious Incompetence

⇩

Conscious Incompetence

⇩

Conscious Competence

⇩

Unconscious Competence

Unconscious Incompetence
This is where we don't know what we don't know. I think it can also relate to people who are not prepared to learn.

Conscious Incompetence
This is when we realize there's something we don't know or a skill we don't have.

Conscious Competence
We have developed knowledge or skill but have to concentrate and deliberately apply ourselves to do it.

Unconscious Competence
Doing things unconsciously, on 'auto-pilot':
>'I know this without thinking about it'.
>'I can do this without even thinking about it.'
>*It's like riding a bike.*

These stages of learning come to life if we think about all the things we can do without thinking, that at some point we had to deliberately learn, like riding a bike, writing, making a cup of tea, using a computer, driving etc.

How We Learn

Tell me and I forget. Teach me and I remember.
Involve me and I learn.
Benjamin Franklin

To optimise our learning it's helpful (and I would say vital) to understand how we learn.

V.A.K. Learning Styles

The original VAK concepts were first developed by psychologists and teaching specialists starting in the 1920's. VAK theory is now valued in the accelerated learning community because its principles and benefits extend to all types of learning and development. I have found it particularly useful in both enabling my children to learn more effectively and to improve communication between colleagues in organisations.

V – visual – sight

A – audio – hearing

K – kinaesthetic – doing / feeling

Research has shown that three of the five senses prevail when it comes to storing information in the brain. These are Visual, through seeing; Auditory, through hearing, and Kinaesthetic, through touch, physical involvement or doing. We use all of our senses to learn, but most of us find it easier to learn by taking in information through one of these senses. If we are motivated to learn, are aware of different learning styles and understand how best we learn, we can make the most of our potential and all opportunities to learn.

Basically, we take in and store information in a way that suits us best. Consider, for a moment, being lost. If you stopped to ask someone how to get to your destination, how would you best remember the information they gave you?

a)   if they just verbally gave you instructions;
b)   if they drew a map for you;
c)   if they either went with you, or described where to go by mentioning some key places with which you could relate e.g. a restaurant, a shop, or another landmark.

You will probably find that one or two of these ways works better than the others, and the same is true for all those with whom we communicate.

We all, therefore, have preferred learning styles, or ways we learn best. There are many ways, in learning and development, of checking our learning style, both in education and in organisations. I have chosen to highlight one of the most popular, the V.A.K. learning styles model, as, from my experience, it is a simple way of helping children make the most of learning opportunities, and helping us all communicate more effectively.

Visual
There are those of us who learn best by seeing things. If we are visual, we prefer to take on board information through sight. There are certain traits that people who are predominantly visual learners share. They may remember faces better than names, or recognise places but have difficulty recalling the street names. They normally talk quite quickly because they are picturing things in their head as they speak. They like their own space to look tidy and clean. They may like their clothes to be colourful, fashionable and co-ordinated. They usually have a good imagination and find it easy to visualise.

Auditory
Some people take in information and learn best through listening. These learners tend to have an advantage in most education systems, where a lecturing mode of instruction often predominates. If people are auditory, they often trust what they hear. If they doubt what is being said, they would want to discuss it. They often talk a lot and sometimes forget that others need to talk, too. This can be a bonus at a party, but not always in group discussions in school and at work. They find it easier to take and give verbal instructions, and can learn effectively without taking notes because they can easily remember what has been said. They often enjoy background noise when working and like to listen to music or have discussions, and may often talk or hum to themselves.

Kinaesthetic
There are many people who learn best by doing. Kinaesthetic people feel emotions very easily and often become emotionally

involved in films, books and events, whether they are happy, scary or sad. Their brain needs time to process information because they are tapping into emotions, relating events to previous experience. This means that they usually talk slowly and can easily be interrupted by visual learners. Predominantly, kinaesthetic learners have a great memory and can often remember events from early in their childhood. They like to get stuck into a new task rather than be told or shown how to do it. Their surroundings and clothes have to feel comfortable and warm and they often like to stretch out and make themselves comfortable wherever they are.

For me, this is about empowering us to be the best learners and communicators we can be, rather than using it as an excuse for not taking on board information if it is not presented to us in a way that best suits us.

Just think about the potential impact this has in communication in everyday life. Think about how this may impact on the way we communicate and receive communication from others at home, at work, in social, coaching and training environments.
Think specifically about:

- how this may affect the way you communicate in various situations;
- how this may help the way you communicate with your children;
- how you may help your children communicate and learn more effectively.

We all learn in a combination of ways, and those with higher-order learning skills have developed ways to learn in all modes, adapting however learning is presented to suit them. When checking preferred learning styles, for example by completing a VAK questionnaire, some people have close scores for all three, and that can indicate that they are able to process information in all three modes – a very strong learning style. For example, whenever I do a learning styles questionnaire, my learning preferences are fairly even, (there is little surprise in that, being an educator and passionate about learning), but there is no doubt that my preferred learning style is predominantly visual. I have always made copious notes, both in school and work environments, and find it very difficult to concentrate when someone is talking in lectures or meetings unless I have a pen and am making notes or doodling. I have very elaborate doodles around my notes during long telephone conversations!

Ways to increase our learning power and improve communication:

If you are predominantly a VISUAL Learner ...

- Write down information.
- Use coloured pens and coloured, unlined paper.
- Use spider charts or mind maps to remember large amounts of information.
- Make mental movies of the facts you need to know.
- Stick post-it notes around the house to help you remember things.
- Illustrate things with pictures, diagrams.
- Use drawings and visual aids to help you remember and when giving talks.
- Use association techniques e.g. my acronym for remembering how we maximise energy, Being D.E.A.R to yourself - Diet Exercise Attitude Rest
- Watch a demonstration or video on how to do something before starting.
- Highlight important information in books and notes.

As a visual learner, Harriet found great benefit from learning to mindmap, and this was particularly helpful when she found aspects of learning very challenging, such as in A-Level Biology.

If you are predominantly an AUDITORY learner...

- Repeat everything in your head over and over to remember it.
- Take part in discussion.
- Ask, ask and ask again until someone can help you clarify and understand.
- Record information you find difficult and listen to it.

- Have background music on while you study or work.
- Discuss what you are going to do with people who can help.
- Make up rhymes to memorise facts.
- Have someone ask questions if you are studying for a test or exam;
- LISTEN well and you will need fewer notes.

If you are predominantly a KINAESTHETIC learner....

- Be comfortable when working.
- Break up times when you need to concentrate every 15 to 20 minutes and move around.
- Volunteer for demonstrations and role-play.
- Get emotionally involved in an activity – this is when you will learn best.
- Walk around as you memorise new information or prepare for anything.
- Play with quiet items, such as Blue Tack (or similar soft, pliable material) or a small soft ball, whilst listening to people, studying or thinking.
- Develop good note-taking skills.
- Use mindmaps and other less conventional forms of note-taking.
- Roll up your sleeves and get involved - Kinaesthetic people learn from being involved – from experiencing success and making mistakes.
- Put information on post-it notes to allow you to manoeuvre it about until it makes sense.

These tips help us to learn more effectively. They also help us get on better with people as we come to understand more about how we all learn and communicate differently.

 Being in the Flow

The quality of a successful person is to flow and not to freeze.
Ralph W. Emerson

Having looked at learning styles, it's worth having a look at the circumstances in which we are likely to learn best: when we're in flow. Imagine, for a moment, that you are running a race. You are absorbed in the movements of your body, the power of your muscles, the force of your lungs, and the feel of the ground beneath your feet. You are living in the moment, utterly immersed in the activity. You have little concept of time. You are tired, but you barely notice. Or, for those of us who can't imagine flow in running, think of something else you might be engaged in that produces that same complete absorption in an activity. Note: this is not a passive activity, such as being absorbed in a book, but actually using our mind and / or body in an activity that demands our full, undivided attention.

According to psychologist Mihály Csíkszentmihályi, what you are experiencing in that moment is known as flow: a state of complete immersion in an activity. He describes the mental state of flow as 'being completely involved in an activity for its own sake. The ego falls away. Time flies. Every action, movement, and thought follows inevitably from the previous one, like playing jazz. Your whole being is involved, and you're using your skills to the utmost.' Flow experiences can occur in different ways for different people. Some might experience flow whilst engaging in a physical activity such as skiing, tennis, golf, dancing or running. Others might have such an experience whilst engaged in an activity such as painting, making something, fixing something, drawing, gardening, playing an instrument or writing.

How Does it Feel to Experience Flow?

According to Csíkszentmihályi, there are ten factors that accompany the experience of flow. While many of these components may be present, it is not necessary to experience *all* of them for flow to occur:

1. clear goals that, whilst being challenging, are still attainable;
2. strong concentration and focused attention;
3. the activity is intrinsically rewarding;
4. feelings of serenity - a loss of feeling self-conscious;

5. timelessness - a distorted sense of time, feeling so focused on the present that you lose track of time passing;
6. immediate feedback;
7. knowing that the task is doable - a balance between skill level and the challenge presented;
8. feelings of personal control over the situation and the outcome;
9. lack of awareness of physical needs;
10. complete focus on the activity itself.

Finding Flow

In his book *Finding Flow*, Csíkszentmihályi explains that flow is likely to occur when an individual is faced with a task that has clear goals requiring specific responses. A game of chess is a good example of when a flow state might occur. For the duration of a game, the player has very specific goals and responses, allowing attention to be focused entirely on the game during the period of play.

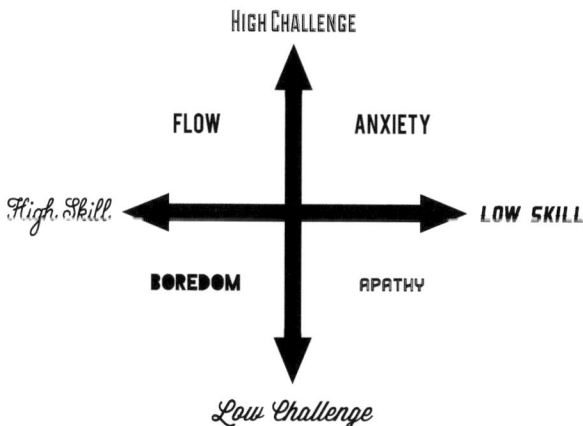

HIGH CHALLENGE

FLOW   ANXIETY

High Skill ←————————→ **LOW SKILL**

BOREDOM   APATHY

Low Challenge

'*Flow also happens when a person's skills are fully involved in overcoming a challenge that is just about manageable, so it acts as a magnet for learning new skills and increasing challenges,*' Csíkszentmihályi explains. '*If challenges are too low, one gets back to flow by increasing them. If challenges are too great, one can return to the flow state by learning new skills.*'

Don't just read the easy stuff. You may be entertained by it,
but you will never grow from it.
Jim Rohn

It is easy for us to see how this applies in learning: in formal education, in interests or activities, such as sports, the arts or computer games. It's therefore important for us, as parents, to take note of when our children are in flow, totally absorbed in what they're doing, find ways to replicate those experiences, and help them reflect on being in flow so they recognize it themselves. If our children say something is boring, then question them to find out why they find it so. It could be that they cannot see the relevance for them or they just don't enjoy a particular subject or activity, or it could be that they are not being sufficiently challenged to stimulate interest and the absorption of flow. This can mean helping our children link the relevance of activities with what they want to achieve, finding different activities, chatting to a teacher or finding a different class. We can all start to spot engaging and effective learning opportunities, and poor learning opportunities, once we understand a little about learning.

As you learn, you develop your appetite for learning.

A pupil from whom nothing is ever demanded which he cannot
do; never does all he can.
John Stuart Mill

 # Multiple Intelligences

Knowing yourself is the beginning of all wisdom.
Aristocle

Most of us are brought up with the notion that someone who is clever or intelligent is good at reading, writing, mathematics and science. Our education system values these above other competencies. However, Howard Gardner's work has helped us to reflect on, and value, different intelligences.

What are Multiple Intelligences?

Howard Gardner's research indicates that our intelligence, or ability to understand the world around us, is complex. Some people are better at understanding some things than others. For some of us, it is relatively easy to understand how a flower grows, but it is immensely difficult for us to understand and use a musical instrument. For others, music might be easy but playing ball sports difficult.

Gardner's work identifies that, rather than having one sort of intelligence, we have several different intelligences. All of us have all these intelligences combined in different and unique ways according to the individual. We may be very strong in one area and much weaker in another. Successful people accept their strengths; they have confidence in them and play to them. They address areas they need to improve as necessary, or work with people who complement their strengths and skills. (Just as a team in sports is made up of people with complementary skills.) There are some intelligences that I suggest we all need to work on, such as knowing ourselves (intrapersonal intelligence), and getting on well with other people (interpersonal intelligence). Much more on this in the *Managing Relationships* chapter.

Here is a brief summary from which you can consider the combinations of intelligence that are found uniquely in individuals and reflect on your own, and your children's, strengths.

Bodily-Kinaesthetic Intelligence
Bodily intelligence means we have control over our bodies and our bodies do what we want them to do. This can include things such as hand-eye co-ordination. Individuals who are bodily intelligent are good at things that require precise movement, such as dance and sports.

Linguistic Intelligence
Linguistic intelligence is being good with words. People who are linguistically intelligent are good at reading, writing and talking about things.

Logical – Mathematical Intelligence

This includes being logical: being good with numbers and scientifically able. People who are logical are good at mathematics and other number activities such as the sciences. They also tend to be good at solving problems with logic.

Intrapersonal Intelligence

Intrapersonal intelligence means knowing ourselves: knowledge of our feelings and range of emotions. It is the capacity to discriminate between our emotions and use them as a means of understanding and guiding our behaviour. Individuals who have intrapersonal intelligence are reflective: know themselves, their strengths and weaknesses. Their view of themselves is also very consistent with the view others have of them.

Interpersonal Intelligence

Interpersonal intelligence means being good with people. Individuals who are interpersonally intelligent are good at mixing with other people and get on well in social networks. They tend to like team games and are good at sharing. I like to think of this as 'tuning-in' with the people around us. Essential if you are going to be good at teaching, training, and other roles that require higher-order interpersonal intelligence.

Musical Intelligence

Being musically able means that we enjoy music and can recognise sounds, and timbre, or the quality of a tone. We can develop our technical ability and express ourselves with music.

Spatial Intelligence

Spatial intelligence is being good at spatial problem-solving. People who have spatial intelligence are good at art, building things, and other activities where you need to create or interpret pictures and diagrams like map reading, finding your way around places, following visual directions for assembling things, and graphs.

Naturalist Intelligence

Naturalist intelligence is a higher-order understanding of the world around us. An individual with a high degree of naturalist intelligence is keenly aware of how to distinguish from one another the diverse plants, animals, mountains and cloud configurations in their ecological environment.

In Howard Gardner's article, *In a Nutshell – Multiple Intelligences*, he concludes:

In brief, Multiple Intelligence theory leads to three conclusions:

1. All of us have the full range of intelligences; that is what makes us human beings, cognitively speaking.

2. No two individuals—not even identical twins—have exactly the same intellectual profile. That is because, even when the genetic material is identical, individuals have different experiences; and those who are identical twins are often highly motivated to distinguish themselves from one another.

*3. Having a strong intelligence does not mean that one necessarily acts intelligently. (*What an individual may choose to do with mathematical intelligence can vary tremendously, from neuroscience to spread betting!)

Harriet and George - Learning and Multiple Intelligences

My children are very different in learning, having different strengths, focus and approach in their formal education. They have been raised to be learners. I have encouraged their curiosity in anything and everything, ensured they know how to learn in a way that best suits them, and encouraged them to become the best they can be in their formal education and individual endeavours and interests. Harriet has used her capacity to learn in her formal education, training and career, and in what she has done outside that. George enjoys words and he's always been a great reader. He, therefore, mainly applied his capacity to learn in English at school (as well as Physical Education, of course!). He has mainly demonstrated his hunger and capacity to learn in his sport.

For the purpose of giving some examples of multiple intelligences and how our children differ, I'm going to do a brief compare and contrast focusing on Harriet and George. They are comfortable with this. I've always tried to engender an attitude to learning that celebrates what we're good at, and gets into perspective the things we find challenging. The important thing is to be comfortable with who we are and what we want to achieve, rather than comparing different achievements in a judgemental way.

Harriet has always be spatially smart, good at art and at building things, creating very impressive models from a very young age. She made incredible Lego models at home and built very impressive working models at primary school. George not so! From a relatively young age, if you gave Harriet a piece of flat-pack furniture, a couple of hours later you would have the perfect finished article. Even now, at 21, you may be waiting many months for George to even start to tackle it. (He certainly wouldn't want to even attempt it on his own.) Sometime later in the year, you may get something that vaguely resembles the picture on the box! He will say, 'That's not my department'.

George has always been linguistically smart, hence finding school a breeze, where being linguistically intelligent is the foundation of so much formal education. Harriet has always found spelling and grammar a challenge. At the age of 7, George found Harriet's (aged 11) spellings easy to learn and couldn't really fathom why she found it challenging. He has always read avidly and quickly, she finds the words jump around on the page and it is really enough for her to do the reading she has to do for study and work; the notion of reading for pleasure is not something she readily relates to. That brings out one of the most important things I've endeavoured to instill in my children: **do not put others down who can't do what you can do; they will have different strengths. Celebrate diversity, what others are good at and what they can contribute.**

Harriet is more naturally mathematically intelligent than George and this has been clearest in their relative interest and grasp of science and technology. He has little interest in technology and petitioned the principal not to have to do an Information Technology Diploma, which was compulsory at his school as an IT Specialist Academy (not the reason he decided to go there!). Harriet did a science degree and George found her dissertation, which was focused on the impact of back strength in medium quick bowlers in cricket, challenging to grasp, even though he was in fact one of the main subjects as a medium quick bowler himself.

Harriet and George are able to use their bodies intelligently, in different ways. She has pursued many different disciplines to a reasonable standard and is expert in training the body for fitness. George has pursued ball sports, namely football and cricket, to a high standard.

In terms of interpersonal and intrapersonal skills, they both know themselves, reflect, and are excellent with people in any context. This is in no small part due to the importance I attach to these intelligences and the things I have done to help them develop these competencies. Reflection and review has been part and parcel of what we have done from a very young age. I have also ensured that they attended schools where they would engage with people from all backgrounds, coached them to handle challenging relationships at school and ensured they experience varied environments.

I believe that one of the most valuable things we can do for our children is to develop interpersonal and intrapersonal intelligence and enable them to get on well with people in any context. In addition to Harriet and George's general interpersonal competencies, there are distinct differences. Harriet is a naturally able teacher, and it is amazing to observe her with individuals and groups. She worked as a 'buddy' supporting children with special needs during summer sports camps from the age of 16, and her impressive work with individuals with complex physical and learning needs led to her managing the 'buddies' over the summer at the age of 19. She has then gone on to be a trainer, on occasion working with less than motivated groups, and achieving impressive results. George has always found it frustrating to work with people who do not share his intellect or drive in areas that are important to him, whether that's supporting a classmate with language at 8, playing cricket with people he didn't think took it seriously enough aged 10, or more recently, coaching younger cricketers. He has no interest unless they are spatially smart at cricket and work hard. The important thing is that he's aware of this.

Our children have innate abilities - or a genetic pre-disposition - in terms of their intelligence in different areas, and I think it's important to recognise that. Those who succeed in any area of life play to their strengths. They also develop in areas that are essential. For me, one of these areas is interpersonal and intrapersonal competencies, and these are areas within which, no matter what level our children are at, we can expose them to opportunities and coach them to improve.

The most important thing is that we empower our children to value their strengths and to not feel down-hearted or inadequate about things they don't excel in. There are only two responses to areas of challenge: accept it or do something about it, and we are in an excellent position to help our children develop this attitude. When we were at Harriet's degree ceremony, George leaned over to me and said, in a positive way, 'Enjoy this, Mum, it's the only one you'll be coming to!'

Building Self-Regard with Learning

An important aspect of learning something new and gaining a skill or capability is how it boosts our self-worth and self-regard. This is explored in the *Believe in Yourself* chapter, but the link between self-regard and learning is worth re-iterating. Being able to do something we couldn't previously do, from reading a book to riding a bike, from learning how to use a computer to making a meal, gives us a tremendous boost, especially if our achievement is reinforced by celebration. Children with low self-regard who have experienced mistakes and failure as something to be criticised, laughed at, or even punished, can gradually learn to fear failure and develop deflection techniques to avoid doing things they may not be very good at. This seriously damages their attitude to learning and capacity to learn. Some of the ways this manifests itself are by not trying, not having a go; saying things like, 'That's rubbish', 'Can't be bothered', 'I can do that but not in the mood' etc. Self-deprecation is another manifestation of this, saying things like, 'I can't do that', 'I'm rubbish at that'. It is therefore vital that we boost our children's self-esteem in learning new skills whenever we can, making a fuss of the weird drawings of people from nursery, acknowledging when our children can do something they couldn't previously do, acknowledging small improvements. We also need to enable our children to look after themselves – valuable for self-regard and valuable for life.

Some people have a view that praising children may result in them being 'big-headed' or getting an exaggerated view of their skills and abilities. This is only the case if it's exaggerated, indiscriminate praise. This very often comes without the other side of the development coin: challenge and the expectation of continuous improvement. I have seen far more damage caused by the negativity of continuously criticising and focusing on poor performance than by giving too much praise.

Expanding Our Comfort Zone

The man who goes farthest is generally
the one who is willing to do and dare.
The sure-thing boat never gets far from shore.
Dale Carnegie

We all like being comfortable. Unfortunately, we can get too comfortable – in our daily routines, in our immediate community, in our relationships, in the places we regularly frequent – and it limits us. It is crucial that we break out of the ruts that we have settled into in order to grow. It takes confidence and courage to try new things, but the moment we expand our horizons, we gain confidence in all other areas of our life.

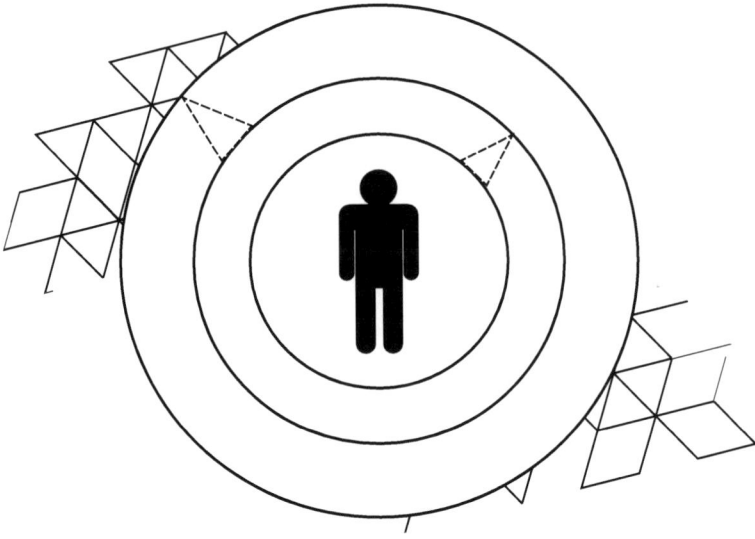

This comfort zones diagram illustrates how this works: you are at the centre, within your immediate comfort zone. This comfort zone is quite small and will start to limit your achievements over a period of time – it is also safe; you know exactly how everything in your life operates. Accepting challenges that help you achieve something new will allow you to break out of your comfort bubble and develop a wider confidence zone that will enable you to cope with even more challenges, and your life will be enriched. Every time you do something new or different, or push yourself to overcome a challenge, you will stretch your comfort zone a little more.

If you do one thing that is new it expands the whole of your comfort / confidence zone. I firmly believe that the moment we stop expanding our comfort zone it shrinks. It is a constant cycle of pushing our boundaries of when and where we are comfortable until we feel confident in all or most situations.

Once you learn to quit, it becomes a habit.
Vincent Lombardi

Successful people expand their learning in areas they are passionate about to support them in achieving their goals, or just to give themselves a new challenge to enable them to think more creatively. They tend to have a helicopter view, and join the dots between things where others just don't see the connections. They use all sorts of learning and apply it to what they want to achieve. Achieving something new brings new insights and ideas to the things you do and want to achieve.

To achieve beyond the norm, we need to soak up new things, try things, but not like a butterfly – flitting from one thing to the next – explore things that really interest us with passion and commitment. Think of Richard Branson and his round the world balloon challenge. And Humphrey Walters, crewing a round-the-world yacht race with no previous experience of sailing because he felt he needed a new challenge.

Successful people are always growing, developing – sometimes reinventing themselves. Continuously improving their knowledge and skills in what they are passionate about, whether that be business, sports, science, music, engineering, the arts etc. They embrace change and challenge rather than fear it.

Be willing to be uncomfortable.
Be comfortable being uncomfortable.
It may get tough, but it's a small price to pay for
living a dream'.
Peter McWilliams

Communities of Excellence

It is no coincidence that we tend to find groups of high achievers together, geographically. If there are a number of people with technical ability, passion and a network of experienced coaches, mentors and the latest learning around them, they learn together and feed from each other. Whether it's Silicon Valley or the British equivalent in Cambridge, groups of athletes, sports teams, academic research, medical excellence, engineering innovation, groups of focused, driven people help each other achieve more through sharing ideas, finding ways to improve, motivating each other, challenging each other and competing. Find your communities of excellence in fields you want to pursue and help your children find those all-important people and networks who can help them excel.

> *Only the curious will learn and*
> *only the resolute overcome the obstacles to learning.*
> *The quest quotient has always excited me*
> *more than the intelligence quotient.*
> Eugene S. Wilson

Affirmations

- I am passionate about learning what I need to in order to achieve my goals.
- I am enthusiastically learning new things from every experience.
- I am exhilarated to be expanding my comfort zone with new experiences.
- I am loving learning from everyone around me.
- I am always improving how I learn.

> *Nothing is difficult that is wholly desired. Trials are but lessons*
> *that you failed to learn presented once again, so where you*
> *made a faulty choice before you now can make a better one*.
> Unknown

 ACTION

The information shared in this chapter can help us communicate more effectively and support our children to improve their ability to learn. The activities below are designed to help you further develop your awareness and better equip your children to learn.

1. How do you learn best?
Download a Learning Styles Questionnaire from the equipped2succeed downloads section of my website to help you and your children reflect on your learning styles.

2. Reflect on your learning and write down:
3 things you've learned in the last week *and* how will you use what you learned.
Regularly ask your children:
'What have you learned at school today?'
'What have you learned from that?'
(successes, mistakes, experiences.)
'How will you use what you've learned?'

3. What are you doing to expand your comfort zone?
Think of something you would like to be able to do but haven't because you are frightened or anxious about it (or have made time excuses!).
Plan, mentally rehearse, enlist support and just do it.

4. What are you doing to help your children expand their comfort zone, *without putting too much pressure on them*?

One of the most powerful ways we can support our children is
to enable and equip them to be
self-empowered, independent learners:
be motivated to learn and know how to learn.
There is nothing more powerful than doing it for yourself
– and knowing you can!

*The things that have been most valuable to me
I did not learn in school.*
Will Smith

Chapter Eleven

Believe in Yourself

We are what we believe we are.
Benjamin Cardozo

 Definitions

self:
- the set of someone's characteristics, such as personality and ability, that are not physical and make that person different from other people;
- the distinct individuality or identity of a person or thing;
- an individual's consciousness of his/her own identity or being.

belief:
- the feeling of being certain that something exists or is true;
- something that you believe;
- a principle accepted as true, especially without proof;
- opinion or conviction;
- trust or confidence, as in a person's abilities.

self-belief:
- trust in your own abilities.

One person with a belief, is equal to ninety-nine who have no interests.
John Stewart Mill

Successful people build and maintain belief in themselves, their goals and their abilities.

Developing and maintaining self-belief is crucial if we are to achieve our goals, and it is one of the most important roles we have, as parents, to empower and enable our children to believe in themselves.

Our self-belief is something we have more individual control over as we grow, and there is always a debate about how much self-belief is a matter of nature or nurture. There is no doubt that some people seem to develop and maintain self-belief much easier than others: as we can recognise from the differences between siblings in the same family, with very similar childhood experiences. There are those who have experienced a very negative childhood who have managed to emerge with tremendous self-belief, and also the opposite is true; there are those who appear to have had a very secure, caring childhood who are riddled with self-doubt. It is also the case that many people who have succeeded in their chosen endeavours will openly say that they have times of self-doubt. The important factor is that they don't allow their moments of self-doubt to paralyse them and prevent them from moving forward. Their self-doubt often comes from humility - a desire to always do better and not settle for mediocrity. Anne Hathaway, in her acceptance speech for the Golden Globe Award she won for her role in *Les Miserables*, said;

Thank you for this blunt object which I will forever use as a weapon against self doubt.

Our self-belief comes from the way we think about ourselves and is affected, positively or negatively, by the people around us. Unless, that is, we are one of those exceptional individuals whose self-belief can withstand being surrounded by negativity and doubters and come out saying, 'I'll show you'. Our self-belief is supported by our 'self-talk' and is linked to the positive, can-do attitude described in the *Be Positive* chapter. To develop self-belief, we need to accentuate what we can do rather than what we can't, and model that with our children. To nurture our children's self-belief, we need to coach them to accentuate what they can do – reinforce what they can do and their limitless potential.

I will become what I deserve is a line from Ben Howard's *The Fear*. In other words, I will become what I think about, what I feel, because that's what I'll attract to me. And it's vital that we believe we deserve our vision and believe in our capacity to realise that positive future for ourselves. In this chapter, we explore maintaining high self-regard and the belief that we deserve, and can achieve, the things we want to be, have, do.

It's crucial, if we are to realise our goals and be, have, do what we really want, to believe in ourselves, and our infinite capacity. A big goal is a light toward which we are heading, and above all else we need to believe we can reach it, taking one step at a time, and believing in our capacity to succeed at each next step along the road, even when things get challenging.

If we find we don't have belief in what we're striving for, we need to change our goals or change our thinking! If we are to develop and maintain positive, affirming relationships - personally, socially, in education and work contexts - we need to have high self-regard and self-belief, or we are in danger of not making the most of opportunities and letting people take advantage of us, or even humiliate and bully us.

Self-belief and confidence are often used to mean the same thing. However, the distinct difference for me is that one is internal and one is external. Self-belief is internal: what we really believe about ourselves, and our capacity to realise our goals. Confidence is what we choose to show to the world. There are people who appear to have great confidence, but who, when we scratch the surface, are actually riddled with self-doubt. Arrogance comes into this mix here and I am always having debates with people about where the line is between confidence and arrogance, especially with those involved in professional sport.

Like confidence, arrogance is what we choose to show to the world. Confidence and arrogance are on the same spectrum; the line between them is sometimes fine, and can easily be crossed. Arrogance may mask self-doubt, rather than indicate self-belief.

confidence	arrogance
trust and self-belief in one's own ability	an exaggerated opinion of one's own importance or ability

People who believe in themselves and are confident appear comfortable in their own skin and are often humble rather than arrogant. As Paul McKenna says in his great book, *Instant Confidence: The Power to Go for Anything You Want,* **Have you ever heard someone say about a person 'they seem comfortable in their own skin'? This is the essence of natural confidence – feeling a level of comfort with yourself that can withstand the slings and arrows of outrageous fortune and carry you forward to the life of your dreams.**

People who are arrogant see themselves as better than those around them and can show this in their language and body-language. They focus solely on themselves and their performance, not recognising others' contributions and value, sometimes putting others down, abdicating responsibility when things go wrong, etc.

Confidence comes not from always being right,
but from not fearing to be wrong.
Peter McIntyre

Self-image - Self-regard - Self-belief

Our self-belief is within and is intrinsically linked to our self-image and self-regard. Definitions of self-image and self-regard vary, but I define them as:

- self-image is your view of yourself;
- self-regard (or self-esteem) is the evaluation of that view.

A positive self-image and high self-regard supports building and maintaining our self-belief.

People with high self-regard, who believe in themselves:

- tell themselves they can – their self-talk is positive;
- are assertive – not passive or aggressive – calmly and strongly state their views and do what is best for themselves and those around them. As Henry C. Link says:

While one person hesitates because
he feels inferior, the other is busy
making mistakes and becoming superior.

We all find that life events, such as failing an exam, failing an interview, losing a friend, performing poorly in something we love, losing a job, ending a relationship or being bereaved – can give our confidence a huge knock. However, high self-regard can act as a buffer to absorb these knocks and help us bounce back.

Signs of High Self-Regard

When asked to do something:	Confidently say you can do it, or say you'll have a go, or say you don't want to do it and give reasons.
How you feel about yourself:	Feel you have value and make a contribution. Feel you can achieve and are learning all the time to do things better.
When you need help:	Are prepared to ask for help and support from people who have the right knowledge, skills and experience to help; without being needy or dependent.
When things go wrong:	Acknowledge when things go wrong and accept responsibility. Learn from mistakes and don't keep making the same mistake.
When you have a difficulty with someone or someone tries to put you down:	Respond assertively with people, being calm and clear with your language, remaining confident in your own value and treating people with polite respect.

Remember, there are no mistakes, only lessons.
Love yourself, trust your choices, and everything is possible.
Cherie Carter-Scott

People with high self-regard also tend to be assertive:

Assertive – being 'for real' and strong	Body language	Actions
Keen to stand up for your rights while accepting that others have rights, too.	Enough eye contact to let people know you are serious.	Lots of listening; seek to understand.
		Treat people with respect.
	Moderate, neutral tone of voice.	Prepared to compromise; solution-focused.
	Moderate, open body posture.	Prepared to state and explain you want.
	Body language in tune with spoken words.	Straight and to the point without being abrupt. Prepared to persist for what you want.

Signs of Low Self-Regard – Two Poles

Quiet (timid)	Loud (brash)
Say can't do things (believe everyone else can).	Say can do things (but not prepared to be tested).
Feel worthless, useless and tell you that.	Have to tell everyone how marvellous they are.
Are constantly needy.	Don't want help – think to accept help is a sign of weakness; people will realise they are worthless.
Don't admit things are wrong.	Constantly reinforce things are wrong. Blame others.
Are frightened to say anything to people who put them down.	Put people 'in their place'. Reinforce their own worth by (often inappropriately) telling people they are in charge.

Low self-regard is evident in a variety of ways, sometimes apparently opposite behaviours showing the same feelings of low self-worth, with timid behaviour at one end of the spectrum and arrogant, brash behaviour at the other. We find these behaviours (and everything in between) in children, young people and adults alike. Low self-regard is a feeling of inferiority or inadequacy. Behavior can include being 'needy' or using avoidance tactics to not let others see your inadequacies. It takes a self-confident person to say 'I haven't got a clue, explain it to me' without feeling inadequate in some way.

The Impact of Praise and Criticism on Our Self-Regard

The praise and criticism of those around us, those with whom we have the strongest emotional bond, those who have some authority over us and those we admire, has the potential to have tremendous impact on our self-regard and self-belief, especially when we are young. One study I read maintained that praise needs to outweigh criticism 15:1 if we are not going to damage an individual's self-regard. However accurate that is, it gives us food for thought as parents. There is no doubt that both can have tremendous impact on individuals, and even greater impact when we add in the uniquely close emotional relationship between parents and children. It works both ways and it can have a huge impact on us when our children praise and criticise us. I certainly feel praise and criticism from my children more deeply than from anyone else. If we also take into account that most of us tend to hear criticism more than we hear praise, we need to be even more careful.

Imagine you are 11, your self-regard has been bruised by something at school and your mum seems to be only finding things to criticise because she's 'stressed'? I have heard myself practising the reverse praise sandwich, criticism with praise in there somewhere, which is totally lost in the mix. I know it's challenging when we're under personal and work pressure, but we are the adults in the relationship with our children and we need to manage ourselves effectively for their benefit. When we are too critical, we need to acknowledge it and apologise. Our children are very forgiving (unless we keep making the same mistakes)!

When praising, we need to think about the purpose and make it as constructive and useful as possible. A pre-occupied 'Well done, dear', when it's obvious we're not paying attention, doesn't do it. Empty praise is almost as bad as thoughtless criticism. It is the same with criticism; it needs to be constructive, useful, and framed in the positive to enable our children to develop their understanding of continuous improvement, of being reflective and using constructive criticism as part of that reflection. If a child is brought up with everyone constantly and indiscriminately telling her or him how marvellous they are, it also doesn't help build their self-belief. Feint praise without the balance of challenge to improve, persist in difficulties etc does not help to equip our children with the resilience necessary to face life's inevitable challenges and failures.

Praise needs to:

be sincere - not just an empty gesture – children spot this a mile away and it has no positive impact, e.g. 'You worked hard and did an excellent piece of homework and really deserve that A grade'.

be specific - praising a specific action or achievement, e.g. 'Your test result is really impressive. I realise how hard you worked and you'll have learned a lot about how to approach tests in the future'.

encourage - particular performance or behaviour, e.g. 'I really appreciate that you've got everything ready for school (or for training)', 'I'm very impressed with the way you helped your school friend'.

promote autonomy - encourage children to take responsibility and be independent, e.g.: 'Well done for getting yourself something to eat'. (It may not have been what we wanted them to eat, but we can address that later by making suggestions.) This can also be praise for helping without being asked, or generally undertaking chores – even if it's expected, we still need to praise.

enhance competence - recognise specific competence and give a pointer for improvement, e.g. 'Your writing is so much easier to read. Perhaps you could try leaving a little more space between words. Your writing is so straight across the page' (an example of the 'praise sandwich').

convey attainable standards and expectations - recognise achievement and reinforce expectations, e.g. 'That was a really well thought out presentation. You presented it confidently and with meaning. Most of us rush when we're presenting so remember always to leave time for your audience to take in what you've said.' We've praised and emphasised things that constitute effective presentation skills and added something to help improve the quality in a way that makes it clear that it's something we all do rather than just them.

celebrate success - success deserves recognition and celebration. I believe in always encouraging and challenging to improve performance. Recognising improvement and celebrating success balances the challenge.

Criticism needs to:

be for our child's benefit - whether that's for them as an individual, or within the context of living with, and getting on well with others, we need to think about the benefit before we frame what we're going to say.

framed in the positive – what we want to see, rather than what we don't want to see. What is the point of criticising unless it's to improve something? We therefore need to recognise positives, effort and prior achievement before suggesting improvements.

come with a solution - the renowned cricket coach Bob Woolmer said to coaches, 'A coach shouldn't say anything about a fault unless he knows what's causing it and how to get rid of it. Otherwise, it causes confusion and frustration.' In other words, if you haven't got a solution, don't say anything at all. I know I've emphasised that coaching is about questioning to help our children to come to their own conclusions, but there are times when we need to act as mentors for our children and use our experience to suggest solutions.

be specific - focusing on a specific area for improvement, not a long list of moans.

come with a question - too many times, criticism comes with 'telling', 'What you should do is .....' Improvement is much more likely to come by starting with a coaching approach, 'What do you think you could do to improve .....?'.

offer help - if criticism is followed by, 'What can I do to help you with this?', it reinforces that we're serious and shows we care and are willing to help.

encourage – a particular attitude, way of thinking, skill, performance or behavior.

promote autonomy - encourage children to take responsibility and be independent.

enhance competence - recognise specific competence(s) that our child needs to develop, for their own benefit and the benefit of those around them. This includes developing emotional and social competence, work ethic, or helping them make a contribution in the home, at school, and in their local community and community of interest.

convey attainable standards and expectations - recognise achievement and reinforce expectations. Ensure that children understand what the standards are, from putting their dirty washing in the linen bin to getting an improved grade.

> *Sandwich every bit of criticism between two*
> *thick layers of praise.*
> Mary Kay Ash

All in all, our approach to praise and criticism needs to be balanced. From my experience as a parent, and experiencing the effects of parenting in so many young people's lives, one thing for me is sure; praise needs to always outweigh criticism in order to help praise outweigh criticism in our children's thoughts about themselves.

Ditch the Doubters

One of the things we need to guard against is having people around us who 'put us down'. None of us need people around us who negatively put us down and limit our ambition from the standpoint of their negativity or fear. This limiting of ambition is often framed or phrased as protecting us – making us 'be realistic'. Others sometimes do this due to their own low self-esteem and need to 'keep you in your place' or 'put you in your place' because of their own insecurities.

If you have friends in your circle like this – move away. If your children have people in their lives like this, help them to guard against their negative impact. If it's their peers at school, coach your children with strategies to guard against the negative impact; counter-balance the negatives with positives, remind them about their protective 'force field' or 'bubble' that lets only the positive in and makes negatives bounce off. If it's our friends, teachers or family members it's up to us to be strong and advocate for our children; challenging their negativity. It is more challenging to limit the impact of family members like this. However, we can mentally move away and limit their negative impact on us and help our children do the same.

The Power of My Self-Belief as a Child

My most powerful memory of self-belief was as a child, aged 11. Most of the country at that time had something called the 11+. Some education authorities still have this, and many independent schools have entrance exams. The 11+ is an examination taken in year 6, the last year of primary school, that decides which secondary school we progress to. I failed my 11+, as did all but one of my year group from the small primary school I attended in the next village. In some families, children were, and are, tutored to pass the 11+. As was usual in my community at the time, my family knew very little about the education system and entrusted our education to the school system. For my parents, providing a secure family environment was their major priority, being the first generation of home-owners in their respective families.

Failing my 11+ devastated me and I cried for a weekend when I opened the envelope and saw the green piece of paper; it was pink if you'd passed. However, after that initial disappointment, I thought they'd just made a mistake. It never crossed my mind that I was not clever enough. I came to terms with going to Mortimer Wilson Comprehensive School and wearing the bottle green uniform rather than grey and red version at the grammar school. My mind was firmly set on being in the 'A' stream at secondary school. The day I started was the first day I'd visited and, after a 20-minute journey on the school bus, I was marshalled into the hall with all other year 7 students ('first years', as we were called then).

We stood in apprehensive silence as a teacher called out the names for each class. I should explain that there was strict steaming in the school as the head teacher, Wilf Dawes OBE, didn't believe in the 11+ and wanted to prove that at least some of his secondary modern students could perform as well as their grammar school peers. So we waited, listening attentively for our names. The names were called in strict alphabetical order for each class, starting with the A stream, who were considered to be the brightest students. A1, A2, B1, B2, C1, C2, D1, D2, etc. You get the idea. I can recollect everything about standing in that hall listening to those names as if it was yesterday. My name is Burton, and they got to R in A2 and I still thought I was in the A stream. I just thought they'd made a mistake (another one), and that they'd say my name at the end. Of course, they didn't, but I didn't have to wait long as I was in B1. It never crossed my mind that they'd put me in the right class. I still believed they'd just made a mistake and I would show them that they had. I was different in that I refused to believe the system's judgement of my intellect and ability. Most children believe teachers' judgements about their ability, especially a child moving from a rural primary school with about 75 children to a secondary school with nearer 1800 children! I spent two terms in B1 and then we had exams. I came top in 7 subjects and went up into A1. That reaffirmed for me that they had made a mistake! But what if I'd believed what they told me?

> *We are each so much more than*
> *what some reduce to measuring.*
> Karen Kaiser Clark

If only I could have maintained that self-belief in everything since! In reflecting on the way my self-belief has ebbed and flowed over the years, and developing my understanding of self-belief from experience and research, I have some ideas about why I had belief in my intellect, despite the test results and teachers' decisions. This, together with the experience of raising my own children, has reinforced for me that self-belief is partly nature and partly nurture. This is also borne out in people's very different reactions to the same adversity as children.

One factor in my self-belief is that, as a young child, I had adults around me who were very affirming. I lived in a small village with very few other children of my age, and therefore most of my time was spent with adults until I started school at the age of five. I am the eldest in the family. I am also the eldest grandchild on my mother's side, and we lived with her father, my grandfather, and her younger sister, my aunt, until I was 3. When we moved into what was to be our family home (and is still where my parents live today), we lived a few hundred yards from my paternal grandmother, whom I also remember spending very positive time with, even though she died when I was 6. I even remember, with affection, sitting chatting to her when she was very sick in bed just before she died. I also had 3 very affirming teachers at primary school, one of whom I remember in particular, Mrs Hill, who stretched my thinking and certainly my vocabulary.

The other major factors I believe are nature. Another factor in my success at school was that I somehow had intrinsic motivation to learn and was passionate about learning from a young age. I was, apparently, a child who asked incessant questions and, of course, I had a variety of adults around to answer them. By today's standards, people may say that I missed out on socialisation with other children and I believe that may have been an issue had I not been an insatiable learner: learning from all my experiences and picking up clues on socially acceptable behaviour from those around me. I was also hungry for new experiences, and went on my first residential school trip, at the age of 9, to Wales for a week, where I remember trying new food etc. (We didn't go on a family holidays, so 'going away' was something completely new to me). I was also quite fearless, as described by my parents and from some of my memories. My personal experience is that siblings in the same family can have very different levels of intrinsic self-belief. This reinforces, for me, that we need to do all we can to enable our children to build their self-belief if they find things fearful and lack the confidence to have a go, or shy away from getting things wrong.

Building Self-Belief in Our Children

There are a number of ways my experience as a child informed my parenting, in terms of nurturng my children to believe in themselves. This has then been added to by what I have learned from experience in my professional life. In addition to what is outlined in the *Praise* and *Criticism* sections above, here are a few things that I believe are really important to help our children develop the self-belief that is essential for them to realise their potential:

- Treating our children as individuals and tuning into how to help them build a positive self-image, high self-regard and self-belief is vital. One child's challenge is a bridge too far for another, and we need to constantly exercise our judgement and knowledge of our children. But if we accept our children's lack of self-belief, and their unwillingness and fear to try new things, and expand their comfort zones etc as a personality trait, we are doing them a serious disservice. We have a duty to do everything we can to nurture our children's self-belief, and especially those who find it most challenging to believe in themselves. It takes time, energy, effort and patience, but seeing our children blossom into self-confident adults, pursuing their goals, is worth every moment.

- We need to ensure that our emotional intelligence is sufficiently developed to tune-in with the situations our children face, and amend our behaviour and approach accordingly, especially with appropriate levels of challenge and support.

- I have always spoken to my children as equals (little people), using pretty much the same language I use with my peers. 'Baby language', such as 'moo cow' for cow, can be very confusing and belittling for children, and has never been part of my vocabulary.

- I have **expected** that they **could** and **would** – in whatever context – and it's amazing what children can do if we expect it of them. There is nothing like achievement in anything to build self-belief, whether that's using a knife and fork, tying shoe laces, riding a bike, walking up Snowden at the age of 3, making a meal for yourself etc.

- The other side of the expectation coin is not burdening our children with disappointment. When we fail at something or just can't understand something, we tend to feel inadequate in some way. If that feeling is compounded by those people with whom we have the strongest emotional connection - our parents - it can do untold damage to our self-esteem and self-belief.

- Failing is an essential learning experience and helps build resilience. We need to support our children to set failure in context; to not see it as something final, but rather as part of the way we grow.

> *Our greatest glory is not in never failing,*
> *but in rising up every time we fail.*
> Ralph Waldo Emerson

I have not always got it right in the way I have endeavoured to nurture my children's self-belief, but I have usually recognised my failures soon enough to apologise and make amends. And I have always learned.

If you accept the expectations of others, especially negative ones, then you will never change the outcome.
Michael Jordan

Michael Jordan is one of the all-time greats of basketball, and yet he was dropped from his school basketball team and told he wasn't good enough. It's a good job Michael Jordan didn't accept the expectations of others!

Courage

To pursue what we really want to do, and achieve anything of worth, we need to be courageous: willing to try and unafraid to fail. When we're young, this can mean being courageous in learning. It can also be embracing new experiences, such as going to a club we want to join when none of our friends want to go, or going on a school trip away from our parents for the first time. As we get older, it can mean challenging someone who is intimidating us, catching the bus on our own, going to University, taking an internship in another country, or getting a job in a city in another part of the country. A big part of our role is to enable our children to overcome fear, expand their comfort zone and be courageous (within reasonable regard for safety, rather than over-protectiveness).

To live a creative life, we must lose our fear of being wrong.
Joseph Chilton Pearce

Affirmations
- I am comfortably handling challenges.
- I am appreciating my skills.
- I am loving how confident I feel.
- I am developing my self-belief every day.
- I am confident in my ability to achieve my goals.
- I am valuing my children's achievements.
- I am promoting self-belief in the people around me.
- I am proud of my contribution.
- I am confidently building my skills and learning every day.

ACTION

1. Reinforce your positive image. Write down three of your:

- best physical attributes;
- best mental abilities;
- best financial moves you ever made;
- most unusual characteristics;
- best general human attributes;
- best social skills;
- most important interests;
- and your single most important value (e.g. health, love, freedom, creativity).

Keep your list where you can see it frequently. This can be adapted to use with younger and older children.

2. Praise v Criticism Diary

Keep a diary for a few weeks in either a notebook or on the electronic device you use most – anything that's going to be handy. The purpose of this is to help you reflect on your pattern of praise and criticism. What we think we do and what we actually do may well be different. It also helps us become more skilled in ensuring that our praise and criticism helps our children. If your children are older, it's really useful to include them in this. I found my children have always been very willing to reflect back to me!

Have a table for each of your children and record briefly your praise and criticism each day, your children's reactions, whether or not you feel it was helpful for them and how you could have done it better, if at all.

Praise v Criticism Diary - Headings

Name .... Date ....

Praise Criticism Reaction Was this helpful? How could I have done this better?

If you do this for a week and then reflect, you can:

- see the ratio of praise to criticism;
- look at the times of day when you're more likely to be overly critical and see how that fits with the stresses and strains you feel;
- consider what sort of praise and criticism works best for your individual children;
- improve your skills.

Whenever I've reflected on this, both myself and my children have noticed particular times of day or circumstances when I've leaned more towards criticism - just getting in from work, when I'm tired and when I'm hungry. This helps you to stop yourself from approaching something until you're in a better frame of mind. One thing it did for me is made me realise I was much better if, on the nights we were not going straight out to training, I went to my room and had 10 minutes of quiet time – deep breathing and relaxation – before we started our evening, reflecting on the day, having a meal, doing homework (mine and theirs!) etc.

3. Being Comfortable Being Uncomfortable

a. Think of circumstances when you feel most comfortable in your daily life: most content and confident.
Think of the feelings you associate with these times.

b. Think of circumstances when you feel least comfortable in your daily life - ill-at-ease, anxious, worried, frightened.
Think of what you can do to overcome this.

Change the circumstances or change the way you respond to the circumstances.

Ask your children these questions and chat with them about how they might increase their confidence in challenging situations. Decide how you can help them with this. The starting point must always be to help and coach them to address challenges themselves. Only step in if there are challenging situations that are beyond their capability or confidence to overcome at this time. It's a balance for us to support without undermining or nannying our children and thereby taking away learning opportunities.

4. Act As If

When we're feeling inadequate and lacking confidence, we can 'act as if'. Act as if we are good at something; act as if we're confident doing something. This makes us reflect on the thinking, language, body language and behaviour associated with what we're working on and helps us build the belief in ourselves. If we take on the thinking, language and the body language of someone who can do something, we start to find we're more comfortable and confident doing it ourselves.

Children are very good at understanding this concept, being just another version of playing make-believe or taking on the persona of role models.

Life is not easy for any of us.
But what of that?
We must have perseverance and above all
confidence in ourselves.
We must believe that we are gifted for something and that
this thing must be attained.
Marie Curie

Marie Curie was a Polish physicist and chemist, working mainly in France, who is famous for her pioneering research on radioactivity. She was the first woman to win a Nobel Prize, the only woman to win in two fields, and the only person to win in multiple sciences. Her name lives on with the Marie Curie Cancer Care Charity.

Chapter Twelve

Manage Stress (better)

Definitions

manage:
- to bring about or succeed in accomplishing, sometimes despite difficulty or hardship;
- to take charge or care of;
- to handle, direct, govern, or control in action or use.

stress:
- the physical pressure, pull, or other force exerted on one thing by another;
- a specific response by the body to a stimulus, such as fear or pain, that disturbs or interferes with the normal physiological equilibrium of an organism;
- physical, mental, or emotional strain or tension;
- great worry caused by a difficult situation, or something that causes this condition.

better:
- of a higher standard, or more suitable or more effective than other things;
- preferable;
- of superior quality or excellence.

Successful people minimise the negative effects of stress; they do it naturally and instinctively or they develop strategies to manage it effectively. Their positive mental attitude and their focus on the future help them to avoid being overwhelmed or paralysed by the anxiety of challenges. They get things in perspective and see beyond the immediate challenge. In this chapter, we consider the impact of general stress in our lives and how we can effectively equip our children to minimise the negative effects of stress to perform at their best, especially when it matters most.

So, what do we mean by stress?

One of the most commonly accepted definitions of stress (mainly attributed to Richard S Lazarus) is that *stress is a condition or feeling experienced when a person perceives that demands exceed the personal and social resources the individual is able to mobilize.*

A growing awareness has meant that stress has become much more widely recognised and talked about. All of us experience it to different degrees, be we parents, shop assistants, sports men and women, computer analysts, teachers, nurses or company directors. Stress affects us all at different times and in different ways, whether we recognise it or not.

In fields of endeavour that involve public performance, such as sports and the arts, stress can manifest itself as performance anxiety, and this is akin to the sort of stress we feel when going into an examination or making an important presentation upon which a lot rests. In the *Develop Your Winning Brain* chapter, I explored how to perform at our best under pressure and when it matters most, and a major contributory factor in this is effectively managing stress and performance anxiety.

Imbalance is usually a feature of stress. A feeling that things are out of control and we can't cope is a major cause of the angst and feelings of paralysis associated with stress. We may have too much to do and too little time: too much freedom and too little direction, too much responsibility and too little power. Change can often create a strong sense of imbalance: we were in control, then things changed and we feel out of control, and our security may seem threatened. The more we know about ourselves, the quicker we are able to define fresh frameworks that make us feel secure again. If a key indicator of stress is feeling overwhelmed and out of control, there is little wonder in the rise of its recognition in recent times. The pace at which we live has changed, with more and more of us juggling infinite numbers of roles and responsibilities. We are bombarded by information, a plethora of communication tools, and are continually trying to find a balance between too little and too much information, and too little and too much communication. This is demanding.

Almost all of us have mobile phones, some of us more than one. We are accessible 24/7 by telephone, text and email for the communication we want to be available for, as well as that which we need to carefully manage and moderate. We can also access infinite amounts of digital information 24/7. Overload is a natural extension of this.

In 2010, Google CEO Eric Schmidt famously said:
Every two days now **we create as much information as we did from the dawn of civilization up until 2003.**
Let me repeat that: we create as much information in two days now as we did from the dawn of man through 2003.

To make it even more personal, in his book *Information Anxiety* (1989), Richard Wurman claimed that,
The weekday edition of The New York Times contains more information than the average person in 17th-century England was likely to come across in a lifetime.

Stress was not used as an expression to describe that state of anxiety - heightened intolerance, feeling overwhelmed or general grumpiness - until relatively recently. Some people still refuse to accept the term stress as an expression that relates to them. Some people recognise it but see it as part of life and don't seek to address it.

Situations and circumstances affect each of us differently, and it's vital that we recognise and address it when things affect us negatively. How we respond as individuals to life's challenges varies. What some will regard as horribly stressful, others will find exhilarating. So perception affects our response and stress levels in different situations.

We also recognise how different situations and circumstances affect our children. We're therefore in the best position to enable our children to develop the tools to handle situations better and perform at their best whenever it's important. This doesn't mean avoiding things that 'stress' them. Sometimes, a continuous avoidance of stressful situations just brings up issues in later life, or puts a limit on them achieving their potential. That also doesn't mean doing stressful things for the sake of it; the old-fashioned approach of forcing young people to do things they find extremely stressful 'because it's character building' can do more harm than good. On the other hand, continuously avoiding things we don't like or find stressful can result in us failing to expand our comfort zones and limits our horizons. That's the last thing we want for our children if we are to give them wings.

A small example that illustrates this was my daughter Harriet's fear of using the telephone with people she didn't know. She would do anything to avoid this, mainly refusing point blank or delegating to her younger brother. This was not an issue of struggling to converse. She was fine face-to-face with new people. Just an anxiety of using the phone with people she didn't know. A notable time was when we were on the way home from a visit to grandparents and she was talking about wanting a 'real' netball to use to practice in her netball net. I said OK, I'd get her one if she called round and found out where they stocked them, and I suggested a couple of stores she may call. I went through with her what she needed to say and we practised it, but she wouldn't make the calls. Neither did I. It was a matter of consistent persistence over a few years to get her more comfortable using the phone to 'strangers', and I persisted in this because it's an important life skill. She only mentioned recently how grateful she was that I persisted rather than complying with her avoidance tactics. This was prior to the online access we have now where she could have just checked online and it would have been trickier for me to find ways for to overcome this fear.

I have learned to recognise that I feel stress when things negatively affect me over which I have some control and choice. Feeling anger or hurt is not the same as feeling stress. I feel anger, sadness or pain over things I can't do anything about: injustice, unfairness, man's inhumanity to man in the world, and when there are people and things that negatively affect my family and friends. The power of empathy means I feel their pain. When my actions and decisions could have been better, when overwhelmed by work that I could manage better, when trying to do too much, juggling work and family and feeling I'm not doing either to the best of my ability, when people I trusted let me down, when trying to keep a business going for the benefit of all involved - swimming hard against a negative economic climate - then I have felt the negative effects of stress. I have needed to use all the tools described in this chapter at different times and, sometimes, all at once.

Of course, there are positive effects from 'stress'; it gives us our motivation, our get- up-and-go and drive to make things happen. Being too 'laid back' can result in not putting in the effort to achieve our goals. A stimulating amount of challenge (or some may use the word 'problem') can make us: work more efficiently; get new ideas; take more risks; have more energy and look better; feel fine on less sleep; feel worthy; feel fit and assertive; have more confidence and more enthusiasm. In short, having lots of stimulation and relishing opportunities can make us thrive and, in general, enjoy life more.

However, when stress becomes too much, we can: become snappy and irritable; make poor decisions; experience mood swings; have trouble sleeping, or sleep more than usual; avoid seeing friends and doing things. As adults, we can: smoke more; drink more alcohol and coffee; eat to excess – or not enough; have a whole range of physical symptoms such as head-, back- and neck-ache, lapses of memory and loss of concentration, stomach upsets and panic attacks. Signs in our behaviour that we may be under stress include: lots of blinking; fidgeting; talking incessantly; frowning unconsciously; repeated swallowing or licking of the lips; making obsessive notes – in our heads or on paper.

I write this as someone who has done all of the above: not recognised stress; suffered from most of the symptoms of stress at some time or other; allowed herself to be overwhelmed by anxiety and stress; allowed stress to negatively affect relationships etc.

I reached a point where I became completely overwhelmed. The doctor diagnosed me as having a virus, but at the time - and in hindsight - I really knew it was my mind and body saying 'enough'. I had been through a marriage break-up, house move, change of child-care arrangements (one of the most stressful bits of all this) and job change in an 18-month period and received plaudits all round for the way I'd 'coped'. When we fail at something as big as marriage, it can bring out strength we didn't know we had, and that can be both a positive and a negative. Feeling we have to take on the responsibilities and demonstrate the competences that you once shared can be very draining. My focus was the well-being of my children and our economic well-being. The Head Teacher of my children's primary school said they wouldn't have known from Harriet and George's demeanour at school what the children had been going through, had I not explained things to their teachers. I had been very open with Harriet's class teacher and George's nursery teacher, as I know how children can act out at school when experiencing trauma at home. I accepted the Head Teacher's comments as a compliment to how we had managed to maintain a sense of security in their lives. My boss had also praised the fact that my work hadn't suffered, and this was at a time when I had a job that required me to work long hours, with late night commitments a few nights a week during school term time. But there was a cost, and the stress I stored eventually came out.

One January, I went to the doctor feeling exceptionally tired - as in having no energy to do anything. This was so unlike me, who seemed to have such a strong constitution and the energy to keep going on all fronts. For about 3 months I kept being signed off work with a 'virus', just keeping a project going one day a week (completely against advice and the rules when we're signed off sick, but I was working with a small group of budding young entrepreneurs who were trying to get themselves off benefit and there was no-one else to cover this!). I got the children off to school, went back to bed, got up when they finished school and went to bed when they went to bed. They were 7 and 11 at the time. Kicking the ball around in the back garden with George was too much for me. The doctor eventually started talking about more serious things and I began my own research. I read that vitamin E was good to recover from viruses, and that acupuncture might help. I started taking big doses of the former and booked in for the latter. I have to say, I had little faith in acupuncture, but as soon as I sat down and started talking to Tony Orridge*, an acupuncturist at our local Natural Health Centre, his calm, intelligent manner and explanations of how it worked started to make sense to me. On my first visit, he took my pulse and said, 'Your energy levels are so low I'm surprised you had the energy to walk in here'. The combination of his wisdom and ability to tune into me as an individual and where I was, and my willingness to learn and follow his advice, started my road to recovery.

I gradually regained my energy levels sufficiently to start reflecting where I was and research how I could prevent this ever happening again. From my research, I realised how my stress may have contributed to the breakdown of my marriage. I needed someone to force me to look at myself and make that wake-up call sooner. My husband had said I should do aerobics classes, but they didn't appeal to me, and I couldn't see when I might do these: with his sporting commitments at the weekend and my work commitments in the week. I wanted to be with the children when I wasn't at work. I should have made time to do something for me that involved exercise!

I had let my stress levels reach unacceptable and unhealthy levels on occasions, prior to my little 'melt down'. This resulted in me overreacting to something the children did as a result of the build-up of pressure from my day. In my role as an Area Education Officer, I tended to stay calm at work, deal with the issues of the day, soak up Head Teachers', excluded pupils' and parents' problems like a sponge, and return home on mental overload. I would then overreact to some minor misdemeanour. I spoke to the children about my role, which was mainly dealing with challenges; schools didn't call their AEO to say they were having a good day with a brilliant teacher and fabulous student! I told them that they needed to reflect back to me when they thought I'd overreacted, which they did. I have to say that George, in particular, soon cottoned on to the fact that he could use this, and there were many times when I had to step back, reflect, and tell him I definitely hadn't overreacted. Having said that, being open with them about the issue and using their reflection was a great help to me.

Are you aware of when you are negatively affected by stress?

Are your own strategies to manage stress well developed?

Are you spotting stress in your children and teaching them how to effectively manage it?

What follows in this chapter is some general information and strategies that have helped me and, in turn, my children, to recognise and effectively manage stress and performance anxiety.

Let's break down what stress is. In my experience, it is always easier to prevent something or address something if we can break it down and reflect on exactly how it relates to us, and those close to us.

The Major Sources Of Stress

Survival Stress
This is when we are in a physically or emotionally threatening situation, and our body adapts to help us react more effectively to meet the threat. However, our brain cannot distinguish between this and other stresses so can put our body into unhealthy survival mode that is designed to get us through a certain incident, over prolonged periods of time!

Internally-generated Stress

This can come from worrying about events beyond our control, from a tense, hurried approach to life, or from relationship problems caused by our own behaviour.

Environmental stress

This can come from:
- crowding and invasion of personal space;
- insufficient working and living space;
- noise and pollution;
- dirty / untidy conditions.

Chemical and nutritional stress

The food you eat may contribute to stress. Examples of stressors are caffeine, sugar from sweets and chocolate, salt. Smoking also puts your body under chemical stress.

Lifestyle and job stress

Examples of these are financial or relationship problems, ill-health, time pressures and deadlines.

Fatigue and overwork

This manifests itself as a constant feeling of tiredness, due to working too many hours, or trying to fit too many things into the hours.

Stress Indicators

Physical Behavioural Emotional

Physical

Tight chest, rapid swallowing / palpitations, indigestion, stomach cramp, shoulder/neck/back pain, persistent headaches, chronic sinus problems, humming in the ears, frequent viral infections, weight loss/gain, skin problems, tired eyes/visual disturbances, body stiffness, attacks of dizziness, frequent pins and needles.

Behavioural:

Poor concentration / inability to listen well, forgetfulness, over activity, restlessness / talking to much, nervous habits / nail biting, unable to make decisions / sort priorities, poor planning, reluctance to delegate, over sensitivity to events and situations, increase in phobic fears, anxieties and obsessions, increase in alcohol / nicotine intake, insomnia / nightmares, loss of libido, unkempt appearance, loss of control over money, over cautious / over protective.

Emotional:
Increase in anxiety / fearfulness, easily hurt or upset, tearful, feeling irritable, lacking in confidence, a sense of worthlessness and apathy, confused / overwhelmed, humourless, getting over excited, generally melancholic or depressed, mood swings, feeling embarrassed / ashamed, feeling controlled by others, gloomy about the future, cynical attitudes, obsessive thoughts, more angry and emotionally reactive, minority have suicidal thoughts.

I include this list as a reminder that it is important to recognize the early signs of stress in ourselves, and our children. In order to manage stress effectively it is most important that we learn to recognize the warning signs.

If you recognise any of these, start doing something about it **now** - there's lots you can do!

The good news is that we can all take control of our responses to stress.

Feeling overwhelmed is like the little dancing
top on the pressure cooker.
It is a safety device that is warning us to take notice.
We can ignore the warning and if we do, something will blow.
Anne Wilson Schaef

Managing Stress Better

Here are some simple ways to improve our ability to manage the stresses of life, all of which we can adapt to coach our children to effectively manage stress.

Remember that every time you think a situation is stressful, your brain tries to help – so it starts the stress responses. Give your brain the right information and manage your brain, rather than letting your brain manage you!

Choosing to

One of the things that has helped me to manage my stress levels more effectively is changing my mindset to 'I choose to...' rather than 'I have to...' We choose to do almost everything we do. We quite often say, 'I have to do this' or 'I have to do that' when really we don't 'have to' at all; **we can choose.**

There are choices and consequences, and we make choices about what we do based on the consequences. I found my stress levels massively reducing as soon as I started thinking that I make a choice about everything I do and consciously saying to myself 'I choose to' rather than 'I have to'. It works with chores, activities with family that we may view as duty, as well as work.

Choices and Consequences

If we don't want to study for an examination, what are the consequences?
With some exams, the consequences of a low grade may be minimal. With other exams, it may mean not being able to progress to the next level of education and study something we really want to, or not being able to follow our chosen profession. We need to help our children distinguish between these and help them decide what's really important to them, rather than blindly following a path!

If we don't like our job, we have some choices

We just need to work through the consequences of all these choices on us, and those around us:

- just stick at it, getting more stressed about doing something that makes us unhappy;
- don't turn up for work;
- do it badly so we get sacked;
- resign without a job to go to;
- set a goal and action plan to change jobs to do something we want to do – use relaxation, visualisation and mental rehearsal to help us see ourselves achieving our goal – and go to work to make the change!

We all need to take control and feel in control of everything we do, and say 'I choose to … do this with my children, do this job, go to work early, help my family, take my parents out, exercise'.

You'll be amazed how liberating it is to adopt the 'I choose to' mindset and how much better you will feel.

Attitude is more important than the past, than education, than money, than circumstances, than what other people think or say or do. It is more important than appearance, giftedness, or skill. It will make or break a company, a church, a home.
Charles Swindoll

Learn to Relax

It is essential that we recognise that relaxation is within our own power and not something that is dependent on external circumstances.

Sometimes, we have very little control over external circumstances, but we always have the power to decide what's going on in our mind. If we systematically learn to positively use that power, we can teach ourselves to be calm and relax at any given moment. When we are calm and daydreaming, the brain goes into a state that makes the body release more serotonin and, thereby, aids relaxation. I have effectively practiced this to lower my stress levels since I learned about it. However, this systematic relaxation is not just important for our general relaxation and wellbeing, it is also essential to maximise our power to perform at our best under pressure when it matters most - in tests and examinations, in interviews etc. When under pressure to perform at our best, we need to be focused but calm, as described in the *Develop Your Winning Brain* chapter. My children have used the ability to systematically relax and focus to great effect for examinations, for sporting trials, for driving tests etc.

As with any other skill or habit, we use it or lose it, so we need to learn to regularly practice relaxation, visualisation and mental rehearsal.

Throughout the day, take mini-breaks (time for yourself) - sit down, slowly take a deep breath in, hold it and then let it out slowly. At the same time, let your shoulders droop down, smile (this is important, as it encourages the release of endorphins, natural tranquilisers) and say something like I - AM - RELAXED. I learned a better breathing technique when someone was demonstrating for me how deliberate breathing can lower our heart rate. I was hooked up to a monitor and told to breathe in, counting internally to 10, and breath out, again internally counting to 10. If we repeat this 5 times, our heart rate lowers and we become more relaxed.

Of course, we also get out what we put in! By this I mean it's important to think about what we drink to aid the power of relaxation. We can't practice effective relaxation if we're pumped full of caffeine. This was a really important factor for me learning to manage stress: limiting my caffeine intake to be able to use relaxation techniques to effectively manage my stress levels.

Alongside relaxation is good quality rest. The importance of good quality rest for our health and well-being is described in the *Maximise Energy* chapter.

Practice Acceptance

To minimise our stress levels it is important to accept the things we cannot change.

Many of us get distressed over things that we can't change, like some else's actions, feelings or beliefs. We can, of course, affect our children's actions and beliefs, but my experience is that being irate and angry as an unmeasured, stressed response does no good for us and makes no difference to what we're railing against. It is only natural to feel distress when faced with things we deem cruel or unfair. Personally, I become distressed by any cruelty or unfairness towards children, whether that's a news report of an atrocity or seeing a parent in a supermarket treating their child cruelly or unfairly. Empowering children is my passion, but I am not going to change the behaviour of one parent or one group of people by getting worked up and ranting. I may feel momentarily better, but have I done any good? What I can do is use all my experience to do all that I can to affect cultural change towards children and young people: contributing to the body of knowledge on how best to nurture our children.

Practicing acceptance can be most challenging with our children. It is often a delicate balance in judgement: deciding what we need to, and can, change in our children's attitudes, thinking and behaviour, and accepting what we don't need to change. We won't always get it right, but a good strategy to reduce the stress is to ask ourselves questions: 'Is it really important? Is it only important to me or is it important in terms of life lessons for my daughter's / son's future?' Asking questions can also be a really useful strategy to help our children practice acceptance. What we're trying to do is teach our children to put maximum effort into what they can achieve: not to accept mediocrity in the things they are passionate about and can excel in, and avoid dissipating their energy on things beyond their control. For example, many children have issues with some school rules (as adults do with some work rules). School rules are generally part of the school when you join. If there is a rule you don't like, ranting and moaning about it will do no good whatsoever. Worse, it will distract you and drain your energy for more important things. If you feel strongly about it, join the student council, get a petition together, write a letter to those in charge etc. Do something within your control about it or accept it and focus your energies on something else. Some of the questions I ask are:

How important is it?
Can you change anything?
Who can help you with this?

In summary, it's vital that we recognise and accept the things we can't change - things that are truly beyond our control - and focus our energies on positively affecting the things we can change.

Talk Rationally to Ourselves

As mentioned above, it's crucial that we get used to having those reflective conversations with ourselves to help get things in perspective. Ask yourself what real impact the stressful situation will have on you in a day or a week, and see if you can let the negative thoughts go. Think through the situation: is it your problem or someone else's? If it is yours, approach it calmly and firmly; planning and setting specific goals and action plans will help with this. Rather than condemn yourself, thinking of past mistakes or 'should haves', think about what you have learned and make plans for the future.

Keep an eye on perfection – seeking perfection in everything limits our forward movement. Set realistic steps towards your goals – remember that everyone makes mistakes; break tasks into smaller units and do important ones first.

Get Organised

I am not the world's best at routine, and am always overly ambitious about how much I can achieve in a day. However, I recognise that having a realistic programme of daily activities that includes time for work, relationships, family, rest and relaxation is really important if we are to achieve our best and manage our stress. For one thing, achievement is a great antidote to the negative impact of stress. Getting things done, tackling challenges rather than leaving things undone, helps us to feel good and relax. There are mixed views on the value of things-to-do lists, but for me they are invaluable; once everything is on a list, it takes away the burden of remembering everything that needs to be done. And ticking things off is great! It is in our nature to focus on the things we like and understand and to avoid the things we find challenging. However, if we can approach those things we like to do least with the attitude of 'I choose to do this' rather than 'I have to', it really helps. We feel tremendous benefit as soon as we tackle some of those challenging things and take steps forward or completely tick them off the list.

Over the years, I have increasingly recognised the importance of our surroundings: tidy room, tidy house, office, workplace, or wherever we spend most of our time. That old adage 'a place for everything and everything in its place' has taken on more resonance. For me, this applies to electronic filing, as well as knowing where we've put things at home. I am not a natural when it comes to filing, and the wasted time and energy looking for documents on the computer, papers in the filing cabinet, or a t-shirt can all add to our stress levels. Straightening things up helps us to use our time and energy as effectively and efficiently as possible, as long as we don't get caught by perfection and spend too much time tidying, and too little time doing those important things that contribute to achieving our goals.

My children are both untidy. My daughter bought a sign for her bedroom door when she was 9, 'My room. My Mess. My Business.' They have both followed this adage with their bedrooms!

However, now my daughter has bought her own place she is far tidier and does realise the significance of that old adage! My son looks after the things that are important to him and for most of the time his bedroom is a mess. I have not helped them tidy their bedrooms since they were young, certainly not since they transferred to secondary school when they were 11. However, getting them to do it has been the harder choice! Letting them take responsibility for their things from a young age has meant they have learned that not being able to find something causes stress, and they have benefitted by being able to manage themselves and their things effectively in their chosen educational and career paths. Certainly, helping Harriet do to-do lists, priority lists, and organise things on the computer helped her as she progressed through education and into work. At times, when she became overwhelmed with the demands of study and exams, the most important thing was to go through with her what she needed to do and help her prioritise and organise herself. When I say help her, I mean coach her to do it for herself, rather than take over. She is now the spreadsheet 'queen', and this stood her in very good stead when managing the renovation of her apartment whilst working full-time.

Exercise

There is no doubt in my mind that physical activity is vital for us in all sorts of ways - health, vitality, thinking - and it is especially important to prevent, and provide relief from, stress. Not only does exercise remove you from the stressful situation, just walking or stretching will help the body recover its normal state. As described in more detail in the *Maximise Energy* chapter, it's important for us to find an exercise regime that suits us, whether that's lots of walking, jogging, sport, dancing, swimming, yoga; we find that our energy levels increase, thereby reducing the cycle of stress.

When Harriet was doing her GCSE exams at 15, it was vital that she maintained her athletics training 3 or 4 times a week. Many of her peers were not allowed to train, or to train as much, when they had exams, but in my view that's a mistake. Exercise not only helps you manage what is a very demanding schedule and stressful time, it also helps your brain function more effectively and helps you sleep better, all of which are vital.

Getting out – walking, jogging, running, cycling – really helps our sanity and ability to think clearly about all that 'stuff' we face. 'Stuff' is a so much less threatening word than 'problems' or 'issues', and **relegates challenges to their rightful place – obstacles that challenge our creativity to get round, over, under or through, but don't stop us!** There are always solutions to 'stuff', and we're good at coming up with solutions and making 'stuff' happen. It's just that when we're in the middle of so much 'stuff', flying at us from all angles, it's hard to use the best of our creative juices or little grey cells! Getting out will help that. I know that one of the effects of stress is feeling that we want to shut ourselves away and sleep.

When we're awake, we just get ourselves back on the treadmill of busy activity, feeling overwhelmed but unable to stop for fear of getting further behind. Taking a walk or some form of exercise helps us break that cycle – just a few kilometres, half an hour a day - makes all the difference. I only wish I'd learned this sooner in my working life!

Reduce Time Urgency

I have always given myself 'just enough' time or, on many (or most) occasions, not enough time, to fit everything in: get to appointments, get home to get the children to activities in the rush hour on a Friday evening etc. I have also consistently overestimated the amount I can achieve in an hour, a day, a week. This causes stress. We deal with it (or not) at the time, but we pay the price - unless we are so laid back that we don't care about being late and making our children late for things. It's crucial that we find ourselves time to do what we've committed to do. Someone who'd sailed round the world as part of a challenge once said that he had a rule, 'Aim to be 20 minutes early at sea and 15 minutes early on land'. This takes away the stress and enables us to deal with any last-minute eventuality.

It's important that we learn to allow plenty of time to get things done: plan and aim to pace, not race. My son is, and always has been, early for sport, training and matches alike. Until he could drive, he would make sure we left early and was always ready to leave on time. I have tried to equip my children with an ethos of 'we do what we say we're going to do, when we say we're going to do it'. We commit to the team, the friend, the activity. They have also learned from me - that is seeing in me, and us discussing, the negative effects of trying to do too much - to pace themselves and focus on what's really important.

Using our personal resources carefully today will make us stronger for what we need to do tomorrow.
How do we marshal our personal resources?
Our wit, our charm, our intelligence, our wisdom,
our clarity of vision, our energy – we have them all.
Anne Wilson Schaef

Disarm Yourself

I find this really difficult. I am passionate about what I do, and have always felt compelled to challenge anything and everything that limits young people (rather than focusing on the specific areas where I am likely to have most impact). This doesn't always get results and, on occasions afterwards, I have gone over and over situations, identifying how I could have behaved differently to bring about a better outcome. This generates stress! It's so much more effective and healthier to approach each situation according to its demands and be very targeted and focused in our efforts. We don't have to raise our voice in every conversation, get our point across to everyone. We can leave our weapons behind when the situation is a lost cause and focus on where and how we can be of most benefit. This approach also really works with our children; calm and measured, but firm, is so much more effective than losing our temper and raising everyone's stress levels.

Chilling is OK

It's taken me years to rid myself of the guilt of just 'chilling'. For example, I walk at pace everywhere. My daughter walks round the boundary with me at cricket and says, 'It's cricket. We're not going anywhere. We're not in a hurry. We can walk at a leisurely pace.' I sometimes get lost in what's happening on the field and my pace quickens, only to look back and see Harriet some way behind, bringing me back to a chilling pace! Having a quiet, undemanding time is important for anyone, and we need to do this for ourselves, recognise the need in our family and friends and, most importantly, teach and coach our children the importance of this. Balance is, yet again, important here, and we need to also ensure that our children don't take chilling to an extreme that means they lose focus on their goals. Chilling is one of the antidotes to hard work, not a replacement for it. We need to model this for our children by balancing our family, social and work life with special events that are private and good for us. They need to see us pursuing our interests and unwinding, taking a walk, soaking in a hot bath, listening to music, watching something (uplifting) we enjoy on TV – these are all good for us. I have not done this sufficiently at times in my life and have allowed work and family commitments to completely take over to the detriment of my wellbeing. My children have learned from this by experiencing me being all things to all people, and from my reflecting on it with them. It's OK to make mistakes and not be perfect for our children as long as we are open with them about where we've gone wrong so they can learn from our mistakes.

Watch Our Habits

Habits, positive or negative, take hold, and it is crucial to develop positive habits to keep us physically and mentally healthy and fit. Eating sensibly is crucial. We all tend to use comfort food, in some form or other, when we're stressed: sweets, chocolate, excess of caffeine, fatty foods, alcohol etc. Our destructive 'Chimp'*, as defined in Dr Steve Peters' brilliant book, *The Chimp Paradox – The Mind Management Programme for Confidence, Success and Happiness*, tells us it's OK as we've had a hard day. This invariably gives us an immediate boost in energy or mood, only to be replaced by feeling even worse. A good diet, as discussed in the *Maximise Energy* chapter, provides the energy we need during the day. We need to minimise alcohol intake as we need to be mentally and physically alert to deal with stress. Excessive caffeine and sugar can cause excitement and can make us hyperactive; that certainly is the case with me. Cigarettes also restrict blood circulation and affect the stress response.

Talk to Friends and Have Fun

Daily pleasant, positive conversations, regular social events, sharing deep feelings and thoughts, aid well-being and reduce stress really well. In his book, *The Outliers: The Story of Success*, Malcolm Gladwell writes about some research undertaken by Dr Stewart Wolf and his friend and sociologist, John Bruhn, in the 1950s, into why the population of a small town, Roseto, Pennsylvania, appeared to be so much healthier than anywhere else. 'In Roseto, virtually no one under fifty-five had died of a heart attack or showed any signs of heart disease. For men over sixty-five, the death rate from heart disease in Roseto was roughly half that of the United States as a whole. The death rate from all causes in Roseto, in fact, was 30 to 35 percent lower than expected'. He goes on, 'There was no suicide, no alcoholism, no drug addiction, and very little crime. They didn't have anyone on welfare. Then we looked at peptic ulcers. They didn't have any of those either. These people were dying of old age. That's it'. The people of Roseto originated in Roseto Valafortore, in the Appennine foothills of the Italian province of Foggia. Their diet wasn't classed as healthy; many smoked heavily and their genetic make-up was similar to their relatives living in other parts of America who did not have the same health profile. They eventually discovered their health was attributed to their social structure: extended families, cooking together, looking after one another, and incredibly impressive social and community structures, 'twenty-two separate civic organizations in a town of just under two thousand people'. This meant people socialised, had fun, belonged and felt secure. '…. the Rosetans had created a powerful, protective social structure capable of insulating them from the pressures of the modern world.' The strong community spirit and social life they had created had incredible benefits on their health, in part, by protecting them from the negative effects of stress.

In my over-active, focused daily routine, it's only in recent years I have truly valued just chatting without a specific purpose and agenda, and learned to feel that it's OK to phone someone for a chat rather than for a particular purpose. It's only now that I properly understand the value of what Wolf and Bruhn found in that Rosetan town: my social network within and beyond my family and informal chat. Laughter is also especially good for reducing stress as this releases endorphins that make us feel better, and having fun with family and friends is crucial (as is learning to laugh at ourselves). We can make anything we do with our children fun, with a bit of imagination, and the benefits are good for us all. The people of Roseta got this and it was the biggest factor in their health, well-being and longevity.

Good friends are good for your health.
Irwin Sarason

Affirmations

- I am positive and feeling great; managing my stress better and better all the time.
- I am loving the feeling of remaining calm and positive.
- I am enjoying the liberating feeling of consciously choosing everything I do in my life.
- I am loving how good I feel after socialising with friends.
- I am feeling tremendous, having fun with my family and friends.

 ACTION

1. Use a relaxation track and process regularly, such as the free download link on the equipped2succeed section of my website, to help you minimise the negative effects of stress.

2. Think of the times you experience feelings or reactions of negative stress.
   Note that our reactions to stress can often be delayed and may come out at other times, e.g. if we're feeling stressed by work we may not lose our temper or 'snap' with our work colleagues, but with our children or partner later.

3. Look at the stress indicators above and use them to help you reflect on your stress levels. Knowing exactly what you're dealing with will help you do something about it.

4. Go to the equipped2succeed downloads section of my website and complete the Stress Quiz: How Stressed Are You?
   What do you think causes your negative stressful reactions?
   So, what are you going to do about it?

5. Look at the Managing Stress Tips and decide which ones are best for you to start implementing.

6. Decide how you might use what you've learned to help your children manage stress effectively.

7. Use the goal-setting templates and guidance in the Set Goals section of the equipped2succeed section of my website. Write a goal and action plan to mange stress / performance anxiety better. You can also use this to help you focus on how you can help your child improve their ability to handle something that they find stressful.

Only the Individual Can Eliminate the Negative Effects of Stress in Themselves, and we are in the Best Place to Coach Our Children to Manage Stress Effectively

relax – take time every day to relax and do mini relaxations throughout the day – even in the toilet;

work on your positive attitude - choose to do everything you do;

look at your diet and make sure you are eating healthily;

exercise your body and your mind regularly – choose the exercise you like;

change what you do and how you do it to eliminate the negative effects of stress;

and

HAVE FUN!

* 'The Chimp' as defined by Dr Steve Peters: *'The Chimp is the emotional machine that we all possess. It thinks independently from us and can make decisions. It offers emotional thoughts and feelings that can be very constructive or very destructive; it is not good or bad, it is a Chimp. The Chimp Paradox is that it can be your best friend or your worst enemy, even at the same time'.* I have used this phrase as it's one to which I think we can all relate.

*Tony Orridge – An amazing acupuncturist whose practice is at the Nottingham Natural Health Centre.

Chapter Thirteen

Maximise Energy

Diet - Exercise - Attitude - Rest

Definitions

maximise:
- increase to the greatest possible amount or degree;
- to make the greatest or fullest use of: *maximize energy by being D.E.A.R to yourself.*

energy:
- the capacity for vigorous activity; available power;
- an adequate or abundant amount of such power;
- an exertion of such power: *She plays with great energy;*
- the habit of vigorous activity; vigour as a characteristic;
- the ability to act, lead others, effect, etc, forcefully.
- forcefulness of expression;
- vitality of action or expression;
- capacity for intense activity;
- vigorous or intense action; exertion.

Successful people have endless energy to pursue their dreams and goals. They have the physical and mental energy to do whatever they need to do to succeed. They are definitely not the people who are 'too tired' or 'can't be bothered' to do the work required to achieve their goals. They have the mental and physical energy to develop a project, take on a challenge, get the grades, build a business, have fun with their partner and children, reach the pinnacle in their chosen career path, do the work required to succeed in any field of endeavour. I use the word energy to indicate that vital, enthusiastic aura that is evident in those who reach the pinnacle in their field and holistic success. Don't we all want the energy to do what it takes to achieve our dreams and goals?

It's vital that we all know how to look after our health and well-being – understand that prevention is better than cure. It is also essential, if we are to realise our goals and perform at our best when it matters most, that we understand how to maintain and maximise our energy levels. We're often taught disjointed bits of healthy eating and the nutritional values of food in school. We exercise in Physical Education programmes without necessarily being taught the value of exercise for us to have the energy to perform at our best – mentally and physically.

Energy gives us vitality, enables us to pursue our passions and, for the most part, is something entirely within our control. As parents, we have a huge responsibility to equip our children with the knowledge, understanding and positive habits to look after their health and well-being and maximise their energy levels. Energy is essential to achieve what we want in life. It obviously links to being healthy, but energy is more than health and makes all the difference in our capacity to succeed. There are people who are healthy but still do not feel energised or radiate energy. On the other hand, there are individuals who overcome massive physical and health challenges and still demonstrates incredible energy, such as Stephen Hawking, a theoretical physicist, cosmologist, author of a number of books, including the best seller, *A Brief History of Time: From Big Bang To Black Hole*, and Director of Research at the Centre for Theoretical Cosmology within the University of Cambridge, and all with motor neurone disease.

Maximising our energy levels has clear links with being able to harness the enormous power of passion and positivity. It's a key factor in being able to 'do the work' required to achieve our goals. Each milestone along the way takes energy, from engaging the right people to help us to spending all weekend packing the boxes to ship out for our fledgling on-line shoe business, from studying long hours for an examination to doing the punishing training regime required to perform at our best in elite sport, dance or music. Energy not only enables us to physically do what we need to, but it's vital if we're going to harness all the power of our brain to learn, create and achieve our goals.

I believe that there are four essential elements to ensuring we have maximum energy, and I created the acronym **D.E.A.R.** to help us remember these and focus on the fact that having energy means looking after ourselves: body and mind. Wellbeing and energy are synonymous, for me, and to achieve both we need to be DEAR to ourselves and get the balance right in our:

Diet   **E**xercise   **A**ttitude   **R**est

Before we look at what being **D.E.A.R.** to ourselves means, let's just remind ourselves about maintaining positive habits.

Habits

Maximising our energy, health and wellbeing is all about developing
INFORMED, POSITIVE HABITS to appropriately balance our
Diet – Exercise - Attitude – Rest

Habits are developed from birth, positive and negative habits, and we all have both throughout our lives. Some of us develop habits very quickly, and some of us take a long time to develop them. All of us take a while to change our habits. Our habits also need to be constantly challenged and re-informed if we are to grow and develop and have the wherewithal to achieve our dreams. Being DEAR to ourselves is all about developing those essential positive habits to look after ourselves and maximise our energy.

Below are some thoughts about how we can be DEAR to ourselves, maximise our energy levels and enable our children to maintain the right balance of diet, exercise, attitude and rest. I am deeply grateful to Harriet for helping me with this chapter with her knowledge and understanding of exercise and nutrition.

Diet

Basically, eating and drinking healthily is vital for our mental and physical wellbeing, and a major contributor to maintaining our energy levels. It is important for us to understand what nutrients we need to stay healthy and have maximum energy when we need it most. It is even more important that we, and our children, know which foods can give us those nutrients. We also need to know which foods make us sluggish and lethargic and avoid them. Let's also not forget the importance of water; our brain utilises 75-80% of our total water intake and therefore water is vital if we're to keep performing at our best - physically and mentally.

The key with nutrition, like exercise, is to get into a regular routine to avoid any spikes and troughs in our energy levels due to what we eat or drink. Things high in sugary carbs, such as sweet foods and sugary drinks, are great for a quick fix, but they will cause energy levels to quickly dip lower than they were originally. Simply, if we maintain a healthy balance of carbohydrate, protein, fat, vitamins and minerals we will feel great and full of energy. It's about doing some research and choosing the foods that suit us.

Food Groups

I think it's important that we teach our children the basics of food groups and the range of different nutrients we need. Some nutrients provide energy, while others are essential for growth and maintenance of the body. Carbohydrate, protein and fat are macronutrients that we need to eat in relatively large amounts in the diet as they provide our bodies with energy, and are also the building blocks for growth and maintenance of a healthy body. Vitamins and minerals are micronutrients which are only needed in small amounts, but are essential to keep us healthy. There are also some food components that are not strictly 'nutrients', but are important for health, such as water and fibre. There is a detailed overview in the Food Groups information sheet on the equipped2succeed section of my website. Below is a summary of what we need to think about in terms of making sure we keep that all-important balance to maintain our health, vitality and energy.

Carbohydrates

We know we need some carbohydrate in our diets, however this should not take over and, again, it's about quality. White bread isn't going to provide you with anywhere near as much energy as wholegrain. The same goes for pasta, rice etc. As with everything, variety is key.

Protein

It's not only carbohydrates that provide us with energy, protein also plays a key role in boosting our energy levels, and it's vital that we boost our energy levels if we're going to maintain the appropriate exercise habits, be ready for that big occasion or make that extra push in study, training, work and leisure activities. Protein is primarily for repair in the body, repairing all bodily tissues vital to keep us healthy and developing. The best way to get all the essential proteins we need is to ensure we eat a good balance of fish, meat and plant sources.

Fats

Despite our obsession with low fat, fat is an essential part of a healthy diet if eaten in moderation. There are, however, different fats, some of which have a positive effect and some of which have a negative effect on our bodies. It is essential that we maintain a healthy level of fat in our diet to ensure effective functionality and optimum health. Fat is essential for the digestion of certain vitamins, maintaining healthy cells including hair and skin, functionality of the nervous system, and much more. We can do this by ensuring we get our fat intake from natural, unprocessed fats, e.g. avocado, nuts and fish, and not pastries, cakes and fried food where the fat has been processed so heavily that our bodies are unable to digest it effectively.

Vitamins and Minerals

Vitamins and minerals are a small proportion of our diet that have a big impact. We can't store most vitamins and minerals. We therefore need to ensure that we eat them every day, the best sources being fresh vegetables, especially green vegetables, and fruit.

We can start young and do all kinds of things to help our children understand the basics of these 4 food groups, and understand that we can store protein, carbohydrates and fat but we can't store vitamins and minerals, so therefore we need to eat them every day – hence things like the '5 a day' campaign. When they were young, I used to ask my children what they'd had for lunch at school and quiz them in a fun way about what was on their plate. By the time they were partway through primary school they had a good grasp of the food groups. They also soon came to realise that I was going to focus on making sure they'd had their vitamins and minerals, which occur in vegetables, salad and fruit.

'Superfoods' are great, and have been scientifically proven to boost energy as well as providing a whole host of other health benefits. One of the latest mainstream treatments for prostrate cancer is a tablet containing some superfoods, including broccoli, pomegranate and turmeric spice. The initial trials have shown a dramatic impact on reducing cancer in those with low-level prostrate cancer. To confirm the importance of these foods, we only have to look at the selection of books on this subject, and search the web to find numerous articles about all the wonderful foods that are now available to us, and the benefits they provide. See the *Some General Superfoods* list on the equipped2succeed section of my website.

Keeping it simple

There are a few simple things that we can do, and teach our children to do, in order to ensure that we keep our diets on track for energy and vitality without making it unduly complicated.

Keep it Fresh

Primarily, we are animals, and it isn't until relatively recently that we have forced our bodies to consume and digest all kinds of processed foods. Most of us have a favourite fast food and have picked up a quick ready meal on the way home from work. But our bodies just don't like it. We've spent thousands of years eating what we could from our environment: fresh, organic food. This is what our bodies are used to and this is what our bodies respond best to. It's easier to digest unprocessed food, meaning our bodies can make efficient use of all the nutrients it provides. By avoiding processed foods, we also minimise the additives and toxins that we introduce into our bodies, and more importantly, into our children's bodies.

In terms of recognising processed food, the basic general rule is to look at the list of ingredients:

Long list of ingredients – BAD
example: a brand of one pot dried meal:
Noodles, Wheat Flour, Vegetable Oil, Firming Agents – Potassium Carbonate, Sodium Carbonate, Water, Vegetables – Carrot, Onion, Peas, Maltodexin (which I assume is a version of maltodextrin), Sugar, Flavourings, Cheese Powder, Low Sodium Mineral Salt (Contains Potassium), Acidity Regulator (Sodium Diacetate), Flavour Enhancer (Monosodium Glutamate), Yeast Extract, Curry Powder, Ground Cumin, Spice Extracts, Chilli Powder, Mango Chutney Sauce (Sugar, Mangos, Salt, Acetic Acid, Spices), Water, Spirit Vinegar, Modified Maize Starch. May Contain Soya.

Long list of ingredients you don't recognise and with lots of numbers – VERY BAD
example: a brand of candy:
Dextrose, Sugar, Malic Acid, Corn Syrup*. Artificial Flavours: Carnauba Wax. Artificial Colours: Brilliant Blue (E133)** Allura Red (E129)** Tantrazine (E102)**
** This may have an adverse effect on activity and attention in children.
Allegan Information: Contains Egg, *May contain GMO (which stands for genetically modified organisms).

Short list of ingredients – BETTER
example: a well-known brand of tinned tomato soup:

Tomatoes, Water, Vegetable Oil, Sugar, Modified Cornflour, Salt, Dried Skimmed Milk, Milt Proteins, Cream, Spice Extracts, Herb Extract, Citric Acid.
No artificial colours. No artificial flavours. No artificial preservatives.

NB – the lists of ingredients above are copied directly from food packaging. The only bits I've added are explanations in italics.

No list of ingredients - BEST
example: there are no lists on fresh food - fresh fruit, fresh vegetables,
fresh fish, fresh meat, dried herbs and spices, home-made food.

We do best if we can avoid foods with lists of ingredients that contain sugar – especially as a main ingredient (often used in low-fat foods to enhance taste), artificial flavouring, artificial colours, numbers; and remember:

> If it doesn't tell you how many calories,
> you know it's better nutrition.

I recognise that we have always needed to preserve things, especially before the times of freezing and importing out-of-season vegetables and fruits, but there are more natural ways of doing this.

Variety

Another important factor is variety. An apple a day may or may not keep the doctor away, but realistically, we need far more variety than this. If we're not sure when it comes to fruit and vegetables, the best way to ensure we get what we need is to just go for as many colours as possible. This will ensure we get all the vitamins and minerals we need, not forgetting those all-important anti-oxidants, which amongst their many benefits, reduce wrinkles and ageing. So even for those odd moments when we are not feeling particularly energised, at least we'll look like we are!

'Kiddie Food' – To Be Avoided?

Food designed and marketed especially for children tends to be the ultimate processed food, coloured, pummelled and packaged to attract little people and full of sugar and salt. Examples include the standard kiddie menu fare in cafes of chicken nuggets, fish fingers, burgers etc. Kiddie food is a relatively new invention and tends to be processed, brightly coloured and designed to be appealing to children. Isn't it more healthy for our children to be eating fresh, unprocessed food containing as few additives and toxins as possible?

I have heard many people say that their children won't eat certain foods, but we tend to build up habits in food - tastes we like and tastes we don't - from a very young age, in just the same way that we develop other habits. I appreciate that some toddlers appear to be 'faddy' eaters, and this can be really challenging as a parent when ensuring that our children eat is one of our most basic roles. However, we need to be firm and not give in to the 's/he'll only eat this'. We need to encourage our children to try things, and be really strict about not eating snacks between meals with those little people who decide, from an early age, that they'll just eat what they want. Some of fussy eating is definitely learned behaviour: habits that quickly become ingrained before children can speak, after which time conversation and rationale becomes possible. Children quickly learn with anything, *'If I make enough fuss s/he'll give in'*. And we all know what a fuss little people can make that can bring about all those difficult emotions in us: hurt, upset, anger, embarrassment, as well as feelings of failure. We also have those people in our ear who say, *'Let them eat what they like'*; *'they'll grow out of it'*, or worse still, *'We can't expect them to eat what we eat'*.

My children have always eaten what we've eaten as a family. When they were very young, I used baby food in jars when we went out purely for ease, but at home they mainly had our food mashed up and from then on ate with us. I understand I may have been fortunate to have two children who would try anything and who ate virtually everything from a very young age. However, I do believe part of this was that I expected them to. People often commented with incredulity when they saw Harriet eating spicy food or olives - or some other food children weren't normally offered - when she was young. The fact that people felt the need to comment indicated to me how hung up we can be on food that is just for children, rather than appropriate nutrition, meal times as an important family experience, and enabling our children to go anywhere, be polite and try any food they are presented with. I lost count of the number of children that came home for tea with Harriet or George and ate what was put in front of them, only to be told later by their mothers that they don't normally eat that. I also lost count of the number of children who stayed over and would only eat white bread.

I endeavoured to prevent Harriet from eating too many sweets, and her Grandma thought I was too strict with this. During one Sunday lunch, which was an institution at their paternal grandparents', she challenged me about grapes having as much sugar as sweets, and if Harriet had a choice, she would eat sweets. We put both on her high chair tray (which gives you an idea of how young Harriet was as she was sitting at the table with us from the age of two onwards), and, much to my delight, she ate the grapes first! She may have preferred grapes, it may have been learned behaviour and she was more used to grapes, but it illustrates how we can influence our children's taste from a very young age.

The beauty of the fruit plate.
When my children were young, they loved a fruit plate. I would cut up a variety of fruit and make it into a face, with slightly different features each time according to the fruit we had. We can get creative and our children find it fun. In hindsight, I should have included more raw vegetables for George as he eats vegetables because of their health value, rather than enjoying them.

Portion Size

Sometimes, the thing I think we all struggle with most is portion size. It's not too bold a statement to say most of us eat more than we need to be healthy. How much should we eat? How much should we put on our plates? How much food should we put on our children's plates? (Or encourage them to put on their own plates as they grow?)

I remember when I was young my father being very against forcing children to eat everything that was on their plate, which was against the prevailing attitude of the time in a small Derbyshire village. He said that forcing people to eat food they didn't want or need was worse than throwing it away. Don't get me wrong, he also didn't agree with snacking between meals, so we couldn't get away with not eating our meal then snacking instead. He also advised us what his Uncle Albert had told him, '*Always stop eating when you could eat just a little bit more*'. Sounds more like current diet advice than wisdom from a farming community in the 1930's! I have followed that, and one exception brought home to me why I should always follow it. We were staying at a friend's and Harriet, 8 at the time, wasn't eating her meal. I encouraged her to eat, which wasn't something I usually needed to do with Harriet, and she wanted to be polite, as my friend had cooked for us all. When I was mopping up the food in the bathroom a little later, I vowed not to go against my father's advice again!

I recently had a look at my diet again, as I think we all need to do periodically as we age, our lifestyles change and we look to prevent health issues in natural ways. I was feeling a little lethargic and couldn't get rid of a cough, and the other elements of D.E.A.R. didn't seem to be the issue. I saw an Ayurveda practitioner, Sharon Jackson*, and made some changes to my diet, much of which was getting back to always fresh, organic, eating regularly etc. (My biggest issue is forgetting to eat regularly because I'm engrossed in something and then suddenly realising I'm hungry and wanting something quick and eating too much at once.) One exercise she carried out with me on portion size was very powerful. Sharon started by saying that nature has a very good way of telling us how much we should eat. She then asked me to hold my hands together and poured dried red kidney beans into my hands until they were about to overflow. The size of our meal should be no more than we can hold in our hands. This makes sense to me, having a son who has been 'big' since he was born and is now 6' 4" with large hands.

When he was about 2 weeks old, I saw the doctor because I couldn't settle him and I seemed to be breast-feeding him for longer and longer. The doctor calmly said, *'He's hungry, Beverley. I know you wanted to breastfeed but I think you need to supplement that with a bottle.'* I had no problem with that. If we are a different size, it makes sense that we need different amounts of food and what we can hold in our hands is a great, natural way of seeing that. How many of us only eat that amount of food at a meal?

Energy Boosts

Energy drinks – now, energy drinks can be misleading. Some people will automatically think of sports drinks, such as Lucazade Sport, and some of the caffeine-filled drinks, such as Red Bull. They all give us energy, but in different ways and with varying degrees of effectiveness.

Coffee, tea (including green tea), and drinks like Red Bull all contain such high levels of caffeine that they can become addictive. The energy they produce also only lasts a short period of time, and then needs replenishing, meaning more cups of coffee which means we are more likely to become dependent on the caffeine for energy. Before we know it, we're stuck in a vicious cycle which is difficult to break out of. In addition, we've got the issue of caffeine being a drug, so once we stop drinking it we feel awful. It can often cause headaches and feelings of extreme tiredness, all of which I have experienced. When I stopped drinking coffee and black tea some years ago, I had a headache for 3 weeks! I replaced that with green tea, which I then drank far too much of in terms of caffeine intake.

Whenever I have been drinking too much caffeine, I recognise the signs and do a complete caffeine detox. I feel unwell for a few days before I became more naturally vital again. You may ask why I don't give up caffeine completely? It's like most things - it's fine in moderation. I do, however, believe people have different tolerances and reactions to caffeine. I can appear to be 'wired', doing things quicker and talking even faster than usual, when I've had a reasonable amount of caffeine, bouncing around like Tigger from *Winnie the Pooh*. Some people, with the same amount of caffeine, would not be nearly so affected.

Sports drinks are different. You have two main types: hypertonic and hypotonic.
The glucose concentration in a hypertonic drink is higher than the concentration in the blood resulting in quick absorption of glucose into the blood, therefore providing an increase in energy levels. However, hypertonic drinks are not the most effective for hydration. Hypotonic drinks contain less glucose concentration than the blood. The body, therefore, absorbs more water resulting in increased hydration.

The Power of Water
And, of course, there's always just plain water, which we know is vital for our bodies in so many ways. How many of us are drinking the recommended 2 litres a day for adults?

Basically, we need different things at different times. In day-to-day life, we just need plain water. With aerobic exercise, we need a mix. If you've ever watched Wimbledon (or any tennis tournament), you might have noticed that all tennis players have 2 or 3 bottles, which they drink from between games or sets. This is to ensure that they get a mix of hypertonic and hypotonic drinks, as well as water. If we're sitting at our desk all day, there is no reason why we need a drink high in sugar or caffeine. If we have a healthy diet, all we need is water. Our brains utilise 75%-80% of the water we drink, and if our brains are working effectively, then so are we. (I do, however, recognise the difference between 'need' and 'want', and sometimes a little of what we want serves a need other than nutritional. That is, if we're conscious of the fact it is a want, rather than a need, we are fulfilling, and there are minimal harmful effects.)

Key themes:

KEEP IT FRESH – as much as possible, eat just fresh food, which naturally avoids the damaging toxins, sugars, fats and salt that is in all processed food.
BALANCE – ensure we're eating food from all the food groups in the right proportion. If we have a mix of colours

from natural food sources on our plate, we're not far off! Remember Uncle Albert's advice, *'Stop eating when we could eat just a little bit more'*.

DRINK WATER

FIND WHAT SUITS YOU

Exercise

Regular exercise is a vital ingredient to maintaining and increasing our energy levels, enabling us to do what it takes to pursue our goals.

Over thousands of years, our bodies have developed to move. Our bodies like movement. Movement is natural to us and it helps keep every bit of our bodies (including our minds) healthy. Exercise is good for us. Period.

Exercise improves our oxygen intake, and the efficiency with which our organs and bodily tissues can use that oxygen, resulting in us being able to function better. It is essential for physical, mental and emotional health. When you consider that 21% of the air we breath is made up of oxygen, and out of that 21% we breath out 16%, we really need to make the most of the remaining 5%. 20-25% of our oxygen intake is used by the brain, which is even more reason to increase the amount of oxygen we take in and use it effectively. Exercise is the best way to do this.

Exercise is essential to maintain our mental, as well as physical, wellbeing. Most of us don't do manual labour, and many of us are in sedentary jobs, that are internally stressful and physically passive, which is the worst combination in maintaining our health, wellbeing and vitality, as well as our energy levels. It is therefore crucial that we find exercise that we enjoy for our own welfare, and crucial that we find some form of physical activity that our children enjoy. It's also important that we help our children to realise that, even if we're not a naturally active, sporting person, we need to do some form of physical activity to develop and maintain a healthy body and mind. The sooner we start to develop these positive habits with our children, the better. I know children do Physical Education at school, but all the statistics point to a big drop in physical activity for most young people during their teenage years, and another drop when they leave school. It's our responsibility as parents to do all we can to ensure that our children develop and maintain an exercise habit that will carry them through their lives. The same principle holds true for our children as for us, the importance of finding the exercise that suits us and we enjoy.

Exercise means something different to everyone. One person may consider walking round the shops a work out, whereas others may need to 'get a sweat on' in the gym to feel like they've done some beneficial exercise. The key is to find the level that suits you. If your heart rate is raised and you get a bit of a 'dab on' (my daughter's expression for getting a bit out of breath and sweaty), then that's exercise, whatever form it may take. There's also exercise, like yoga, that specifically links mind and body, and is good for strength and suppleness.

If we are going to maintain our exercise regime we are probably going to need to enjoy it. Our time is precious and we often feel time-pressured. If it doesn't come naturally to us, finding something we enjoy and doing it with a friend is the best way to establish the habit. If we enjoy the activity, recognise the benefits, make it social and enjoy the environment, we are much more likely to maintain it. If we feel awkward and uncomfortable in a gym, we won't go and won't enjoy it when we do.

It's helpful to try alternative exercise or sports that we can do at varying venues and environments to find what we enjoy. When it comes to choosing exercise, the key is just to have a go and not put off if our first experience of exercise is challenging. There is so much available, from parks where we can set little challenges for our children (and ourselves) to add fun and fitness to a walk, great family fitness activities which work for busy parents, and a plethora of 'new' sports or dance activities, as well as the ones we all know. Local neighbourhood or regional websites have lots of information and the governing bodies of the various sports give information on where we can join in locally. Being part of a group helps those of us who have not maintained the enjoyment and motivation to use our bodies.

Basically, if we find some form of exercise following which we feel satisfied, like after a good meal, and mentally energised or calmed after a stressful day, then we've found what works for us. The more often we can exercise and the sooner we get into the habit of exercising regularly, the better. You eat a pack of sweets with 'e' numbers, or drink a pot of strong coffee, and you get an almost instantaneous burst of energy. But it doesn't last! You go for an early morning walk and feel energised and refreshed for the rest of the day.

We've all heard of endorphins, known as 'happy hormones', which are released in the body when exercising. Current research suggests that, in order to get the additional release of endorphins, you need to exercise at a high intensity, eg anaerobic exercise: putting your body in a state of stress where there is insufficient oxygen to meet the demands of the body. This isn't to say that there is no benefit from low-intensity exercise. There is major benefit. However, to get the true 'runner's high', you need to train hard. Endorphins are released whenever the body is put under emotional or physical stress, so if you jump out of a plane, you will get a huge boost of endorphins; if you really push yourself out of your comfort zone and speak to an audience of 1000 people, it has the same effect. For most of us, it seems much easier to work up a sweat in the park to get that good feeling!

I noticed the positive impact of exercise on my daughter's mood from a fairly young age. Harriet reached the 'terrible twos' early and the moody teens early. Thankfully, the difficult teens were relatively short-lived, between 12 and 13, but her brother and I remember them well. I recall George and I whispering to each other when she was 12, 'She'll be all right when she's been training!' Invariably, she was. George has always played lots of sport and even though he's very even-tempered, he has always become very frustrated when unable to practise or play, even for just a few days. He really hasn't enjoyed the fitness training side of sport as much as Harriet, in the gym and running, but he does whatever is needed and has taught himself to focus on the benefits of 'doing the work'.

Over the years, I have participated in a variety of fitness activities, trying to do whatever I found time for around work and family commitments. To be frank, I haven't prioritised my own fitness and exercise as much as I should have over the years. My naturally high energy levels have got me through juggling life's demands: that, and walking at pace! Having said that, I have got into much better exercise habits in recent years and, with me, variety is best. A friend from New York put the time pressure excuse I used in perspective when she said, *'If you can't find time for exercise you had better find time for fatigue and illness'*. I do some yoga every morning, walk wherever I can, and do a combination of classes, swimming and gym. I am also continuously improving my golf! However, I am a firm believer in getting exercise where we can, finding ways of being active in our daily lives, such as taking the stairs rather than the lift, running up stairs rather than walking and, of course, walking at pace. (The speed at which I walk is a standing joke with family and friends!) When having renovation work done at home that I was managing, I used carrying tiles up and down stairs, slabs from the front to the back of the house etc as a good way of naturally exercising. When I do go to the gym, music is really helpful, and I have different tracks for different activities.

It is with exercise as it is with everything:

**Those who want to do something find a way;
those who don't find an excuse.**

Attitude

You Get Out What You Put In.

Do your work with your whole heart,
and you will succeed; there's so little competition.
Elbert Hubbard

Our attitude has a big impact on our energy levels. Successful people can keep going when others may be feeling tired, and this has a lot to do with their positive mental attitude. A positive attitude and approach is crucial to maintaining enthusiasm and high energy. The importance of a positive attitude is explored in the *Be Positive* chapter, so I am only highlighting a few things specifically linked to energy in this section. The power of the mind is incredible in enabling us to gather the energy we need to do the things that are important to us, e.g. when we say that we are tired, then we will think that we are tired, so we will be tired. Having goals we are passionate about and staying positive and focused on achieving our goals helps us maintain the energy we need for gruelling training programmes, essential study, and long meetings into the night.

Others reflect back to us our energy and positivity. It's therefore vital that we are energy givers rather than energy sappers. We've all met them, and I'm sure you can think of the people in your life who give you energy and those who sap it – if you allow them to. It's what you might call a virtuous cycle. Positive words and a smiling face can give energy to us and those around us. They then reflect that energy back to us in a smile, a gesture or positive words that give us even more energy. You can see the impact of this en masse in a sports stadium when the mass energy of fans gives the team extra impetus.

Try smiling more – at home, at work, in the supermarket – you'll be amazed at the results! Laughter is also proven to boost positive endorphins and energy, so it's important to laugh: to find humour and use humour for our own benefit and the benefit of those around us. By humour, I don't mean the negative, put-down, sarcastic type that can belittle and sap energy, but the kind that makes us all chuckle.

Laughter is the sun that drives winter from the human face.
Victor Hugo

We have all had times when we've not had enough rest, but enthusiasm and desire keep us going to pursue things we are passionate about. We don't let our babies cry in the middle of the night because we're too tired; we don't miss important deadlines because we're too tired; we don't let friends down because we're too tired; we don't let our team down because we're too tired. There's a saying in sport, 'Don't leave anything on the pitch', which means give every last bit of energy you've got - physical and mental energy – to obtaining the result you desire. Those who succeed in anything find the energy to go that extra step, dig deep and find a bit more when others are only prepared to work well within their physical and mental limits. This applies in anything: doing the work necessary to achieve the grades you want in school; successfully completing a project; starting a business; making that important breakthrough in science, IT, engineering; becoming elite in sport, music, dance or any area of the arts.

This, the last of human freedoms; to choose one's attitude in any given set of circumstances, to choose one's own way.
Victor Frankl

Harriet's efforts to get a First Class Degree, after being very sick in her second year at University, showed this sort of grit. Her training for Tough Mudder, an extreme assault course over twelve miles, was a combination of physical and mental training. She knew that completing the challenge would take both, and completing the challenge within a target time would take even more mental toughness. I have seen George lead and energise his school football team - when they have been losing and teammates' heads have started to go down - with sheer positive energy and will power, putting himself all over the pitch and encouraging his teammates. I have also seen him bounce back from failure with a tough, resilient, positive attitude, whilst others have let failure overwhelm them.

Maintaining a positive attitude and energy includes not allowing others' negativity to drain our energy levels. We need to surround ourselves with positive people who help us maintain our energy levels and help our children to do the same.

How we think we feel has a definite effect on how we actually feel physically. If your mind tells you that you are tired, the body mechanism, the nerves, and the muscles accept the fact. If your mind is intensely interested, you can keep on at an activity indefinitely.
Norman Vincent Peale

Rest

The best bridge between despair and hope is a good night's sleep.
E. Joseph Cossman

What do we mean by rest? Rest can be both sleep and relaxation, or just changing our routine. Most of us need an average of 7 hours' sleep a night to maintain our energy levels and be at our best when we need it most. We see what sleep deprivation does with our children from the moment they are born, and it continues. In simple terms, tiredness prevents us from being at our best. We learn to mask tiredness as we get older, but it is no coincidence that a quick nap is called a 'power nap'. Many successful people use short naps to top-up their energy levels at key times, for example, just before an important presentation or meeting, or just before a sporting performance. Athletes plan their essential rest times into their training programme. It doesn't need to be for a long period of time to benefit us. Ellen McArthur, the round the world sailor, and Richard Branson are great examples of what a power nap can do for us!

From trying to establish a consistent sleep pattern when our children as babies to being patient with our teenagers when they sleep half the day, as parents, our children's sleep is a constant consideration for us. No matter what age, sleep is important to us.

Appropriate sleep and rest contributes to:
- mental alertness
- ability to handle stress
- good memory
- ability to concentrate
- healthy appetite with appropriate portion size
- best use of our eyes
- best use of our motor skills
- ability to manage relationships
- health and vitality
- ability to be calm and measured in our approach

Lack of sleep contributes to:
- fuzzy thinking
- inability to handle stress
- poor memory
- inability to concentrate
- increased appetite
- vision problems
- poor decision making
- diminished motor skills
- relationship troubles
- medical problems
- mood swings

Think about what impact this may have at every stage of our lives in:

- school
- work
- relationships

Think about what impact this may have in pressure situations – when we really need to perform at our best in:

- exams
- trials
- sports performances
- music exams
- driving tests
- interviews

At any given time, one in five people feels unusually tired, and one in 10 have prolonged fatigue, according to the Royal College of Psychiatrists. Women tend to feel tired more than men. Tiredness that is not linked to lack of rest or genuine physical tiredness can mean that we don't sleep well, which can turn into a vicious circle. Most of the time, fatigue is linked with mood and the accumulation of lots of little stresses in life. We are then back to exercise to get that 'good' physical tiredness that means we rest well, making sure our caffeine intake isn't keeping us from high quality rest, and using relaxation techniques to calm our minds and rest well.

Teenagers Need More Sleep

At this point, it is worth mentioning the debate we all have about sleep with our peers and our children during their teenage years. As parents, we go through forgetting what a 'lie-in' is when our children are young, to wondering when our children are going to surface in their teen years. We experience our children having trouble getting up on school days, marathon lie-ins at weekends, and sleeping on the sofa in the middle of the day.

In fact, sleep experts say teenagers do need more sleep, and today's teenagers are sleeping less than they ever have. This is a worry, as there's a link between sleep deprivation and accidents, obesity and cardiovascular disorders. Physiological changes, social pressures and external factors such as TVs and other stimulating gadgets in the bedroom contribute to late nights and the potential for the sleep-deprived mood swings they can bring. Lack of sleep can also affects teenagers' education, as it can leave them too tired to concentrate in class and perform at their best in exams.

Our sleep patterns are dictated by light and hormones. When light dims in the evening, we produce a chemical called melatonin, which gives the body clock its cue, telling us it's time to sleep. *'The problem is that society has changed,'* says Dr. Paul Gringras, consultant paediatrician, and director of the Evelina Paediatric Sleep Disorder Service at Guy's and St Thomas' Hospital in London. *'Artificial light has disrupted our sleep patterns. Bright room lighting, TVs, games consoles and PCs can all emit enough light to stop the natural production of melatonin.'* Other distractions include mobile phones and instant messaging, which young people (and many of us) may use well into the night. These all worsen the usual changes taking place in the body during adolescence, which means teenagers fall asleep later in the evening. *'That wouldn't be a problem if there was no need to get up early in the morning for school,'* says Dr Gringras. *'The early-morning wake-ups mean they're not getting the average eight to nine hours of sleep.'* We can thereby end up with teenagers suffering from all the negative consequences of lack of sleep outlined above at a crucial time in their education.

The clear message for those with teenage children is that we, as parents, need to be mindful of this and do all we can to avoid the communication and stimulation overload that can have such detrimental affects on our children's sleep patterns and resulting performance. We also owe it to our children to ensure that they have a diet and exercise regime that allows them to develop and maintain healthy patterns of rest.

Being DEAR to ourselves is a lifestyle choice we can all implement. We can also support our children to develop these positive habits and have the health, vitality and energy to realize their goals and potential.

Affirmations
- I am feeling great; maintaining the physical and mental energy for everything I want to do.
- I am exercising regularly and feeling energised.

- I am eating and drinking to maximise my mental and physical energy.
- I am relentlessly positive and have the energy to do what it takes to succeed.

ACTION

1. One of the things we can do to check that we're maximising our energy, health and wellbeing is to keep an **Energy Diary** for a couple of weeks: something very simple, so it's easy to maintain. Complete it 3 times a day, at the same times each day. Use a simple table, something like the one you can download from my website, or make your own. You can turn it into a sticker version for your children. These are the headings you need

Day.................. Time.......... Time.......... Time..........

Eat

Drink

Exercise

Rest

Attitude

Energy Level

(score our of 10)

2. Use the Energy Diary to check when your energy levels are at their highest, and when they dip, and reflect:

High Energy / Low Energy

Why?

Which of the four key factors was in / out of balance in the last 24 hours?

Did you eat energy-giving foods? Or foods that make you lethargic?

Have you drunk plenty of water?

Did you do any exercise?
Did you rest enough?
What was your attitude like?
What was the attitude of those around you like?
Are you remaining positive?
Are you allowing others to give you energy or drain your energy?

You can also use this with your children by teaching them, in simple terms, about **D.E.A.R.**, and then asking them questions so they can learn for themselves how they can feel vital and energetic for the things that are important.

Once we are in tune with our energy levels and the reasons for energy dips, we find it much easier to maintain high energy.

3. Set a goal and action plan to increase your energy levels or maintain high energy levels to achieve your goals.

When setting your goal and creating your action plan, think about the four key elements to developing and maintaining high energy and decide what the priorities are for you.

4. Encourage your children to try new foods – turn it into a game of deciding what it tastes like, looks like etc.

Reference – British Nutrition Foundation - nutrition.org.uk
*Sharon Jackson – ayurvedallifestyle.co.uk

Chapter Fourteen

Manage Relationships

The most important single ingredient in the formula of success is knowing how to get along with people.
Theodore Roosevelt

Definitions

manage:
- to bring about or succeed in accomplishing, sometimes despite difficulty or hardship;
- to take charge or care of;
- to influence (a person) by tact, flattery, or ingenuity;
- to handle, direct, govern, or control in action or use.

relationships:
- a connection, association, or involvement;
- an emotional or other connection between people;
- the way in which two or more people or groups regard and behave towards each other.

To achieve success in all areas of our life, we need to understand ourselves, manage ourselves effectively, and form effective relationships with those around us.

The title of this chapter ought to be *Manage Ourselves Well, Our Emotions and Behaviour, Individually and Within Relationships,* but of course that's far too long! However, it's a far more accurate description of what we can seek to equip ourselves, and our children, to do. We can learn to effectively play our part in relationships and we can influence others, but just as we can't manage time, we can't really manage relationships. What we can do is learn to manage ourselves, and tune in to and influence others. With our children, I feel that we need to be focused on enabling and equipping them to behave appropriately in their many and varied interactions and relationships when we're not there, which means coaching rather than controlling.

In personal relationships, social situations and most work situations, it is vital to recognise how important it is to understand ourselves and manage ourselves effectively in order to achieve the best outcomes. This is especially true when it matters most: being a good friend when we're really needed; in those differences with friends in the playground (at any age!); in that all-important interview; playing our role in the team; leading our team; and behaving appropriately in those important and challenging situations at home, school and work. Successful people (that is, those who could justifiably rate themselves highly across the whole Wheel of Life spectrum) realise how important it is to manage themselves effectively and get on well with others: forming positive relationships and behaving appropriately to bring about beneficial outcomes. They are also aware of the power of emotions and reflect on their behaviour with others.

In my view, there are three essential elements to managing yourself effectively and managing relationships for the benefit of all:

Emotional Literacy – understanding emotional intelligence and constantly improving our emotional literacy;

Being Assertive – understanding the importance of assertive behaviour and developing our capacity to be assertive, rather than passive or aggressive, to develop healthy relationships;

Teamwork – understanding the essentials of teamwork and learning how best to contribute to, and lead, teams.

There are obviously some specific fields of endeavour where relationships with people are exceptionally important, and those where they are less so. For example, if we start a retail business, we have many relationships that we need to effectively manage and be good at: to lever support from those from whom we require help to set up; customers; employees; suppliers; premises landlord – the list is endless. Even if your performance and success is less people-focused, such as scientific research and individual pursuits, we all need to engage with and elicit support from people at some point, and it is always helpful if those relationships are positive.

The People Stuff Is Important!

If your emotional abilities aren't in hand, if you don't have self-awareness, if you are not able to manage your distressing emotions, if you can't have empathy and have effective relationships, then no matter how smart you are, you are not going to get very far.
Daniel Goleman

Successful people (remember, we're talking about holistic success) know themselves: are aware of their emotional temperature and are able to manage their internal states; are empathetic (aware of others' emotions) and develop to become comfortable in all situations. They are able to 'tune in' to the people they meet, at work and socially, through interpersonal skills and 'doing their homework' – finding out what's important to others. This is crucial, and something I've spent so much time on with my children and the young people with whom I've worked. Emotional literacy, social literacy and assertiveness are not systematically developed in most school curricula. It is therefore very dependent on us, as parents, to help our children develop these capabilities.

Part of my vision for my children was that they could engage appropriately with people in any context and form positive personal, social and professional relationships. My decision about where to raise Harriet and George, and where they went to primary school, was very influenced by this: Nottingham being a diverse city and

Carrington Primary School being a small microcosm of society.

This chapter focuses on the three things that I regard as the most essential aspects of knowing yourself and getting on well with those around you. If we know ourselves and can tune into and manage our emotional state, we can reflect accurately on our behaviour and modify it appropriate to the situation. If we get on well with others and can manage relationships effectively in all contexts, we reap the rewards in so many ways. I am still learning, and still get things wrong - say the wrong thing at the wrong time in the wrong way - as we all do, but the important thing is that we are aware enough to know when we get things wrong and what to do about it.

In all aspects of managing ourselves effectively with others, for me, there are the 3 R's:

Respect:
Treat everyone as an individual and respect them as individuals, their micro and macro culture:
- micro culture - their home, their way of doing things, what they can do (rather than what they can't);
- macro culture - in society, their contribution, their heritage, their customs, their religion.

Reflect:
It is only by systematic reflection that we learn the complexities of getting on well with people in all sorts of contexts and learn to amend our behaviour appropriate to the situation. In this way, we learn from situations where we've handled things well and where we could have handled things better.

Review:
Make changes; amend our behaviour as we grow and learn. 'I'm just like that' is not acceptable if our behaviour stands in the way of us having mutually affirming, rewarding and beneficial relationships.

Pretend that every single person you meet has a sign around his or her neck that says, 'Make me feel important.'
Not only will you succeed in sales, you will succeed in life.
Mary Kay Ash

Constant And Never-ending Improvement applies in relationships, as with anything else – if we are always learning, we have the capacity to make our personal, social and professional relationships richer all the time. The alternative is not learning, growing or adapting, and then our relationships are likely to become more impoverished and continuously challenging.

Emotions and Behaviour

How well we interact with others boils down to **emotions** and **behaviour**:

- what we feel
- what others feel
- what we say and how we say it
- what others say and how they say it
- how we receive what others say - how we feel and how we respond
- what we do and how we do it
- what others do and how they do it
- how we receive what others do - how we feel and how we respond

Just looking at this list gives us an insight into the complexity of managing ourselves and managing relationships effectively. If we add into that mix how we need to amend our language and behaviour appropriate to the context, the mix gets more complex. A small example springs to mind when George was in the final year at primary school. I heard him use inappropriate language at home one day. I recognised that this language was probably commonplace in the school playground and I also realise the importance of certain aspects of fitting in with your peers in the playground. I simply said, 'Playground language. Would you say that in front of your grandparents?' The answer came back, 'No', in that tone we all recognise as, 'Don't be stupid, of course I wouldn't'. 'Why wouldn't you?' Again, in that exasperated tone, 'Because they wouldn't like it'. 'Exactly! The same applies to me.' That was a very brief exchange, but gives a clear example of recognising what's important for our children's social relationships when we're not around, and reinforcing with them the importance of adapting to circumstances. Avoiding the word 'don't', which often comes across as controlling or a challenge, and coaching rather than telling, is almost always more effective. In all this we always need to remember that:

Nothing is perfect. Life is messy. Relationships are complex. Outcomes are uncertain. People are irrational.
Hugh Mackay

However, once we are more aware of ourselves, we can then develop our skills and competencies to make the most of relationships with others, learning to:
- manage ourselves better;
- be more assertive, rather than passive or aggressive;
- be better at working with others: teamwork – participating in, and leading, teams.

 Emotional Literacy

Anyone can become angry – that is easy. But to be angry with the right person, to the right degree, at the right time, for the right purpose, and in the right way – this is not easy.
Aristotle

Emotional literacy enables us to be self-aware and to accurately self-reflect: constantly improve our ability to manage ourselves, and improve our interactions and behaviour with people. We need to understand ourselves, be positive with ourselves, and behave appropriately and positively with others to achieve successful relationships in all areas of our life: with family, with friends, in work – anywhere we need to get on with people, and that's pretty much everywhere! Developing emotional literacy is about understanding emotional intelligence and becoming more competent in managing our emotions.

What is Emotional Intelligence?

Much of our current understanding of emotional intelligence has come from Daniel Goleman's work. Daniel Goleman is an internationally-renowned psychologist whose 1995 book, *Emotional Intelligence – Why it Can Matter More Than IQ,* was on *The New York Times* bestseller list for 18 months, with more than 5,000,000 copies in print worldwide in 40 languages. He has written a number of further books expanding our whole understanding of the way we manage our emotional state and effectively relate to others. His books, *Working with Emotional Intelligence* and *The New Leaders – transforming the Art of Leadership into the science of Results* with Richard Boyatzis and Annie McKee, have had a major impact worldwide on our view of effective management and leadership, and how leadership has needed to change to meet the demands of our changing economic and social environment. For me, Daniel Goleman's work has enabled me to put what I have learned from experience into context. It gives us a clear framework to help us reflect on, and develop, our emotional literacy.

Daniel Goleman's **Emotional Competence Framework** from *Working with Emotional Intelligence* is broken down into personal and social competencies. I have used this below as I believe it is the most comprehensive, straightforward framework for exploring how we can reflect on our own emotional intelligence and enable our children to develop their emotional literacy and competence.

Personal Competence
These competencies determine how we mange ourselves.

Self-Awareness
Knowing our internal states or emotional temperature, our preferences, our personal resources, and our intuitions.

> *Emotional awareness:* recognising our emotions and their effects on others.

Accurate self-assessment: knowing our strengths and where we need to improve.
Self-confidence: a strong sense of our self-worth and capabilities.

Encouraging and enabling our children to be self-aware is vital if they are to feel empowered to recognise and understand their feelings and trust the accuracy of their interpretation. This is the fundamental building block for us to be equipped to effectively manage ourselves, and our relationships with others. As I have explored elsewhere, accurate self-reflection is a vital tool for improvement in any area, and it is the most valuable tool when it comes to managing our emotional state, mindset and behaviour.

Self-Regulation
Managing our internal states or emotions, our impulses, and our personal resources.

Self-Control: keeping disruptive / negative emotions and impulses in check.
Trustworthiness: maintaining standards of honesty and integrity.
Conscientiousness: taking responsibility for personal performance.
Adaptability: flexibility in handling change.
Innovation: being comfortable with innovative ideas, approaches, and new information.

Regulating ourselves - taking control and managing our emotions - is one of the most challenging aspects of emotional literacy. Breathing deeply and reflecting, taking that moment to consider our response and responding appropriately - especially in difficult situations - is something most of us find challenging. It is essential that we help our children to develop this competence to enable them to realise their potential.

Anger is never without a reason, but seldom a good one.
Benjamin Franklin

Motivation
Emotional tendencies that guide or facilitate reaching our goals.

Achievement drive: striving to improve or meet a standard of excellence.
Commitment: aligning our goals with the goals of the groups or organisations of which we are members.
Initiative: readiness to act on opportunities.
Optimism: persistence in pursuing goals despite obstacles and setbacks.

This summarises the 'get up and go' required to consistently move forward with whatever we are pursuing. It also emphasises how we need to 'tune in to' the environment and people around us, personally, socially and in our chosen fields of endeavour. Motivation is a recurring theme and different aspects are explored in other chapters.

Social Competence
These competencies determine how we handle relationships.

Empathy
Awareness of others' feelings, needs and concerns.

Everything that irritates us about others can lead us to an understanding of ourselves.
Carl Gustav Jung

Understanding others: sensing others' feelings and perspectives, and taking an active interest in their concerns.
Developing others: sensing others' development needs and bolstering their abilities.
Service orientation: anticipating, recognising, and meeting customers' needs.
Leveraging diversity: cultivating opportunities through different kinds of people.
Political awareness: reading a group's emotional currents and power relationships.

Empathy is one of the essential traits we need to challenge stereotypes and overcome prejudices.
Roman Krznaric

Social Skills

Adeptness at responding appropriately to others and bringing about desirable responses in others.

Influence: wielding effective tactics for persuasion.
Communication: listening openly and sending convincing messages.
Conflict management: negotiating and resolving disagreements.
Leadership: inspiring and guiding individuals and groups.
Change catalyst: initiating or managing change.
Building bonds: nurturing mutually helpful relationships.
Collaboration and co-operation: working with others towards shared goals.
Team capabilities: creating group synergy in pursuing collective goals.

I will not waste my life in friction when it could be turned into momentum.
Frances Willard

Most of us constantly strive to improve our social skills from a young age, realising the importance of being happy in our personal relationships, feeling comfortable and enjoying, to the full, varied social situations, and having a fulfilling experience with peers in education and colleagues in work. We also recognise how vital our social competency is to gaining the help we need to achieve our goals. However, we all know people who are skilled and knowledgeable in all sorts of ways, but who are uncomfortable with people, show little empathy, fail to pick up social clues on behaviour and fail to engage appropriately in social and work situations. [1] They miss out on realising their potential. They have technical ability, experience, and are competent in many ways, but never learn those essential people skills that enable them to use their other skills and knowledge to best effect.

I think that much of our failure to equip our young people with the necessary social competencies is as a result of a commonly-held belief that we learn social skills by osmosis. We pick them up along the way and if we don't, it's held against us as some personal flaw, or those around us just say, 's/he's just like that'. Daniel Goleman's, and others', research, our own experience of the changing, complex nature of the educational environment, social interaction and the working environment, clearly point to the fact that this is not enough.

We owe it to our children to equip them with the personal and social competencies to establish and maintain mutually affirming personal relationships and mutually beneficial social and work relationships. The fact that many of us now work in smaller organisations, where it's even more important that we get on with our colleagues, adds to the importance of this. The main challenge we have in making this explicit within the school curriculum is that emotional intelligence cannot be taught like facts and knowledge in the traditional sense, beyond the basic framework, which gives young people a language and context on which to hang their experiences and feelings. We need to facilitate children and young people to learn personal and social competencies, mainly through coaching and experiential learning – exploring real-life experiences and scenarios. It is therefore largely down to us, as parents, to equip our children with the essential competencies they need to manage themselves and manage the many and varied relationships they will need to form to realise their potential.

> *It is not our differences that divide us.*
> *It is our inability to recognize,*
> *accept, and celebrate those differences.*
> Audre Lorde

At this point, it's worth mentioning that word 'relationship'. Most of us use it predominantly to refer to personal, intimate relationships, whereas we have a relationship with everyone with whom we engage, from our children to our work colleagues, from partners to bank managers, from relatives to our coaches. An example of recognising the importance of emotional literacy and emotional competence was a discussion George and I had when he was young. When he was in Year 3 at school (8 years old), there was a girl in his class who, for the purpose of this illustration, I will call Ruth. Ruth and her mother were living in a nearby women's refuge at the time, and she had special educational needs in her capacity to learn and behave appropriately. She liked George, and took to asking him for help a lot in the classroom and following him around the playground. He was agitated with this, and I remember one evening him complaining about Ruth. I pointed out that it was his responsibility to manage his relationship with Ruth. He immediately said, in a horrified tone, 'I don't have a relationship with her'. I pointed out that they were in the same class, and would be for the remainder of the year. He would spend more time with her, in one way or another, than many other people. Therefore, he did have a relationship with her, a 'working' relationship. He continued to say how she annoyed him. We then had the following dialogue in order to enable him to understand what I meant by saying he was responsible for his relationship with Ruth and needed to find ways to manage it:

Me: Who's more able at spelling, you or Ruth?

George: Me, of course. (In the tone that said – are you dumb?)

Me: Who's more able at maths, you or Ruth?

George: Me. (In the same tone – are you dumb?)

Me: Who's more able at sport, you or Ruth?

George: I am. (In the tone – now you're just being silly!)

Me: Who gets on better with the other children in your class and in the playground, you or Ruth?

George: Me. (Again in the tone – now you're just being ridiculous.)

Me: Therefore, if you're more able in all those ways, you are responsible for effectively managing your relationship with Ruth.

George had nowhere to go as he realised that it was his answers that had led me to that conclusion, and so we then had a meaningful conversation about how he could manage his relationship with Ruth, without hurting or belittling her, so that he did not become as frustrated with her behaviour. Much of that was accepting the situation and his role within it, and then practicing assertive behaviour and deflection.

For every minute you remain angry, you give up
sixty seconds of peace of mind. (Or happiness!)
Ralph Waldo Emerson

On the other side of the coin, I made a notable mistake in expecting too much of Harriet in a relationship challenge. She was 5 or 6, and told me about a girl at school who was verbally bullying her. From my work, I could empathise with the girl's situation and recognised the signs of low self-regard and the resulting aggressive behaviour that can often result when a child has had a challenging time. I tried to coach Harriet, taking the role of the bully and getting her to decide how she would respond, and encouraging her to be assertive in terms of how she said it and her body language etc. We tried this for about a week or so, and Harriet was becoming more distressed by the behaviour of the girl. I then went with Harriet to see her teacher. Harriet talked through what had been happening and we shared what we'd tried to do so far. The teacher sorted it and afterwards, I made a note to myself – watch the balance between empathising with others and expecting too much of my children in those situations.

At the other end of the educational journey, a classic example of someone who had not learnt many or any of these emotional literacy lessons earlier in life was a young woman we had on work placement during the summer, just before the final year of her degree. Again, I will change her name. We were a small education organisation and Caroline had just completed her second year of a science degree. We had a clear project for her to work on which would be beneficial both to the organisation, and to her development. Within days, she had offended and/or upset everyone in our small team, with her propensity to tell everyone what she thought and imply, or even say, she knew better than them. This was not just an issue of how to behave appropriately in the workplace, but also one of generally poor social competence. The consequence was that I spent a great deal of time with her, working through emotional intelligence, pointing out situations where her approach had caused issues and coaching her to improve her social skills. I took this route rather than saying 'Goodbye' at the end of the

285

first week partly because I knew we could help, and partly because I felt it was a sad indictment of our education system that a young person could get to 20 without any idea of how to behave appropriately with others, whether in the workplace or anywhere else. Caroline responded well to coaching. We saw vast improvements in her social skills at work, and she fed back how it had helped her socially.

All the way through their school careers, Harriet and George demonstrated that they could effectively manage situations and teachers in a way to assert their own rights whilst avoiding angering teachers: challenging at the right time, appropriately, and in the right way. George was not a studious, unquestioning, compliant scholar. He said there were often occasions when friends were disciplined for challenging a teacher about a similar issue to him, but he wasn't disciplined. To paraphrase Aristotle, **challenging the right person, to the right degree, at the right time, for the right purpose, and in the right way.** Harriet has repeatedly demonstrated her emotional literacy at school and, latterly, in her work with colleagues and clients: 'managing' people as they need to be managed rather than taking the view that 'one size fits' all when dealing with people. George's ability to get on with people, and contribute to, and lead, the team has been consistently demonstrated and commented on in his sport by teammates, teachers and coaches alike.

As our children are unlikely to find many formal opportunities to develop their emotional literacy as children, young people or adults, it's down to us as parents to do all we can to equip them with the self-reflective, personal and social tools they need to continuously develop their emotional intelligence.

Being Assertive

The aim of assertive behaviour is to communicate productively
with another person, achieving what is often described as
a win-win outcome.

Being assertive is an aspect of emotional competence, and I want to highlight it as an important part of equipping our children to effectively engage in mutually beneficial relationships, expressing their thoughts and feelings in an appropriate way and standing up for themselves. From my experience with young people, I think many of the behaviour issues and confrontations that arise at home and in schools could be avoided if we taught our children to be assertive, and coached them to consistently practice it. Over the years, I have used a wide variety of sources to help me put together workshops and coaching that enables young people and adults to become more able to assert themselves. In this section, I share a few of the insights that have guided my approach in both my professional life, and with my children.

Assertive People Believe they have the Right to:
- have their own values, beliefs, opinions, and emotions;
- tell others how they wish to be treated;
- express themselves and say, 'No,' 'I don't know,' 'I don't understand';
- take the time they need to formulate their ideas before expressing them;
- make mistakes;
- stand up for themselves and for what they believe and want;
- be treated with respect.

Many assertive people also do not feel compelled to justify or explain their actions to others, and may become irritated at having to do this, even when it's appropriate to do so! This may be a positive or negative according to the context and your perspective. However, when challenged, the assertive person will explain themselves clearly and without the negative traits of defensiveness or aggression.

Behaving Assertively
To behave assertively we need to pay attention to our eye contact, tone of voice and body language, as well as the words we use. There are variations on eye contact and body language, according to culture, and we all need to remember to check cultural norms when we are travelling.

DIRECT EYE-CONTACT	**CALM CLEAR TONE OF VOICE**
OPEN BODY LANGUAGE	**CAREFULLY CHOOSING THE WORDS YOU USE**

The Four Behaviour Types

It is generally recognised that there are four main ways of behaving: passive, aggressive, passive/aggressive and assertive. The following table provides a summary of the four behaviour types and the behaviour, voice, speech pattern, facial expressions, eye contact and body language we associate with them.

Most of us behave in all these ways at some time – often behaving differently in different situations – but we can all change and continuously develop our assertive behaviour to improve all of our relationships. We can also enable our children to develop assertive behaviour by teaching them about society's norms and expectations, and about the elements of assertive behaviour. We can reflect back to them the way they've said things and how that makes us feel, or might make someone else feel, coaching them in appropriate responses and how they should ask for what they want in an appropriate manner.

The Pros and Cons of the Four Behaviour Types

It's clear to see from the summary of the pros and cons and of the four behavior types in the table below why it's important to equip our children to be assertive.

Behaviour Type	Voice	Speech Pattern	Face	Body Language	Actions
Passive Keen to avoid confrontation, often by supressing their own needs; hopes people will 'know' what he or she wants; excessively concerned with what other people think of him or her.	Sometimes 'wobbly'. Tone may be whining. Very soft, quiet or childlike. Often dull or monotonous. Drops away at the end of a sentence.	Hesitant, many pauses. May stress 'you' words. Frequent throat-clearing. Gives up when interrupted.	'Ghost' smiles when expressing anger or being criticized. Eyebrow raised in anticipation (of rebuke, for example). Expressions change frequently grimace / smile / frown / lowered eyes - within a few seconds	Minimal eye contact. Evasive. Furtive glances. Often looks down or away from the other person. Wrings hands. Hunches shoulders. Steps back. Covers mouth with hand. Nervous movements – shuffles feet, if holding anything, fiddles with it. Arms crossed for protection	Self-blame. Goes round the issue. Avoids the issue. Over-justification. Permission-seeking statements. Gives in easily. Generates sympathy. Makes people feel guilty in order to get what he or she wants.
Aggressive Keen to win, if necessary at the expense of others - stand up for your rights but also violate the rights of others. Involves expressing your needs, wants, opinions, beliefs and feelings in inappropriate ways, often ignoring or dismissing the rights and opinions of others.	Tone cold, may be sarcastic. Hard and sharp. Strident, may be loud. Voice may be raised at end of a sentence. Often the loudest voice.	Fluent and very conficent / arrogant. Often abrupt and clipped. Often interrupts, shouts down if interrupted. Stresses blaming words and 'you' words. Often very fast.	Smile may be wry or disbelieving. Scowls when angry. Normal expression is set and unfriendly. Jaw set firm, teeth clenched. Chin thrust forward.	Eyes narrowed and cold. Tries to 'stare you out' and dominate. Looks 'over' you. Challenging posture - fist clenching /thumping. Finger pointing. Sits bolt upright or leans forward (invades personal space). Strides around impatiently. Folds arms unapproachably.	Quick to blame others. Criticises person, not his or her behaviour. Interrupts frequently. Authoritarian. Uses sarcasm, criticism and ridicule to win the point. Makes requests sound like orders. Escalates a situation to confrontation easily.

Behaviour Type	Voice	Speech Pattern	Face	Body Language	Actions
Passive / Aggressive A mixture of behaviour combining passive and aggressive behaviours. Keen to get even without the risk of confrontation.	Sometimes passive and sometimes aggressive tone of voice and can swing between the two.	Mixture of passive and aggressive.	Mixture of passive and aggressive.	Minimal eye contact but looking away rather than down. Tight-lipped, impatient sighs. Exasperated or 'I don't believe it' expression. Closed posture.	Indirect responses. Sarcastic asides. Barbed humour. 'Gets even' indirectly.
Assertive – being 'for real' and strong This involves standing up for your own rights without violating those of the other person. To do this, you need to express your needs, wants, opinions, beliefs and feelings in a direct, honest, clear and 'adult' way.	Steady and firm. Tone – middle-range, full and warm. Clear, sounds sincere. Neither too loud, nor too soft.	Fluent and confident. Pauses are intentional, not awkward. Key 'action' words are stressed. Even pace. If interrupted, waits, then repeats calmly. Use of 'I' phrases, rather than (accusing) 'you' comments.	Smiles when pleased. Frowns when angry. Normal expression is friendly, approachable and open.	Meets other person's eyes. Does stare them out. Open hand movements, inviting others to speak. Sits upright or relaxed, does not slouch or cower. Stands with head held up. Makes firm and definite movements. Does not fidget.	Lots of listening - seeks to understand. Treats people with respect. Prepared to compromise - solution-focused. Prepared to state and explain what he or she wants. Straight and to the point without being abrupt. Prepared to persist for what he or she wants.

The Benefits of Being Assertive

Assertive behaviour enables us to state clearly our thoughts, feelings and views, and to stand up for our rights whilst treating people with the respect they deserve - family, friends, people in our team, coaches, tutors, colleagues etc. It may not guarantee that we achieve what we want, but it does provide three very useful benefits:

- It gives us the best chance of achieving what we want
- It provides us with the reassurance that we positively played our part in the conversation.
- It helps us to maintain our self-regard and confidence.
- It gives us the best chance of effective relationships and increased capacity to continuously improve in our relationships.

As we interact with others, it's useful to focus on the four essentials of assertiveness:

I'M OK

| WIN/LOSE | WIN/WIN |
| AGGRESSIVE | ASSERTIVE |

YOUR'E NOT OK ──────────────────── *You're ok*

| PASSIVE/AGGRESSIVE | PASSIVE |
| LOSE/LOSE | LOSE/WIN |

I'M NOT OK

How people feel about us is largely a direct result of the way we behave towards them; the more positive our behaviour, the more valued we are by our family, friends, work colleagues, tutors, team mates etc. (Of course, we are often very forgiving of the way our children, parents and those closest to us behave towards us. We recognise that our children can take out their frustrations on us when they don't feel able to with anyone else. However, that doesn't alter the principle that we have more fulfilling relationships when we behave in a positive, affirming way with each other.)

In summary, assertiveness is the ability to get our views, wants and needs across to others in a calm, rational manner, to stand up for ourselves and say how we feel, when we feel we need to. It includes:
- expressing our own opinions and feelings.
- saying 'No' without feeling guilty.
- setting our own priorities i.e. choosing how we spend our time.
- asking for what we want.
- being able to take reasonable risks.
- choosing not to assert ourselves at times when we feel it would be better to say nothing.

Teamwork

You can have everything in life you want if you'll just help enough other people to get what they want!
Zig Ziglar

Developing our emotional literacy and assertiveness are essential for us to work effectively with others, including contributing to, or leading, a team. We may live in an age of high technology, but we also live in an age when the impact of the way we get on together, in work and in life generally, has never been more important. Most of us need to contribute to, and lead, teams: productively co-operate in order to achieve individual, team and organisational goals. Teamwork is a key element of what employers emphasise in any list of what they're looking for in young people's employability skills, and there is always an emphasis on this in organisational learning and development programmes.

The world-renowned expert on teams in the workplace is Dr Meredith Belbin, author of *Team Roles at Work*, *Management Teams - Why They Succeed or Fail*, and for young people starting out in work, *The Belbin Guide to Succeeding at Work*, amongst many others. I had the privilege to meet him in early 2013 and hear, first-hand, his insight into enabling people to work effectively to achieve shared goals. Dr Belbin maintains that fitness for purpose is crucial if we are to consistently make the most of people's talents and skills in organisations; that is, bringing the most appropriate people together to work on specific tasks and projects rather than confining people in inflexible job roles. I don't intend to go into teamwork in the workplace here, but mention it to reinforce the importance of enabling our children to contribute to, lead and manage themselves effectively within teams, whether that's sports teams or medical teams, business teams or charity teams, our 'domestic' team (at home), or the school Young Enterprise team.

Elements of Effective Teamwork

Here are the elements of teamwork that I view as essential for young people to understand. As you read through this list you'll be able to think of ways we can help your children develop these understandings and skills in everyday life, and you'll see how they tie in with the earlier sections of this chapter.

Co-operate with others
Fundamental to effective teamwork is co-operation. We don't always like the people we need to work with, at school, at work, in sports teams etc, but a mark of someone who is a good team member and team leader is working productively with people, as necessary, to succeed in achieving the goal.

Actively listen
Show that we are listening by our body language and ensure we hear what people say, reflect on it, question it, and use it in our

thinking.

Ask questions
Ask questions to gain clarification and seek further understanding for ourself and the team. Avoid passively agreeing.

Encourage others
Use affirming language and body language to encourage contributions. Acknowledge others' skills, experience and potential contribution. Ask for others' views.

> *We cannot hold a torch to light another's path*
> *without brightening our own.*
> Ben Sweetland

Tolerate other people's ideas
There will be disagreements and heated debate in any high-performing team.

Be positive
Positive language and body language create an environment where people are more likely to contribute. A positive, yet challenging, atmosphere energises people and enables creativity to flow.

Come up with solutions
We all know the '1001 reasons why not' people in teams: those who always produce issues, but no solutions. They drain everyone's energy. Teams need those who come up with ideas and seek solutions: who find ways forward and help others find ways forward.

Justify opinions
We must expect to justify our opinions and respond to challenge without taking it personally.

Consider other people's views
Listen, hear and reflect on others' views.

Critically evaluate ideas and contributions
All ideas and contributions need to be scrutinised, questioned and evaluated rather than just accepted. This doesn't mean delaying

progress by unnecessarily pedantic behaviour. That is simply energy sapping and deflating for a team. Also, don't accept ideas just because of who they come from!

Be willing to change if appropriate

If we listen and are open-minded, we are able to see when changes can achieve better outcomes.

Agree strategies and solutions

Gain agreement and ensure strategies and solutions are actively shared.

Take responsibility

Teams look for team members and team leaders who take responsibility – delivering on their role and helping the team deliver. The 'pass the buck' person is an energy sapper, and soon becomes resented by other members of the team.

Show commitment

Whatever the team task, role or project, team members and team leaders look for commitment from their fellow team members. Commitment is essential to maintaining focus and drive towards shared goals.

Only the guy who isn't rowing has time to rock the boat.
Jean-Paul Sartre

Organise

Organisation is vital to enable teams to achieve their aims, and those with organisational skills should be valued and listened to just as much as those with technical and creative input.

Decide who will do what

Whether it's a school sports team, a complex work project, or 'Young Enterprise' business team, individuals need to know what their role is and who is doing what if the whole team is to function effectively. If two people are doing the same job, they get in each other's way and, more than likely, another job isn't being done; this applies whether the task is organising a party or implementing a project.

Motivate others

There are times in any team when some members are not at their best, and it's important that members of the team help to motivate each other. Team members need to challenge and support each other to perform at their best to effectively and efficiently achieve goals or win!

An example of this that sticks in my mind is a Cup Final when George was captaining his school football team.

The team were losing 3-1 at half-time, and some of the players' body language indicated that they had accepted defeat. At the start of the second half, George led by example, shouting encouragement and demanding players to show commitment and fight, challenging hard for every ball and running with the ball straight into the heart of the opposition at every opportunity. You saw the body language of the team change and their energy levels rise as they started to fight back. They won!

Support the team

Team members expect support from each other and from their leaders support (as well as leaders expecting support from their team.)

The miracle is this - the more we share, the more we have.
Leonard Nimoy

Trust

To perform at their best, teams need members who trust each other: trust they'll see it through and trust each other to do what they say they're going to do, when they say they're going to do it.

Make it happen

Teamwork is sometimes mistaken for just being nice to each other: getting on well, coming up with creative solutions. They are all aspects, but what the team has to do is deliver the desired outcome! Get it done on time, get it done within budget, win the match etc.

A Recurring Theme

Energy is a recurring theme in the elements of teamwork (above). Energy givers are crucial to help the team perform at its best, and if all team members are energy givers, the team has an edge. Likewise, energy sappers detract from the team's propensity to perform at its best. Energy-giving behaviour is encouraging, positive, affirming and enthusiastic. Energy-sapping behaviour is detracting, negative, unduly critical and highlights problems without offering solutions. When we watch a sports match, we support one or other team, and it's very usual for teams to say they felt the energy from supporters which boosted their performance.

Successful people relate well to others, develop their emotional literacy and understand the power and value of emotions in engaging others. People who achieve personal, social and economic goals are assertive. They feel comfortable in their own skin and gain the respect of those around them. Through constant reflection and a desire to improve, they recognise their strengths and limitations and effectively contribute to, and lead, teams.

Affirmations
- I am feeling energised from the marvellous, mutually beneficial relationships.
- I am loving the way we are getting on as a family.
- I am always improving my understanding of my feelings and the feelings of those around me.
- I am making a positive contribution to the team and I'm humbled by their trust in me.

ACTION

Over the years, I have developed a number of self-reflection tools, which I call C.A.N.I.'s: tools to help us maintain Constant And

Never-ending Improvement. There are a couple of these that are relevant to help us reflect on managing relationships. All of the suggested actions below can be adapted to give us a framework to help us reflect with our children. I have young people's versions of most of the reflection tools, but the main value of this is to improve our understanding and tool-kit as parents. It is a matter of our judgement to know when it's appropriate to use any of these frameworks and reflection tools with our children.

1. Emotional Literacy

a. Complete the **Emotional Literacy C.A.N.I. (Constant and Never-ending Improvement)** on the equipped2succeed downloads section of my website.

b. Think of times when you may not have used your emotional intelligence and reflect on how you may have acted differently. Write these events in your self-reflective diary and include alternative suggestions for handling the situations differently. Find an opportunity to share these with another person and see what other perspectives you gain. Another person's view is often affirming.

c. Use the outcomes of activities 1a and 1b to identify areas for improvement. Set a goal to further develop your emotional competence, perhaps in specific situations, and resolve to practise developing these competencies.

2. Being Assertive

Complete the **'How assertive am I?'** questionnaire on the equipped2succeed downloads section of my website, and use the descriptions of assertive, passive and aggressive behaviour to reflect on how you can become more assertive in all situations. We can then use the young person's version of this with our children. It gives us the language and framework to then support our children to reflect, and enables us to coach them to be more assertive.

We can use 'The Four Behaviour Types' summary to help us reflect on our behavior and improve assertiveness in all situations. We can reflect to what extent the descriptions apply to us in different situations, and what we can do to be consistently more assertive. We can also use it to help our children be consistently more assertive.

- Highlight the main behaviours you recognise in yourself and talk to your children when you recognise different behaviours in them.

- Highlight, from the assertiveness description, the ones you would like to exhibit more often.

The questions below are something we can use ourselves, and to support our children to reflect when they are facing a challenge in their behaviour and need to be more assertive:

- List the situations when you are assertive.
  What does being assertive entail in these situations?
  How does it feel?
  What can you do to behave like this more consistently?

- List the situations in which you behave passively.
  What does being passive look like in these situations?
  How does it feel?
  What can you do to become more assertive in these situations?

- List the situations in which you behave aggressively.
  What is aggressive behaviour in these situations?
  How does it feel?
  What can you do to become more assertive in these situations?

Coach your children to be more assertive by going over scenarios and helping them find alternative, more assertive ways of putting things, whether that's asking for something, making a contribution to a discussion, or responding to others.

3. Teamwork

Encourage and enable our children to take every opportunity to work with others, be part of a team, and reflect on how well they contribute and manage relationships with others.

Use the **'Teamwork C.A.N.I'** on the equipped2succeed downloads section of my website to focus on where your strengths are and where you need to improve.

In all this 'people stuff', be prepared to acknowledge and accept your mistakes. Don't beat yourself up about mistakes - apologise, promise yourself and those around you that you will improve in the future, and move on. This is crucial to developing a positive relationship with yourself and others.

You don't have to be perfect to impress people.
Let them be impressed by how you deal with your imperfections.

What's really important is that we recognise the importance of the 'people stuff' and develop our children's ability to understand and manage themselves, and work well with people in their many and varied relationships.

We must learn to live together as brothers or we will perish together as fools.
Martin Luther King

*1 In this, I acknowledge and recognise the challenges this poses for people on the autistic spectrum.

Chapter Fifteen

Be Persistent

📖 Definitions

persistent
- continuing firmly or obstinately in an opinion or course of action;
- persisting, especially in spite of difficulty, opposition, obstacles, discouragement, etc;
- lasting or enduring tenaciously.

resilient
- (of a substance or object) able to recoil or spring back into shape after bending, stretching, or being compressed;
- (of a person or animal) able to withstand or recover quickly from difficult conditions.

There's Only One Thing More Painful Than Carrying On and That's Giving Up

Being persistent and resilient in the face of adversity is essential if we are to achieve those things that are really important to us. Successful people demonstrate relentless persistence, that 'stickability' and 'never give up' attitude that is essential to do what it takes to attain elite performance in any field of endeavour. There are few better examples of persistence and resilience than two British athletes that have won seven Olympic Gold Medals between them, rower Sir Steve Redgrave and athlete Dame Kelly Holmes.

Sir Steve Redgrave won an incredible five Gold Medals in five successive Olympic Games from 1984 to 2000, as well as a bronze, not allowing diabetes, age or any other obstacle to stop him. Having been diagnosed with diabetes in 1997, he took the same resilient approach to that that he took to any other set-back, '*I decided very early on that diabetes was going to live with me, not me live with diabetes*', and he went on to win his fifth gold medal.

Harriet, George and I were privileged to see one of Britain's most successful and celebrated female athletes, Dame Kelly Holmes, win Gold Medals in both the 800m and 1500m events at the 2004 Athens Olympic Games. She set British records in numerous events and still holds the records over the 600, 800, 1000 and 1500m distances. Kelly took up athletics in 1982 at the age of 12 and it was a very long journey to her success in Athens. Having entered professional sport quite late, after a successful career in the army, her dedication, drive and never-give-up attitude enabled her to overcome many injuries and set-backs in her career. Her persistence paid off, with numerous records and successes in major competitions, culminating in double Olympic victory at the age of 34.

There are many words and phrases that can be used to describe the relentless pursuit of getting to where we want to be that these athletes demonstrate:

strength of mind   determination

doggedness   pushiness

willpower   resolve

purpose   grit

hard work (working smart as well as working hard)

Individuals who excel in their field persist: they carry on when the going gets tough, when others give up or don't try quite as hard. In education, business, sport, career, maintaining a relationship you value, dance, music, earning the money to buy your dream house, in any area of life, persistence is a crucial part of succeeding.

We are determined and persist in the things that are important to us and that we are passionate about. So it's important to decide what we want, decide what we need to do to get there, decide what we're prepared to pay in time, energy and effort, and persist. If we're passionately working towards something, persistence is an essential ingredient in success. When there are challenges, as there will be, those who are persistent find a way through, round, over – keeping their sights firmly on their goals.

Resilience is the other side of the persistence coin, enabling us to overcome setbacks. It is that inner self-belief and outer protective coating that equip us to persist in pursuing our goals through any manner of hostile environments. That all-important persistence and resilience doesn't happen by accident. My experience is that young people often need to be helped to develop the sort of persistence that is essential to keep going when the going gets tough, and the resilience to handle difficult times and maintain their self-belief.

> *Patience, persistence and perspiration*
> *make an unbeatable combination for success.*
> Napoleon Hill

Persistence and resilience often means taking what other people view as risks, and having the self-belief to see it through. If you ever feel like giving up on pursuing your goals, just watch the film *The Pursuit of Happyness.* I could have just said watch that film at the start of this chapter and left it at that! It is a 2006 biographical film starring Will Smith, about the - at one time homeless - salesman-turned-stockbroker Chris Gardner.

The film begins in 1981 in San Francisco. Linda and Chris Gardner live in a small apartment with their son, Christopher. Chris has invested the family's life savings in a franchise, selling portable bone density scanners. These scanners provide slightly denser pictures than X-rays, but Chris finds that most of the doctors he visits think they are too expensive. Linda works in a dead-end job in a local hotel laundry. The tension between them mounts as financial pressures increase with unpaid rent and bills continuing to accumulate. Chris often parks his car in 'no parking' areas so he can make scheduled appointments on time, and an accumulation of unpaid parking tickets mean that their car is impounded. After missing a shift at her job, Linda finally leaves with their son Christopher, returns briefly, then departs for a better job in New York City, leaving behind Christopher with his father (at his father's request).

Chris accepts an unpaid internship brokerage firm Dean Witter Reynolds that promises employment to only one trainee. His lack of salary, and his lack of scanners to try to sell, leaves him riddled with debt, and he and his son eventually become homeless. After spending several nights riding buses and sleeping in subway restrooms, saddled with their meagre belongings, they begin lining up at a Church on a daily basis in an effort to secure accommodation for the night. Sometimes they succeed, other times they are literally left out in the cold. As he struggles to provide a semblance of family life for his son under the most difficult of circumstances, Chris becomes more determined to complete the intern program and become the sole trainee the firm will hire.

In the end, Chris gets the job, and in 1987 starts his own brokerage firm, called Gardner Rich. In 2006, he sells a minority of it for a multi-million dollar deal. It's a stark example of relentless pursuit of a goal and the pay-off for persistence. This film should be compulsory viewing for all teenagers, with appropriate discussion afterwards bringing out the learning and how they can apply the lessons in their own lives. The following quotation could easily have been used in this film:

Four steps to achievement: plan purposefully, prepare prayerfully, proceed positively, pursue persistently.
William Ward

Balancing Challenge and Support

We return to the recurring theme of balance. On the one hand, we need to raise our children to stick at things, on the other hand, we need not to force them into sticking at things we 'think they should do' rather than things that they are interested in. However, there are a few examples of very successful people who have been driven by a parent rather than their own passion. A notable example of this is Andre Agassi. He hated tennis, but couldn't stop playing partly because of his father's early influence and partly because of something inside him that made him persist. *'I play tennis for a living, even though I hate tennis, hate it with a dark and secret passion, and always have.'* His Dad, Mike Agassi, a former boxer who fought for Iran in two Olympics, decided Andre was going to be tennis player.

In a passage from the book *Open*, Agassi details how his father made him play a match for money with American football legend Jim Brown, in 1979, when Agassi was 9 years old. Brown was at a Vegas tennis club complaining to the owner about a money match that was canceled. Agassi's father stepped in and told Brown that he could play his son and he would put up his house for the wager. That shows incredible faith, as well as putting incredible pressure on young shoulders. Brown countered with a $10,000 bet, but after he was warned by the club owner not to take the bet because he would lose and be embarrassed, Brown agreed with Mike Agassi that they would set the amount after he and Andre played two sets. Brown lost those sets, 3–6, 3–6, declined the $10,000 wager, and offered to play the third set for $500. Brown lost 2–6.

At age 13, Andre was sent to Nick Bollettieri's Tennis Academy in Florida. His father could only afford for him to go for 3 months. After thirty minutes of watching Agassi play, Bollettieri called Mike Agassi and said: *'Take your cheque back. He's here for free,'* claiming that Agassi had more natural ability than anyone else he had seen. Agassi dropped out of school in the ninth grade and, as they say, the rest is history. Despite his avowed continued hatred of the sport, he persisted. When reflecting on that before his match with Bogdatis in his final tennis tournament, the 2006 US Open, when looking in the mirror he reflects: *'Somewhere in those eyes, however, I can still vaguely see the boy who didn't want to play tennis in the first place, the boy who wanted to quit, the boy who did quit many times. I see that golden-haired boy who hated tennis, and I wondered how he would view this bald man, who still hates tennis and yet still plays.'* Those thoughts came at the end of a legendary career that included eight Grand Slam Championships and 60 titles overall. That is persistence!

I am not judging Agassi's father. We all have seen examples of parents deciding what their children are going to pursue, from medicine and law to simply going to university, from sports to running the family business, and they ensure that their children persist each step of the way, with little thought of whether or not it's their children's passion. We are all, in our own way, doing what we think is best for our children, and despite the examples like Agassi, I am firmly of the view that we need to empower, enable and equip our children to pursue their path. However, purposefully pursuing a path towards a goal or goals is non negotiable. As I have quoted in the *Set Goals* chapter, **those who aim at nothing are sure to hit it**, and it's vital we enable our children to purposefully pursue something.

Agassi's is a high profile example of a parent initially 'forcing' persistence with outstanding results in terms of the life Agassi has been able to create for himself. There are many more modest examples of parents insisting on an appropriate study regime to enable their children to get the grades to progress to the next level of education etc. There are also many examples of parents supporting their children to pursue their dreams, against the prevailing accepted wisdom, educational or otherwise, with outstanding results.

I have endeavoured to maintain a balance of challenge and support with Harriet and George in a number of ways, from education to chores. I have sought to enable George to pursue his passion in sport, helping him stand up to the 'be realistic' brigade, being the perennial taxi service and ensuring he has appropriate kit etc, whilst insisting that he takes responsibility for preparing appropriately to perform at his best. For example, he doesn't naturally like breakfast, but you can't perform at your best without appropriate fuel. Therefore, from the age of 6 when he started playing competitive football for a local U8's team, I have insisted he eat appropriately before training and matches. When he said he didn't want anything first thing in the morning before a match, my answer was always, *'What has whether or not you like breakfast got to do with it? If you want to perform at your best for your team you need appropriate fuel'*. He also knew that this was non-negotiable. As George got older, he recognised the importance of this for himself, but the early discipline came from my insistence. He has always worked hard at training and given his all in matches, but there are other young people he's played with who have not and, sadly, there are parents who have condoned this, reinforcing a poor work ethic and/or an excuse culture in their children. What you learn in one context also carries over to other contexts, so those young people who are brought up with that 'only if he / she wants to' ethos in one context take it through to others and don't learn the work ethic, persistence and resilience to 'dig in' and succeed when the going gets tough, as it always does at some point.

> **Opportunity is missed by most people because it is dressed in overalls and looks like work.**
> Thomas Edison

It's vital that we raise our children to commit to whatever they take on, whether that is their team, or courses and examinations that give them choices for their future, or commitments they make with their friends. Those who 'let others down', in whatever context, soon get a reputation that sticks with them and leads to people not committing to them.

Another important aspect of this is to not give up when the going gets tough, but rather find ways to overcome challenges. This links to the *Take Responsibility* chapter, in that we need to enable our children to take responsibility for finding solutions to challenges, whether that's with appropriate help from others or on their own. This solution-focus and belief in their own capacity to solve problems can be encouraged through systematic review and genuine, question-based coaching, especially when things go wrong. Knowing we're there for them is essential, but the other side of that is appropriate, non-judgemental challenge that helps build persistence and resilience.

Open questioning, rather than telling, enables our children to take responsibility and builds their persistence and resilience by helping them learn from success and failure, and *learn that they have solutions.* (See *The Coaching Spectrum* on the equipped2succeed section of my website.)

Reviewing Success and Failure - Supporting and Challenging Our Children to Persist

There are many ways that we can help our children persist, but one way is encouraging and enabling them to join groups or clubs, in and out of school, whether that's sports, dance, drama, art etc. We then need to ensure that they keep going, at least for a certain period of time. I realise that this can be more challenging if our children prefer individual pursuits, but this is one area where I would force the issue and do my best to find something that suits them. Otherwise, we are in danger of our children just doing 'what's compulsory', in terms of school, rather than having any experience of taking responsibility for committing to something voluntarily, outside that prescriptive environment. It's also important in terms of developing social intelligence and learning to engage with people in different ways. Committing to a group and sticking to that over time, even if it's only a term, semester or year, is really important.

There will be times when our children don't want to attend and I can empathise with those parents who take that as an opportunity to have a break from their part-time taxi service. However, it is crucial that we encourage our children to go until it becomes very clear that they are simply not benefiting from the experience. It may be that they want to do something else, or that they have 'out grown' it in some way. This happened with my daughter as, over a year or so, she changed ballet and gymnastics to netball and athletics.

Another way we can help build persistence and resilience, and build our children's self-belief in their capacity to learn and find solutions, is by helping our children to systematically review. This brings out what they have learned and enables us to help them build on success by pinpointing the elements that have enabled them to succeed. It also helps them address the doubts and fears that come from failure. If failure is viewed as a learning opportunity rather than something to be ashamed of, we can enable our children to address the things they need to work on in a positive way. The importance of seeing failure as a learning opportunity is reinforced in Alistair Arnott's book, *Positive Future: Understand how embracing failure is a tool for development.*

In the following, it is important that we act as parents, rather than teachers or technical coaches, helping our children to reflect for themselves. The sorts of questions we may ask, appropriately adapted for the age of our children:

> What went well?
>
> Why do you think that might be?
>
> What didn't go so well?
>
> Why do you think that might be?
>
> What have you learned from that?
>
> How may you use what you've learned in other areas?
>
> What can you do to improve ....?
>
> How can I help with that?

Whatever the situation, we then drill down into the specifics of the situation, not just accepting generalities. This helps our children recognise their capabilities and skills, and the ways in which they can continuously improve. Timing is important. Immediately after a success or failure is not the right time. A week later is probably too late. The following day is just about right. The right place is also important – formally sitting in front of each other often isn't conducive to an open conversation. However, that may be necessary if there is a specific, persistent issue. What is usually more useful is an informal conversation, whilst doing something together. (We've had many good conversations in the car.) This helps enable our children to understand the value of reflection and review in continuous improvement. It also helps our children build their self-belief, persistence and resilience through recognising their strengths and realising that their progress is within their own control.

Please note – 'why' questions can come across as threatening and can produce defensive, rather than considered, responses. We therefore need to be really careful when using these. Adding the word 'might' can soften the question, such as, 'Why do you think that might be?' rather than, 'Why is that?'

See *A Coaching Approach for Parents and Carers* on the equipped2succeed downloads section of my website.

Discipline

> *Now and then a man stands aside from the crowd, labours earnestly, steadfastly, confidently, and straightway, becomes famous for wisdom, intellect, skill, greatness of some sort. The world wonders, admires, idolizes, and it only illustrates what others may do if they take hold of life with a purpose. The miracle, or the power, that elevates the few, is to be found in their industry, application, and perseverance under the promptings of a brave, determined spirit.*
> Mark Twain

The discipline of study, the discipline of practice, the discipline of doing whatever we need to do on a daily basis to achieve our goals is a form of persistence that we can learn and turn into a habit. Above all, this requires discipline of thought and, as Dr Steve Peters may say in his brilliant book, *The Chimp Paradox – The Mind Management Programme for Confidence, Success and Happiness*, not allowing our 'Chimp' to take us off track. Discipline means systematically dismissing those thoughts that lead us to deviate from the journey to our goals:

'I can have a day off exercise today. I know I didn't go yesterday but I have ….(whatever we can convince ourselves is more important) … to do. I'll go for a walk tomorrow.'

'I'm really not in the right frame of mind to study. I'll just watch this programme first.'

'I can just have another half hour in bed.'

'Another slice of cake won't hurt.'

Successful people systematically manage their 'Chimp'. They maintain their discipline in the things that are important to them and what contributes to their achievement, no matter what that is. Losing discipline doesn't always mean taking a lazy, line of least resistance route. I've lost my discipline when I've worked too long hours. I've lost my discipline when I've spent too long with colleagues who needed to talk, which has caused other challenges and time-pressures for me, rather than arranging a better time.

Discipline with our children is usually talked about in relation to us imposing discipline, and our children being disciplined in what we think is important, whether that's being polite, table manners, doing chores, studying etc. Those are important. However, just as intrinsic motivation is much more powerful than extrinsic motivation, enabling our children to be self-disciplined is infinitely more important than 'doing as they are told'. Another important factor is enabling our children to understand the importance of self-discipline in pursuing their goals, not just in the things that are standard norms, such as doing homework. Discipline is a habit and therefore practicing it in one context enables us to use it in other contexts. However, just as we can be determined in some things and not in others according to our interests, passions and motivation, we can be disciplined in some things and not in others. It's a matter of aligning our discipline with what matters. And yes, we need to model disciplined behaviour for our children!

My children have seen my disciplined work habit. They have also experienced how disciplined I have been in getting home from work to get them to their various activities, and I hear myself saying, *'Because you need to commit to things you do, stick at it and don't let yourself and others down'.*

As I've mentioned, both my children are untidy and I'm not naturally the tidiest person (although I have become less and less tolerant of cluttered, untidy spaces!). The tidy bedroom challenge has been on-going since they were young, but it has never been a 'deal breaker'. It has never been something that I have used in terms of, 'do that or you can't do this'. Whether their bedrooms were tidy or not has not prevented them from applying the discipline required in what's important to them. One thing I haven't done is tidy their rooms for them. The consequence is that they may not have been able to find things and then realised the importance of everything in its place. However, they never arrived at a cricket match or athletics tournament without the right kit (and I didn't pack kit bags for either of them). And they were always ready to go to training when I arrived home from work.

Harriet disciplined herself to do what she needed to do to get the grades she wanted in examinations with minimal guidance and help from me. Having said that, by the time she was taking examinations, she had done quite a lot on how we learn, how we study, how our brain works, how we manage our mind in stressful situations, setting goals etc. She understood that her first serious examinations at 15 were not an end in themselves, but doing well would give her maximum choices in the next phase of her education. I did everything I could to enable her to be self-determining and self-disciplined, applying what she'd learned, rather than setting her a study schedule and policing it.

In discipline, like many other aspects of parenting, we can only judge our success by how our children behave when we're not around.

Allowing Our Children to Learn from Experience

I am not discouraged because every wrong attempt discarded is another step forward.
Thomas Edison

The most valuable learning comes from experience: from general experience, and from success and failure. I know that it is so challenging to allow our children to learn from failure. There was one notable example of this with George, which I think had great significance going forward. He was in the Notts County Football Club Centre of Excellence for a couple of years when he was young. He had an amazing left foot and had been spotted when he was nine, scoring free kicks and being consistent in accurately passing the ball. When he was 11, we were called to a review meeting with coaches. I had done quite a bit of work with Notts County, especially workshops for parents on supporting their children in that environment, and therefore one of the coaches wanted to alert me to what was to happen at the review meeting in case I wanted to prepare George. He was to be released: that is, basically told that you're not good enough and you'll leave tonight and not come back. I immediately said, *'I won't take this learning experience away from him'*. The coach was surprised and said it was refreshing as it wasn't the approach most parents would take. I called George's father and told him. He thought we should prepare George but I was firm on this. We went into the meeting; George sat between his father and I on one side of the table, with two coaches on the other side of the table. They went through the review process and ended by saying, although George had very good skills, his sprinting speed was an issue, and he wasn't quick enough to take forward, and therefore they were releasing him. I was emotional. George was fine. We shook hands, thanked them for the way they had handled it and left. We then reinforced the positives with George and he said it had probably showed that he was starting not to enjoy it as much as he might. Cricket was already beginning to take over, and little did we know at that time how helpful this experience would be in helping him build his resilience to handle the disappointments that were to come in cricket. (Failure is an inevitable part of sport, and most fields of endeavour.)

When George trialled for the Nottinghamshire age group cricket (County age group cricket is the pinnacle of regional cricket for young players), he failed each year in under 11s, under 12s and under 13s. However, he had already started to build his resilience and simply said each time, 'What do I need to do to get in next year?' He got in at under 14s, but only played one match. (Most of the boys who were in the squad when they were young tended to keep their place). He wasn't discouraged but merely kept training, playing club cricket and improving. He was then a regular in the side from under 15s and is one of the few young people from that age group cricket who is still on the journey to play professional cricket.

That wouldn't have been the case if he'd given up when rejected the first, second or third time. It also wouldn't have happened if he'd not had the resilience to overcome poor performances and continue to improve year on year. The resilience, persistence and self-belief that he has developed from bouncing back from failure enabled him to handle his release from Nottinghamshire County Cricket Club two days after his 21st birthday and pursue his goals to play professional cricket elsewhere. He didn't see it as a reflection of his ability, just one of timing and getting to be in the right place at the right time. He has built his self-belief and resilience through times of failure, poor performances, and moments of doubt.

Decide what you want, decide what you are
willing to exchange for it.
Establish your priorities and go to work.
H.L. Hunt

Persistence enables us to achieve our potential.
Lack of persistence means we can end up settling for something less than our dreams.

Affirmations
- I am persistently pursuing my goals.
- I am relishing my achievements one step at a time.
- I am feeling energised, breaking down barriers to my success.
- I am having fun, reaping the rewards of my persistence.
- I am feeling fantastic, working persistently towards my goals.
- I am feeling powerful and resilient.

ACTION

Find out what your children have the potential to enjoy and be good at by letting them try things. If they take an interest in one, sign them up to the club or similar, and ensure they stick at it, whether that be rehearsals or training or simply joining in and attending for a minimum period of time. Also, ensure that they learn to prepare appropriately so that they can perform at their best.

Find something that your child wants to do, some form of activity or project that they can do themselves, over a considerable period of time. Support them to plan it and establish milestones and times for review along the way. You may also need to add some stimulation at times to help keep them going. The finished project, whatever that is, will give them a great sense of achievement and is one way of getting them to appreciate the value of staying with something or persisting.

When our children want to 'give up', no matter what that is, question them about why and explore with them the choices and consequences of giving up or staying with something. Sometimes, getting through a challenging time in a particular pursuit can be a turning point to persistence.

Be persistent with the things you think are important. If children are expected to help with chores, or as I put it with my children, to contribute, they must be expected to contribute consistently. I know it's much easier to do it ourselves sometimes, but this is where <u>we</u> need to be persistent.

* *The Chimp* as defined by Dr Steve Peters:
'The Chimp is the emotional machine that we all possess. It thinks independently from us and can make decisions. It offers emotional thoughts and feelings that can be very constructive or very destructive; it is not good or bad, it is a Chimp. The Chimp Paradox is that it can be your best friend or your worst enemy, even at the same time'. I have used this phrase as it's one to which I think we can all relate.

Chapter Sixteen

Develop Technical Ability

I have been impressed with the urgency of doing.
Knowing is not enough; we must apply.
Being willing is not enough; we must do.
Leonardo da Vinci

Definitions

develop
- to bring out the capabilities or possibilities of; bring to a more advanced or effective state;
- to cause to grow or expand.

technical
- belonging or pertaining to an <u>art</u>, science, or the like: *technical skill;*
- characteristic of a particular art, science, profession, trade, etc;
- skilled in or familiar in a practical way with a particular art, trade, etc;
- technically demanding or difficult.

ability
- power or capacity to do or act physically, mentally, legally, morally, financially, etc;
- competence in an activity or occupation because of one's skill, training, or qualification.

Successful people become experts in their field. They do the work, study and gain experience, to develop their knowledge, understanding, skills and technical ability.

Bill Gates, 'Mr Microsoft', spent thousands of hours learning about computers. When he was in the eighth grade, the Mothers' Club at his school used proceeds from a jumble sale to buy a Teletype Model 33 ASR terminal and a block of computer time on a General Electric (GE) computer for the school's students. Gates took an interest in programming the GE system in BASIC, and was excused from mathematics classes to pursue his interest. He wrote his first computer program on this machine: a version of tic-tac-toe that allowed users to play games against the computer. Gates was fascinated by the computer, and how it would always perfectly execute software code. After the Mothers' Club donation was exhausted, he and other students sought time on other systems. One of these systems belonged to Computer Center Corporation (CCC), which banned four Lakeside students, including Gates, for the summer after it caught them exploiting bugs in the operating system to obtain free computer time. At the end of the ban, the four students offered to find bugs in CCC's software in exchange for computer time, which they did for some years, whilst also writing programmes for other companies and the school's administration. Gates went on to Harvard but did not have a definite study plan and spent a lot of time using the computers, whilst working on various research and commercial activities. Having easily done his '10,000 hours', Bill Gates eventually dropped out of Harvard to start his own company and the rest, as they say, is history.

Much is known of David Beckham and the iconic status he has in the football world. As a youngster, he practised relentlessly, working hard on the things he was good at to become the best. When he was fourteen, he wasn't considered fit enough or strong enough so he worked harder than ever on his fitness and strength, continuously coming top of fitness tests going forward. He was renowned for training as hard as than anyone whilst at Manchester United, practising free kicks over and over again at the training ground after others had finished, and on school fields near where he lived in 'time off' in the summer.

Mary Kay Ash spent over 25 years working in sales for different companies, firstly part-time as a young married woman to supplement the family income and then full-time. From 1939 to 1962, Mary Kay Ash worked full-time for two different companies and left the second one in 1962 after watching yet another man whom she had trained get promoted over her and earn a much higher salary than her. She started her cosmetics company, Mary Kay Inc., in 1963, aged 45, with her 20 year-old son, using incentive programmes and other strategies to give her employees the chance to benefit from their achievements. The marketing and people skills Mary Kay had learned soon led her company to enormous success. Her goal was to provide women with an unlimited opportunity for personal and financial success. She used her 'Golden Rule' as a guiding philosophy and encouraged employees and sales force members to prioritise their lives according to this simple motto: 'God first, family second, career third'. This was designed to be empowering for women juggling caring responsibilities with work, and was very different to most other company philosophies of the time. Her philosophy was based on years of experience, her deep understanding of sales, the barriers facing women and the infinite potential of women in the workplace.

Richard Feynman, Nobel Prize-winning physicist, showed, from a very young age, an insatiable curiosity for how things worked, improving things and solving puzzles. He was heavily influenced by his father, who encouraged him to ask questions to challenge orthodox thinking, and who was always ready to listen and teach Richard something new. As a child, he had a passion for engineering, maintained an experimental laboratory in his home, and delighted in repairing radios for people in the neighbourhood and making radios from old discarded ones. Once, he created a home burglary system while his parents were out, activated by someone entering his room. When he started working in a hotel as a teenager, he was always seeking to find better ways of doing things, much to the irritation of the owner and staff when things went wrong. (It is interesting to note that his parents saw working as an essential part of his 'education', especially for someone so academically able, who later became a leading academic of the 20th Century.

There are too many young people who are channelled through an academic route, with their parents thinking getting a part-time job is too much for them, only to then find they haven't gained the appropriate experience, skills and general broad perspective on life to take them successfully into their working life). At college, Richard did older students' physics assignments to expand his grasp of the subject and relentlessly solved puzzles, informally and formally training his mind for what was to come. He continued to pursue knowledge and broad experience outside his main field of endeavour throughout his life, which informed his physics and contributed to his exceptional achievements.

Marissa Mayer also showed an early interest in maths and science. Whilst at high school, she worked at a local grocery store, where she memorised the prices for hundreds of items in order to streamline the checkout process. Her journey to be President and CEO of Yahoo probably started just after high school when she was selected by the Wisconsin Governor as one of the state's two delegates to attend the National Youth Science Camp in West Virginia. At Stanford University, Mayer developed a passion for computers and went on to earn both a Bachelor of Science degree in symbolic systems and a Master of Science degree in computer science, both with a specialisation in artificial intelligence. During her studies, Mayer also taught undergraduate courses in computer programming, earning two teaching awards for her contribution. However, it was her research internships at Stanford University and the Union Bank of Switzerland's research lab in Zurich that helped her gain 14 job offers straight out of University, including one from a small company called Google. She joined Google in 1999 as their 20th employee and was the company's first female engineer. During her 13 years with the company, she was an engineer, designer, product manager and executive, holding many key roles across the company. She had certainly done a long and detailed 'apprenticeship' by the time she took over at Yahoo.

Sir Richard Branson is one of the most successful entrepreneurs of recent times. He is best known as the founder of the Virgin Group of more than 400 companies, but he started his business life very young. His first real business venture (after many earlier entrepreneurial activities) was a magazine called The Student at the age of 16. In 1970, he set up a mail-order record business from the crypt of a church where he ran The Student. Branson advertised popular records in the magazine and it was an overnight success. Trading under the name 'Virgin', he sold records for considerably less than the high street stores. Branson once said, 'There is no point in starting your own business unless you do it out of a sense of frustration.' The name 'Virgin' was suggested by one of Branson's early employees because they were all new at business. At the time, many products were sold under restrictive marketing agreements that limited discounting. In effect, Branson began the series of changes that led to large-scale discounting of recorded music.

Oprah Winfrey had a very challenging childhood (to say the least!), which is well documented. However, from a young age, she played games, interviewing her dolls and the crows on the fence when living with her grandmother. Winfrey acknowledges her grandmother's positive influence, saying it was her who had encouraged her to speak in public and 'gave me a positive sense of myself'. As a teenager, she went, for the second time, to live with Vernon Winfrey, whom she viewed as her father. He was encouraging and made her education a priority. Winfrey became an honours student and joined her high school speech team at East Nashville High School, achieving second place in a national 'Dramatic Interpretation' competition. She also won an oratory contest, which secured her a full scholarship to Tennessee State University where she studied communication. Her first job as a teenager was working at a local grocery store. She also worked at a local black radio station in Nashville, which hired her to do the news part-time. She continued to work there during high school and her first two years of college. Working in local media, she was both the youngest news anchor and the first black female news anchor at Nashville's WLAC-TV. Oprah's story reminds me of this quote:

Life is a grindstone.
Whether it grinds us down or polishes us up depends on us.
Thomas L. Holdcroft

Whatever our chosen field of endeavour, if we want to succeed, we need to develop appropriate and specific knowledge, understanding and outstanding technical ability in that field. If we want to achieve elite, out of the ordinary performance, we need to develop elite, out of the ordinary technical ability.

Only a mediocre person is always at his best.
W. Somerset Maugham

The '10,000 Hours Rule'

The 'Ten Year rule', or '10,000 hours rule', refers to the prolonged, systematic, deliberate practice that is essential to achieve elite performance. It is usually used in a sports context but is relevant in any field of endeavour, whether that's Marissa Mayer's knowledge, understanding and ability to optimise search engines, or Richard Branson's knowledge and insight in business, or Baroness Susan Greenfield's knowledge of the brain (author of *The Secret Life of the Brain*).

One of the best books about developing elite performance is Matthew Syed's, *Bounce - The Myth Of Talent And The Power Of Practice*. He uses research, first-hand experience and many examples to demonstrate that elite, world class performance is not about 'talent' but opportunity, environment, hard work, dedication and purposeful, deliberate, high-quality practice. One of the examples he uses is the Polgar sisters.

An extreme example of systematically developing technical ability is the Polgar sisters' experience. Laszlo Polgar advertised for a wife to collaborate with him to test out his theory that, 'Geniuses are made, not born'. Chess Grandmaster Susan (Zsuzsanna) Polgar and her two younger sisters, Grandmaster Judit and International Master Sofia, were part of their father's educational experiment; he sought to prove that children could make exceptional achievements if trained in a specialist subject from a very early age. He and his wife Klara educated their three daughters at home, with chess as the specialist subject. At age 4, Susan Polgar won her first chess tournament, the Budapest Girls' Under-11 Championship, with a 10–0 score. In 1982, at the age of 12, she won the World Under 16 (Girls) Championship. Despite restrictions on her freedom to play in international tournaments (due to Hungary being within the USSR at that time), by 1984, aged 15, Polgar had become the top-rated female chess player in the world. In January 1991, Susan Polgar became the first woman to earn the Grandmaster title through tournament play, and she is renowned for breaking a number of gender barriers in chess. In 1992, Polgar won both the Women's World Blitz and the Women's World Rapid Championship. She is the only world champion, male or female, to win all three forms of world chess championships. She is also an Olympic chess champion. Susan is now a chess teacher, coach, writer and promoter and the head of the Susan Polgar Institute for Chess Excellence (SPICE) at Texas Tech University. Her father's experiment of focused, deliberate practice and pursuit of excellence certainly worked in attaining elite performance. It's certainly a similar model to the one followed by Richard Williams and Oracene Price with their daughters, Venus and Serena, and Lewis Hamilton's and Andre Agassi's parents.

As a parent, I have reservations about this as a model for our children's childhood. I have always believed it important to empower, enable and equip my children, as rounded individuals, to pursue their dreams, not mine. However, I also think that only the children involved in such intense programmes have the right to judge. Whatever else, there is no doubt that such examples demonstrate how vital it is to develop the necessary knowledge, technical ability and experience if we want to perform at an elite level in anything.

> *You must work very hard to become a natural golfer.*
> Gary Player

C.A.N.I.
Continuous And Never-ending Improvement

Excellence requires a **growth mindset** and a C.A.N.I. approach. Continuous And Never Ending Improvement is an essential part of achieving success in any field.

I Can do Better Philosophy

All successful people are constantly asking themselves – *'How can I do better? How can I improve?'* They practice C.A.N.I.:

>Constant
>And
>Never-ending
>Improvement

When you ask yourself, *'How can I do better?'*, the creative power of your mind is switched on and ways to do things better suggest themselves. When you ask others, experts in your field, *'How can I do better?'*, they are inevitably willing to help. They are impressed by your attitude, appreciate that you value their experience, and are pleased to be able to help. There are a number ways those who succeed achieve elite performance and continuously improve:

Formal Learning

Progressing through educational and training routes in their specialist field, focusing on a specific or niche area, and excelling at each stage. Doing everything they can to go beyond the normal expectations: further focused, deliberate practice, further research, finding ways to communicate with leaders in their field, internships and other opportunities for specialist work experience – searching out ways to access those special opportunities that set them apart from others in their field.

Informal Learning

Making the most of informal learning opportunities, such as; watching a documentary; taking every opportunity to talk to people in the field; exploring relevant on-line sources of information and inspiration; reading relevant books and reading autobiographies of people in their field. When working with young sports people it always amazes me how few of them have read autobiographies of, or found out about, people who've become elite performers in their sport. What better way to learn than from those who have been there and done it?

Teachers, Mentors, Coaches
Those who succeed are open to improvement, to being taught, coached and mentored. They make the most of learning opportunities, not in a compliant, passive way, but in a discerning way, gaining what they need and what's important for their development. They gain all they can from those with relevant experience and expertise from insightful questioning, intelligent challenge and focusing on what's important to them.

Systematic Reflection
Winners in any field; those who achieve the pinnacle in their profession, out-perform others in business and win in sports systematically reflect all the time. They review every step of the way to ensure they are on track. Winners constantly de-brief: every step, every event, every milestone, success and failure:

      A. What did I want to happen?
      B. What actually happened?
      C. What caused the gap?
      D. What am I going to do about it?

Winners expect and positively use feedback. They want those whose opinion they value to critically appraise their performance. They accept or question advice for further understanding and act on it as appropriate.

Winners strive to be at their best <u>all the time</u>
Whatever the field, on a potential scale, if potential is 10, winners consistently achieve 10 and constantly seek to go beyond 10. They appreciate that there are no short cuts to As becoming A+s and they seek to maximise their potential at any given moment. Whether their A is in education, career, business, sport, academic research,

leaders in any field are always trying to convert their As into A+s.

Every success is built on the ability to
do better than good enough.
unknown

Marginal Gains

The concept of Marginal Gains is currently very much associated with Dave Brailsford, who became Performance Director of British Cycling in 1996. He has developed and led a culture of constant improvement and increasingly remarkable performances during that time. He spoke openly about the simple concept of marginal gains when interviewed on BBC Breakfast during the London 2012 Olympics.

'The whole principle came from the idea that if you broke down everything you could think of that goes into riding a bike, and then improved it by 1%, you will get a significant increase when you put them all together,' he explained.

'There's fitness and conditioning, of course, but there are other things that might seem on the periphery, like sleeping in the right position, having the same pillow when you are away and training in different places.'

'Do you really know how to clean your hands? Without leaving the bits between your fingers? If you do things like that properly, you will get ill a little bit less.' (NB As athletes train at such high intensity, their immune system can often be suppressed which makes them prone to illness.)

'They are tiny things but if you clump them together it makes a big difference.'

You get from this how important it is to look at every aspect of how to improve.

Britain won two bronze cycling medals at the Atlanta Olympics in 1996. They won seven out of 10 track cycling gold medals in London 2012, matching their achievement from Beijing 2008.

What could you do to make marginal gains in
all areas of your life?
What could you do to make marginal gains in your
quest to realise your goals?

Take and Make the Most of Opportunities

Successful people spot, take and make the most of opportunities. Opportunities to learn, work, pursue their passions, seek out the right contacts and talk to people who can help them, take onboard coaching and demonstrate the sort of work ethic that 'goes the extra mile'. They are the ones who study that bit longer, are first there at training and last to leave, take that internship hundreds or thousands of miles from home and make the most of it, are first to set their stall up on the market or keep their shop open later than everyone else.

Box of Tools

Many people who attain elite performance or become leaders in their field talk about their tool-kit, or box of tools, that has helped them to develop and maintain excellence. This book is about developing your generic tool-kit, but there are things we need to do that are specific to developing our technical ability in our chosen field of endeavour. The contents of our box will be many and varied, with unique elements that we, as individuals, need. Successful people learn, adopt and adapt tools from many and varied sources; their tool-kit goes beyond the norm. These tool-kits include all of the elements mentioned above, tailored specifically for their needs, relevant to their field and them as an individual. Whatever we pursue, it's vital that we find out what we need in our specific tool-kit and do everything we can to develop the excellence essential for success. As parents, we are best placed to help and support our children to develop their tool-kit. We need to do all we can to help them develop the generic tool-kit all successful people need and also find ways to help them to develop the tools specific to their chosen field of endeavour.

The foundation of lasting self-confidence and self-esteem is excellence, mastery of your work.
Brian Tracy

I have supported Harriet and George to the best of my ability to achieve in their chosen fields each step of the way. I have succeeded on most of the core, generic capabilities described in this book. In hindsight, I could have done much more in terms of helping them develop their technical ability in their chosen fields. It is no coincidence that dynasties arise as knowledge and expertise and a powerful network of contacts is passed from one generation to another. If we don't know the field and are not in that particular network, locally or regionally, we need to find out how best to support our children, Who are the best people to talk to? Who can give you up-to-date advice? Who's the best person to tutor or coach in that field? Which is the best school for that? Looking back, I realise I scratched the surface of expertise in their fields and should have done much more to find the right sports coaches.

Financial Capability (or Financial Literacy)

One of the essential technical competencies I feel it is vital to enable all of our children to develop is financial capability. It doesn't matter what their particular interest or the endeavour they decide to pursue, all our children need to be financially competent. I like the phrase financial literacy because it is a concept we can easily understand. We can all relate to the importance of essential basic literacy. We need to equip our children with an understanding of the value of money and the capability to effectively manage their money. My financial mistakes over the years have reinforced the importance of this for me.

Although finance, in some form, is on most school curricula, as parents, I believe we owe it to our children to ensure they develop basic financial capability. By that, I mean the knowledge, skills and attitudes necessary to start to become self-sufficient as adults and then enabled to create the wealth they need to achieve the life they choose. The first stage of that is learning the importance of economic self-determination and the basics of money management. This includes the ability to manage their finances effectively and become questioning and informed consumers of financial services. Financial literacy can be divided into three interrelated themes:

Knowledge and Understanding - familiarity with a range of concepts such as money, credit and investment and banking basics;

Skills and Competence - budgeting, financial planning and personal risk management;

Attitudes – thinking through, and taking responsibility for, the wider impact and implications of money and their financial decisions, which includes the following topics:
      saving for the things they want;
      understanding their attitude to money – risk v reward;
      deciding whether something is a want or a need;
      prioritising saving and spending;
      earning their own money.

For me, this also includes making informed decisions about investing in their own knowledge, understanding and skills through formal and informal education and learning.

One of the ways I helped Harriet and George develop their financial capability is by instituting an allowance system. From when they went into year 7 at the age of 11 they had an allowance, paid directly into their bank accounts, each month. This was increased going into year 9 at the age of 14, and then going into year 12. At each stage, I was very specific about what the children needed to buy for themselves from that allowance. It was designed as an introduction to managing money for themselves: deciding what to spend their limited resources on and realising how much things cost. It also helps our children understand that you can only buy things if you have the money, and if you want to buy something you can't afford, you need to save or do some work to earn more money, whether that's earning money doing more than your allocated chores or getting a part-time job.

In conclusion, I think the following quote, from one of the all-time greats of golf, succinctly sums up that disciplined, hard work and developing our knowledge and skills is essential to attain elite performance in our chosen fields.

The harder I work the luckier I get.
Gary Player

 ACTION

Do your research in your passion / chosen field of endeavour:

> Explore relevant on-line sources of the latest experience and research in your field;
>
> Read books by people who have achieved success in that field;
>
> Find out what examination grades are required in your field.
>
> Find out whatever statistics / records there are that apply to elite performance in your field.
>
> Find people nearby who can help you; who can act as a coach or mentor.

Help and support your children to do this. This tends to start with us doing much of the research and gradually moves to enabling our children to do the work for themselves.

How Can I do Better Today?

Each day, before you begin to do anything, devote 10 minutes to thinking 'How can I do better today?'
Ask yourself:

How can I encourage my friends, family, work colleagues, people I lead, class-mates?
What special favour can I do for my friends?
How can I increase my personal efficiency – how can I get things done better and quicker?
How can I do something positive to take another step forward towards my goals?

Do the Work, day-by-day, to improve your technical ability in your chosen field through constantly improving your knowledge, skills and capabilities to achieve elite performance and become your best.

Chapter Seventeen

Being the Best Parents We Can Be

The Most Amazing Journey of Our Lives!

Parenting is a journey that contains all the contours of the most loving, exhilarating, challenging, exciting, comforting and awe-inspiring relationship journey. I hope that this book is a small contribution towards enabling parents to make the most of that journey and bring about the positive outcomes that we all want for our children.

In the introduction I said I wanted the book to be affirming, and I truly hope that you have found it affirming of the love, care and joy you have in empowering, enabling and equipping your children to be all they can be.

The equipped2succeed framework is, in itself, a journey of continuous improvement that is relevant for us all. Simultaneously holistic and compartmentalised, we will be better at some bits than others at different times, both individually and with our children. The important thing is that we are always learning and improving: growing with our children. We start by being there for them for everything and we gradually change our role: enabling them to become more self-determining as they grow until we're there for them, as and when, for celebrations, sharing family time and those inevitable challenges.

My sense of success as a parent lies in the fact that my children, as adults, want to talk to me about the important stuff and don't feel they need to edit it for my ears. When they directly ask my advice they generally get a lot of questions back in true coaching style. When they come to a decision on anything they know that I will back them and not judge them on the outcomes. I'll be there to celebrate successes or be the helping hand to comfort and help them learn from failure. Whether they want to discuss practical matters or they need to touch base in an emotional quandary, what's important is that they still feel I'm there for them. When I look back at the vision I had for my parenting when Harriet was born, I can see successes and failures, incredible highs and heart-wrenching lows along the way. Being a parent is without doubt the most rewarding, awe-inspiring journey of my life: raising two amazing, self-determining young people.

I feel that relationships are always a work in progress, and no more so than with our children. I wish you continuous growth, fulfilment and happiness in the journey of empowering, enabling and equipping your children to be all they can be.

Printed in Great Britain
by Amazon